CONTENTS

About this book

This book is designed to support students who are studying on the Edexcel, BTEC First Diploma in Caring course. The BTEC First Diploma is a National Qualifications Framework level 2 qualification. The book may also provide a useful resource for other Care courses of a similar level.

Assessment

Most learning is assessed through tasks or assignments designed by teachers at the college or centre where you are studying. Teachers will provide you with guidance on how to evidence the assessment criteria and grading criteria for each unit. Unit 3, Care Practice Foundations, is assessed through an Integrated Vocational Assignment (IVA) which is designed and set by Edexcel. This assignment is first marked by teachers in your centre and then re-marked by Edexcel. This unit has double the points value towards the overall grading of the qualification. For further details and examples of the IVA assessment, readers should access the Edexcel website at www.edexcel.org.uk

Features of the book

This book is designed to be easy to access. Extensive use is made of section and sub-headings for easy reference. Throughout the text there are a number of features that are designed to encourage reflection, relate theory to practice and assist you to use concepts. These features are:

What you need to learn:	a list of points that set the context for the unit in relation to Edexcel's standards
Think it over:	questions designed to encourage individual reflection or discussion with others
Did you know?:	information that might act as a stimulus for reflection or discussion
Case studies	examples which might help to explain a concept or help to link theory with practice
Diagrams and tables	some theory is presented in diagrams in order to make it more accessible, easy to use in class activities and easier to remember
Bullet points	some key issues are expressed using bullet points in order to make a theory accessible and easy to use in class activities or in assignment preparation
Assessment activities	activities designed to support achievement in relation to unit outcomes.

The authors of this book hope that you enjoy your BTEC First in Caring course and that you will enjoy using this book and find it informative. We wish you every success in achieving this qualification and in your future career.   **Neil Moonie, April 2003**

£15.99

Heinemann Educational Publishers
Halley Court, Jordan Hill, Oxford OX2 8EJ
Part of Harcourt Education

Heinemann is the registered trademark of
Harcourt Education Limited

© Neil Moonie, Yvonne Nolan and Siân Lavers, 2003

First published 1999
Second Edition 2003

08 07 06 05 04
10 9 8 7 6 5 4 3

British Library Cataloguing in Publication Data is available
from the British Library on request.

ISBN 0 435 40146 7

Designed by Carolyn Gibson
Typeset by Techtype
Printed in the UK by CPI Bath

Acknowledgements
The authors and publishers would like to thank the following individuals and
organisations for permission to reproduce photographs:

Alamy pages 67, 107 and 241; Bubbles page 178; Corbis page 87; Gareth
Boden page 289 and Oxfam page 129.

Every effort has been made to contact copyright holders of material reproduced
in this book. Any omissions will be rectified in subsequent printings if notice
is given to the publishers.

Tel: 01865 888058 www.heinemann.co.uk

UNIT ONE

VALUES AND INTERPERSONAL SKILLS

This unit explores the social and political factors that influence service user needs and the role of care workers. The values, rights and responsibilities that are central to care work are studied during this unit. The unit also focuses on the skills that care workers need in order to be able to work effectively.

Public services are experiencing a period of rapid change and the Government's modernisation agenda is included as a focus for study

This unit is internally assessed and ideas for evidencing the grading criteria are presented.

In this unit you will learn about:

- factors that influence diversity and equality
- skills required of a care worker
- responsibilities of the individual carer.

Social care work is 'working with people' – and people are all different from one another. Examine your fingerprints – there are about 6000 million people in the world today and yet it is very unlikely that you will have exactly the

Figure 1.1 *There are approximately 6000 million people in the world, but each person's fingerprint is different*

same fingerprints as anyone else. Each person is different from other people physically, and each person also has different life experiences.

The great thing to enjoy about care work is getting to know so many different people, with their different views of life. Although each person is special, there are patterns which mean that some people are similar in some ways to other people – they may share similar life experiences. This unit will explore some of the social and political factors that influence people's lives, making us different from each other but also creating patterns we can recognise.

Because people have different life experiences, it is very important that people are not treated as if they were all the same. Each person who needs care will have his or her own individual, social and cultural needs. If people are to receive a fair and equal service, their different needs have to be understood. This unit will explore the risk of discriminatory practice. Discrimination can happen when people are seen as being 'all the same'.

Factors that influence diversity and equality

The range of differences between people is called 'diversity'. It is important that people working in care should recognise diversity and treat people with equal respect whoever and whatever they are. Many factors make people different from one another. These factors include:

- social class
- geographical location
- culture
- gender
- financial viability
- family structure
- ethnicity
- age.

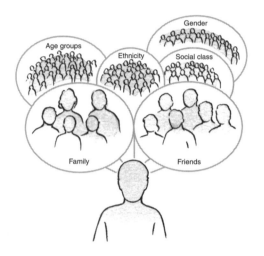

Figure 1.2 *Most people feel that they belong with groups such as their family and friends — but people also belong with other groups such as their social class, age group and ethnic group*

The groups we belong to can have a strong influence on how we think, what we value, how we act and what we do. When people are with their friends they will behave differently from when they are at work. People say and do different things when they are with family than when they are with people they have not met before.

The wider groups that people belong to also influence how they behave. It is important not to make assumptions that other people will have the same views, attitudes or needs that we do. Men often react to things differently from women. Older people do not necessarily see things the same way that younger people do. Ethnicity can influence your life experience, and social class can make a big difference to the experiences and opportunities an individual may have.

Social class

> ### Case Study – William, Mischel and Sean: Schools
>
> **William** is 16. His father works in the diplomatic service as a senior civil servant. He boards at a private residential school, which charges fees of £12,000 per year. In the holidays he stays with his parents on their five-acre estate in the country. He is studying four A-levels and has advanced skills in sailing. He is not sure about his career, but after completing his degree he may choose to take a post within the civil service. If he chooses this option he would expect to achieve a senior post by the age of 30.
>
> **Mischel** is 16. Her father is a senior teacher at a comprehensive school. Mischel attends a different school three miles away from the semi-detached home where she lives with her family. Her mother takes Mischel to school each day by car – and will do so until Mischel is old enough to take her driving test. Mischel hopes to stay on at school and take A-levels. She would like to get the qualifications to work as a journalist.
>
> **Sean** is 16. His father is currently working as a technician at a tyre-fitting company. Sean walks or catches a bus to school each day. Sean lives on a large housing estate in an urban area which is very congested with traffic. He is not sure what he wants to do when he leaves school, but hopes he can get bar work or some sort of hourly paid employment locally.
>
> These three people are the same age – yet they have very different lifestyles. One boards at school, one travels by car to the best school in the area, and one walks to the local school. Their lives will be different in many other ways. The friends they mix with, education, career opportunities and future income will probably be very different. Sociologists would explain these differences in terms of **social class**.

Social class is a way of classifying the social status that different occupations have. In other words, some jobs are seen as high status or high class, while other jobs have less status. Your social class is concerned with the way other people think about your job – not just about the money you have.

Social class is a term that has been used to describe different groups of people for a very long time in Britain. Mostly, people are used to the terms 'upper class', 'middle class', and 'working class'. Upper-class people have more power, influence and status than middle-class people, but middle-class people have more power, influence and status than working-class people. Before the 1960s, class differences were open and obvious. People usually wore different clothes which showed the class they belonged to and they usually only mixed socially with members of their own class.

Historically, social class was often seen as being like a pyramid, the upper class at the top and depending on the work of the other classes.

Between 1971 and 2001 the official system for grading jobs contained five 'classes' in order to grade different occupations. The system was known as 'The Registrar-General's Social Class Index'. The five classes in this system are set out below:

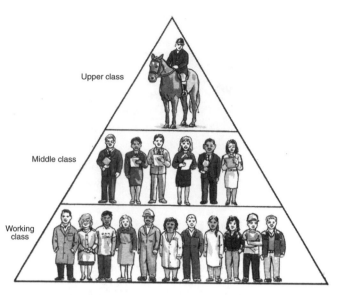

Upper class

Middle class

Working class

Figure 1.3 *The social class pyramid*

Class Level	Definition	Examples of occupations in each class
Social Class I (1)	*Professional occupations*	Company secretary, doctor, judge, lawyer, university teacher, solicitor, scientist
Social Class II (2)	*Intermediate occupations*	Aircraft pilot, police or fire brigade officer, teacher, manager, farmer
Social Class III N (3 Non-Manual)	*Skilled non-manual*	Cashier, clerical worker, estate agent, sales representative, secretary, typist
Social Class III M (3 Manual)	*Manual occupations*	Bus driver, bricklayer, carpenter, electrician, hairdresser, baker, butcher
Social Class IV (4)	*Partly skilled occupations*	Agricultural worker, bar staff, hospital porter, street trader
Social Class V (5)	*Unskilled occupations*	Road sweeper, kitchen labourer, refuse collector, window cleaner, office cleaner

Since the 2001 census, a new system for classifying social class has been used in all official statistics and surveys. This system uses eight classes to classify occupations and is called the National Statistics Socio-economic Classification. The whole system is very complex and can be viewed at www.statistics.gov.uk. The eight 'analytic classes' used in the system are set out overleaf:

The National Statistics Socio-economic Classification – Analytic Classes

1	Higher managerial and professional occupations. This class is split into:
	1.1 Large employers and higher managerial occupations
	1.2 Higher professional occupations.
2	Lower managerial and professional occupations
3	Intermediate occupations
4	Small employers and own account workers
5	Lower supervisory and technical occupations
6	Semi-routine occupations
7	Routine occupations
8	Never worked and long-term unemployed

Case Study – William, Mischel and Sean: Money

William comes from a wealthy family, and mixes with people who are used to taking money for granted. If William wants extra tuition to help him with his studies, the money is there. If he needs a car, it will be bought for him. William can expect to travel widely – expense isn't an issue. If he wants books or sailing lessons, he gets them. William mixes with other people who have very high expectations of life. William listens to people who have direct experience of how government and business work. He is very clear about the possibilities for his future. He works very hard – but he knows what he is working for. He would describe himself as middle class – but his father's occupation and his family's status would fit Class 1.

Mischel's parents are buying their house on a mortgage. Mischel can get the latest clothing and music and she has her own computer. She has a Saturday job which gives her a small income. Mischel's parents can pay for little extras, but money is always an issue that has to be talked about. Mischel mixes with people who do not know much about government or business, but she gets advice on careers from the local school. Mischel is interested in her future career and her parents put pressure on her to do well in exams, telling her that qualifications are very important. People similar to Mischel's parents are likely to fit Classes 2–4.

Sean's parents live on a crowded housing estate. Sean goes to a school similar to Mischel's, except that many of the students there don't believe that school is important. Most of Sean's friends say that school is boring and that what matters is getting out and earning money. Once you get some money you can be independent – you can do what you want. Sean hasn't got a job yet, but he is looking forward to getting the latest clothes, CDs, etc. when he can get one. Sean's parents often worry about money and are looking forward to Sean going out to work so that he can contribute to the household budget. Sean's parents might fit into Class 6 or 7.

THINK IT THROUGH

What are the differences in lifestyle for these three people?
What will happen to each person in the future?

Does social class matter?

Social class can make a difference to how people live their lives – whether they think about social class or not. One reason social class matters is that class can influence the attitudes and values that people have.

People whose work roles place them in Social Classes 1 and 2 often believe that they control their own lives. They expect to choose where to buy their own house or flat, they choose entertainment, what they eat and what they wear. People in classes 1 and 2, or children with parents in classes 1 and 2 may not see themselves as being wealthy, but often they do not worry too much about the cost of items, or about getting into debt.

Some people in lower status occupations feel that they cannot control their income, their jobs and housing needs. Some people in 'routine occupations' may feel worried about money. If you are short of money, you have to be careful what clothes and what food you buy. Money worries can limit where you can go out – where you can go on holiday and what social life you can have. If you have to rent a house or flat, you may feel that you have less choice of where to live than if you can afford to buy your own property.

Sociologists explain that people who belong to the higher social classes often feel they can choose their own lifestyle, whereas people in the lower classes may have less chance to choose how they live and what they do.

Does social class influence happiness?

Happiness is a very personal issue, and happiness comes and goes each day. In 1994, the psychologist Michael Argyle published a book on social class and happiness. He came to the conclusion that a large range of studies showed that people in the higher social classes are generally 'somewhat happier' than people in the lower social classes. Why does higher class lead to more happiness for many people?

- **Money** Lower social class jobs often don't pay very well. People in the lower classifications may have less to spend and less savings than people in the higher classes.

- **Enjoyable work** The more prestigious jobs, like lawyer or accountant, may often be more enjoyable than routine or boring jobs.

- **Respect** People with high-status jobs may be treated with more respect than people with low-status jobs.

- **Self-esteem** People who feel they have been successful and have developed their abilities may feel good about life.

- **Stress** People who have money worries, or who live in poor-quality housing – in areas of crime and so on – often feel that life is difficult and full of stress. Upper-class people may be more free of this stress.

- **Holidays** The higher classes take more holidays and more days out from home than working-class people.

- **Sport and exercise** Generally, people in the higher classes enjoy more sport, exercise and social activity than people with occupations lower down the scale.

- **Health** On average, people in the higher classes had less chronic (or long-term) illness, less sickness and even lived longer than people in lower classes during the last century.

- **Job security** Unskilled people are ten times more likely to be out of work than people with a high level of education and training.

Naturally, not every person who is in a job of high social class is happy, and not every person who is in an unskilled job is sad. All sorts of things can go right or wrong for anyone, but the evidence suggests that people with high-status jobs do seem to have more chances of being happy over their lifetime.

Lifestyle

In modern Europe, it seems that you are what you buy. Whenever you read a newspaper, watch TV, look at the Internet or just walk down the street, you see advertisements. Adverts don't just tell you about things you can buy – they often invite you to join in a way of life. Adverts offer a lifestyle.

Some sociologists say that it's not so much the work you do that matters, it's more how you spend your money – what lifestyle you buy into.

Many people now buy four-wheel-drive cars, yet rarely use them in the way they are intended to be used – in the country. Most of the time they may sit in traffic jams. But owning a four-wheel-drive says 'I'm part of the sporting outdoor set'. It's the image or lifestyle that people spend their money on.

When it comes to spending money, people are not equal – some have far more money to spend than others.

Figure 1.4 *A four-wheel-drive being used in a town*

DID YOU KNOW?

On average financial managers earn over five times more per week than people like hairdressers, catering assistants and bar staff. (Source – Social Trends 2002)

Financial viability

People who get less than 60 per cent of the income that an average person expects may be considered to be at risk of poverty and social exclusion. Financial viability means having enough money to live on. In 2001 an estimated 10.7 million people (18 per cent of the population) in Britain lived on or below the 60 per cent of average earnings poverty line; in 1979 only 4.4 million people were estimated to live in poverty. The number of people who can be considered to be poor increased dramatically between 1985 and the early 1990s. The proportion of people with low income (18 per cent of the population) has remained the same for the last few years.

Key groups of people who have to live on very little money include one-parent families, people who are unemployed, elderly people, people who are sick or disabled, single earners and unskilled couples.

People who are poor may have enough money for food, for some clothes and for heating, but poverty means that there is little money for interesting purchases and exciting lifestyles. People who depend on benefits have limited life choices. The latest clothes, nice reliable cars, the latest electronic equipment, digital TV and so on, may not be choices for people on low income. People with little money have to restrict what they can buy when they visit a supermarket or shopping centre.

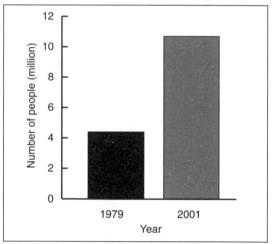

Figure 1.5 Poverty has more than doubled since 1979

Many lifestyles are not possible for people in poverty. Belonging to a sports club is not possible if you cannot afford the membership fees. Even jogging is not possible if you feel your neighbourhood is not safe to go out in.

In 1999 the government published a report called 'Opportunity for All'. In this report the government states: 'Our aim is to end the injustice which holds people back and prevents them from making the most of themselves'. The government says that their goal is: 'that everyone should have the opportunity to achieve their potential. But too many people are denied that opportunity. It is wrong and economically inefficient to waste the talents of even one single person'.

The 'Opportunity for All' paper states that:

- People living in households with low incomes have more than doubled since the late 1970s.

- One in three children live in households with below half average income.

- Nearly one in five working-age households has no one in work.

- The poorest communities have much more unemployment, poor housing, vandalism and crime than richer areas.

The government report, 'Opportunity for All', says the problems which prevent people from making the most of their lives are:

- **Lack of opportunities to work** Work is the most important route out of low income. But the consequences of being unemployed go wider than lack of money. It can contribute to ill-health and can deny future employment opportunities.

- **Lack of opportunities to acquire education and skills** Adults without basic skills are much more likely to spend long periods out of work.

- **Childhood deprivation** This has linked problems of low income, poor health, poor housing and unsafe environments.

- **Disrupted families** Evidence shows that children in lone-parent families are particularly likely to suffer the effects of persistently low household incomes. Stresses within families can lead to exclusion; in extreme cases to homelessness.

- **Barriers to older people living active, fulfilling and healthy lives** Too many older people have low incomes, lack of independence and poor health. Lack of access to good-quality services are key barriers to social inclusion.

- **Inequalities in health** Health can be affected by low income and a range of socio-economic factors such as access to good-quality health services and shops selling good-quality food at affordable prices.

- **Poor housing** This directly diminishes people's quality of life and leads to a range of physical and mental health problems, and can cause difficulties for children trying to do homework.

- **Poor neighbourhoods** The most deprived areas suffer from a combination of poor housing, high rates of crime, unemployment, poor health and family disruption.

- **Fear of crime** Crime and fear of crime can effectively exclude people within their own communities, especially older people.

- **Disadvantaged groups** Some people experience disadvantage or discrimination, for example on the grounds of age, ethnicity, gender or disability. This makes them particularly vulnerable to social exclusion.

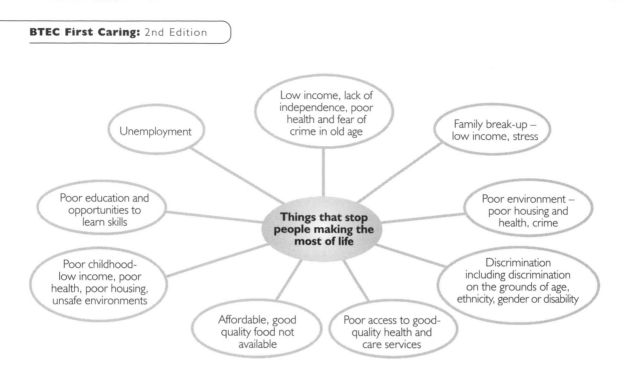

Figure 1.6 *Factors that affect whether people are able to make the most of their lives*

Geographical location

People who feel confident about their future income and finances can choose their lifestyle. They can also choose where they would like to live. People in the higher social classes tend to live in more expensive housing, areas with good facilities for travel and education. People with lower incomes tend to live in more densely occupied housing areas. People on lower incomes are often forced to rent rather than buy their homes. Different social class groups often live in different neighbourhoods. Marketing companies can use postcodes to work out what advertisements to send to different areas.

Does it matter what kind of location you live in? Many people would say that the important thing is to get on with the people you live with and that money, or the size of your house, does not matter. But there can be disadvantages to living in poor-quality or high-density housing. These can include noise, pollution, overcrowding, poor access to shops and other facilities, and stress from petty crime. When people are on a low income, household maintenance can become a problem. Poorly maintained housing can create health hazards.

If you live on a low income in a crowded block of flats or high-density housing, you may get:

- noise from neighbours

- more chance of being woken up in the night

- stress from neighbours' behaviour

- nearby busy roads where traffic fumes create pollution

- a number of children or relatives crowded into one bedroom

- more burglary, car crime and personal attacks

- poor car parking and travel facilities.

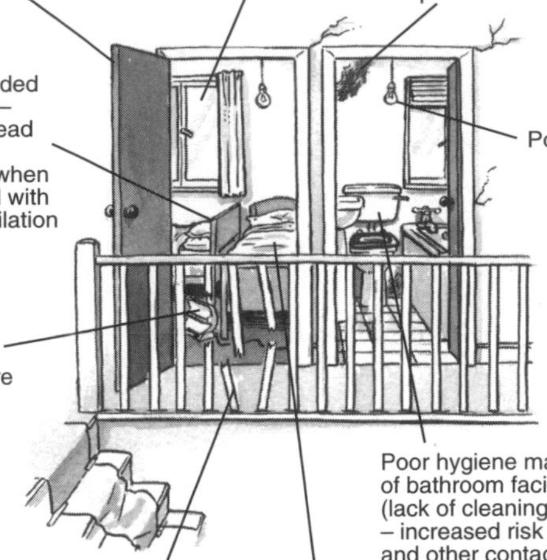

Door hinged outward to create space (safety hazard)

Windows kept shut to conserve warmth – resulting in poor ventilation

Damp patch on wall from broken gutters outside – risk of infection from fungal spores

Overcrowded bedroom – helps spread airborne infection when combined with poor ventilation

Poor lighting

Portable radiant electric fire (safety hazard)

Poor hygiene maintenance of bathroom facilities (lack of cleaning agents) – increased risk of skin and other contagious diseases

Poor maintenance of building – increased accident risk

Overcrowding may increase interpersonal stress and, coupled with other stressors, may lead to poor mental health

Figure 1.7 *Poor housing may contribute to a wide range of hazards to health and social well-being*

Low income and poor housing are a source of stress to many people. The table below lists the percentages of householders who said they had problems with the issues listed in the left-hand column. In general, people with money appear to have fewer problems compared with people who live in low-income areas. Living in the suburbs or in the country may also cause less stress than living 'in town'.

Problems in the area that you live	People in wealthy suburban or rural areas	People in council or low-income areas	People in wealthy urban areas	Overall percentages
Crime	49%	66%	59%	56%
Litter and rubbish	26%	58%	49%	42%
Vandalism and hooliganism	25%	58%	42%	40%
Dogs	22%	37%	25%	29%
Noise	16%	31%	35%	23%
Graffiti	11%	36%	32%	22%
Neighbours	7%	18%	17%	13%
Racial harassment	1%	8%	9%	4%

Source: Adapted from *Social Trends 2002*

THINK IT THROUGH

Explain what is meant by social class and the relationship to geographical location. Look at a map of your local area. Work out if the housing is different in different areas on your map. You may need to walk around the streets to note what kind of housing exists. What lifestyles do people have in the different areas? How do you think lifestyles and stress levels might vary between areas of housing in your area? What conclusions can you draw about social class in different areas?

Family structure

People differ from one another in the kinds of families or groups that they live in.

THINK IT THROUGH

Try watching the TV adverts on a typical evening. Many adverts for food products and cleaning products will show actors in a family setting. Just looking at these adverts, it would seem that most houses are occupied by 30-year-old couples with two children, and perhaps some cats and dogs. Is this image really how most people live?

Looking at the homes that people lived in in 2001, 29 per cent of homes were occupied by single people; 23 per cent of homes were occupied by couples with dependent children and 6 per cent were occupied by single parents with children. In 2001, 29 per cent of homes were occupied by couples with no children and only 1 per cent of homes housed more than one family.

Many people do live as couples with their children, but it would be a mistake to imagine that all people are born into and grow up in small families.

A family is a social group made up of people who are 'related' to each other. This means that other people (society) recognise that this group is related. In British society, 'family' is the word used to describe groups where adults act as parents or guardians to children. Belonging to a family can have many advantages. Family relationships can provide a safe, caring setting for children. Family groups can guide and teach children, and they can provide a source of social and emotional support for adults and older family members as well as children.

Modern sociologists identify four different types of family:

- extended families
- nuclear families
- reconstituted families
- lone-parent families.

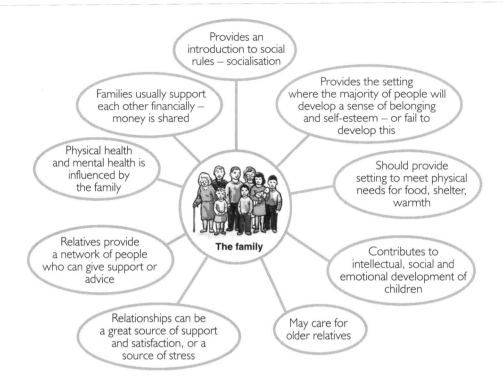

Figure 1.8 *What the family does for people*

Extended families

An extended family is where parents, children and grandparents all live together or near each other, so that they are often together. Between 1800 and 1900 in England, many families lived in this way. The extended family can have many advantages. Parents can work all day without having to worry about who is looking after the children – the grandparents might do this. If the grandparents needed care, then the parents or even the older children could help. The extended family provides a network of people who can support each other.

Ross lives with his brother and his mother and father on the top two floors of a very large semi-detached Victorian house near the centre of a city. Ross's mother's parents live on the ground floor of the building. They have their own bathroom and kitchen, although the whole family sometimes eat together at the weekend. Ross's parents were able to buy such a large house only because the grandparents sold their home to

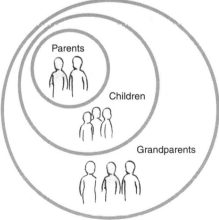

Figure 1.9 *The extended family*

make it possible. The grandparents own part of the new house, but they have left their share of the house to Ross's parents in their Will.

Nuclear families

A nucleus is the centre of a living cell, and the nuclear family is like the centre of the extended family on its own. By the 1950s, many people in Britain no longer lived with grandparents. The term nuclear family was invented to describe this new, smaller family. The original nuclear family was usually a husband who would go out to work, a wife who would look after the children while they were young, and the children.

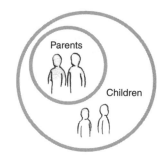

Figure 1.10 *The nuclear family*

Nowadays many couples no longer fit this description. Often both parents will have full-time work and the children are cared for by childminders, nannies, or nursery services. Male and female roles have been changing – men and women are now usually seen as equally responsible for household tasks. However, studies suggest that women still undertake the majority of child care and housework tasks.

Meena lives with her sister, mother and father in a three-bedroom, semi-detached house. Meena's grandmother (her mother's mother) lives in the Caribbean and she has not seen her for two years. Meena's father's parents live about eighty miles away, and she sees these grandparents about five to eight times each year. Meena's family moved to the house they live in three years ago when her father got a better job.

Reconstituted families

Approximately one marriage in every three now ends in divorce, and some people think this figure will increase. Many young people live together before marriage and have children, but there is evidence that a large number of these couples split up too. Over a third of marriages each year are likely to be re-marriages, and about one million children live with a step-parent. Roughly a quarter of children might experience their parents divorcing before the age of 16.

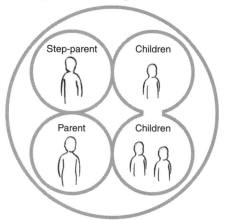

Figure 1.11 *The reconstituted family*

The reconstituted family is where the couple are not both the parents of each child in the family. One partner might have been divorced from an earlier marriage, and has now re-married to create a new family. Sometimes children from different relationships may be included in a new, reconstituted family. One partner may have been single but is now married to a partner who has children from a previous relationship.

Sarosh lives with his mother and stepfather in a modern terraced house in a small town. His mother and stepfather have been married for two years. Sarosh's 'real' father calls every other Saturday to collect him for a visit. Sarosh's mother and father divorced four years ago. His new stepfather has a daughter, Zara, who lives with her mother over two miles away. Sarosh has met Zara and they like each other, but Sarosh thinks his stepfather cares more about Zara than him.

Lone-parent families

Nearly a quarter of all families with dependent children are lone-parent families. Twenty per cent of families with dependent children are lone-parent families led by a lone mother, with just 2 per cent led by a lone father.

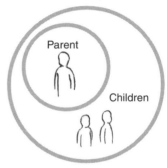

While some lone-parent families may be well off, many are disadvantaged. A family expenditure survey in 2000 showed that twice as many lone-parent families live on low incomes compared with couples with dependent children. Many lone parents rely on benefits or receive low income wages.

Figure 1.12 *The lone parent family*

Janice is a single mother with an eight-year-old son, living in a fourth-floor flat on a large housing estate. Janice is looking for part-time work, but her son has an attention problem at school and the school often telephones her to ask her to come and collect him or to calm him. Janice depends on Income Support to get by. She doesn't have enough money for holidays or to take her son out for the day. Janice cannot afford leisure activities which cost money. At night Janice usually stays in and watches TV. There is a high drug-related crime rate on the estate and Janice worries that her flat may be broken into.

The type of family that a child lives in can change. An extended family can turn into a nuclear family if the grandparents die or move away. Families can become 'reconstituted' if one partner leaves and is replaced by a different person. Few people can guarantee a family style for life. When people leave their partners, divorce or die, a lone-parent family may be created. If the remaining parent finds a new partner, the lone-parent family becomes a reconstituted family. The same child might live in different family structures during childhood and adolescence. Some advantages and disadvantages of different family types are given below.

Extended families

Advantages

Children	Parents	Grandparents
You have grandparents to look after you, as well as parents. You learn from a wider group of people. Security and stability. There is usually someone at home all day	Grandparents can look after your children. Shared financial resources; parents and grandparents may be able to afford a bigger home. There is someone at home all day	You feel that you belong and are needed. Both children and grandchildren can help you and talk with you. Shared financial resources

Disadvantages

Children	Parents	Grandparents
Adults might boss children about. Children might feel they have less freedom	You may have to look after your parents as well as your children. It may be difficult to move house and relocate for work reasons. Larger houses cost more to run. Smaller houses may become crowded	You have to get on with your children. You may have less independence

Nuclear families

Advantages

Children	Parents	Grandparents
Close relationship with parents. Security and stability	Family can prioritise one parent's career. Family can move house to further a career. Family may have two incomes	Independence from children. No unwanted pressure to look after grandchildren

Disadvantages

Children	Parents	Grandparents
May tend to receive care from one person only (often the mother)	The division of work may not satisfy both people. Child care may be needed if both parents work full time	May lose contact with children and grandchildren. May become lonely or have insufficient social support

Reconstituted families

Advantages

Children	Parents	Grandparents
Similar to nuclear family	Similar to nuclear family – may have two incomes and financial security	Few responsibilities

Disadvantages

Children	Parents	Grandparents
May have difficulty making relationships with a new parent or with new brothers and sisters. May have to live in, or make visits to, more than one home	Similar to nuclear family	Possible feeling of being cut-off from grandchildren or from a child's family. Risk of isolation. May have to establish new relationships

Lone-parent families

Advantages

Children	Parents	Grandparents
Only one parent to relate to. Possible freedom from stressful or even abusive relationships	Independence and control of own life	Similar to nuclear family

Disadvantages

Children	Parents	Grandparents
Only one parent to guide and help	Generally more risk of low income. Responsibilities for home and child care fall on one person. Managing an independent lifestyle might be stressful on a low income	Similar to nuclear family

Changing family patterns

In the past 45 years there has been a gradual change in the way people live. Fewer people now live in extended families than at any time in the past century, fewer people live in nuclear families than in the 1960s and 1970s. There are more reconstituted and lone-parent families with dependent children than there were 20 years ago.

There are many issues that influence people's lifestyles, but it is important to understand how money and economic factors influence family patterns. People do not simply 'choose' their pattern of family life like picking clothes from a catalogue.

When people worked on the land as farmers and farm labourers, the extended family was a very effective way to live. There was little reason for children to move away from the village when they grew up – the work went with the house where they lived. The more people that lived together, the more they could help each other and share the work.

When most people stopped working on farms and worked instead in businesses and factories, it was hard for young people to stay in the same area as their parents. If a new factory opened 20 miles away, it was best to move to the area where the new work had developed. Because younger people moved away from their parents to get work, fewer extended families existed and more nuclear families developed.

We live in an information age where each person may do individual work – men and women increasingly share employment opportunities. Running a home can be done much more easily than forty years ago. People may not need to live as a couple in order to cope with the dual pressures of employment and running a home.

Economic pressures no longer encourage or force people to live in traditional types of family to the same extent as in the past.

Culture

The way we behave, the language we speak, the diet we eat, the way that we dress and our lifestyle are all part of our culture. Culture includes the things which make one group different and distinctive from another.

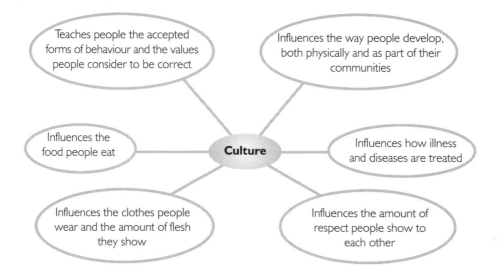

Figure 1.13 *How our culture can influence us*

Culture gives us a set of rules or expectations which help us to understand each other, and to know how to react in certain situations. Very often we do not even understand the culture we are surrounded by; we just do 'what is normal' and fit in. Because society is made up of different sorts of people, brought up in different circumstances or places, and following different beliefs and religions, different people's cultures can be different. We all tend to follow the way we were brought up and the influences of the people around us. Not everyone shares the same culture. There are many different cultures in Britain.

Ethnicity

For many people their race is of vital importance and it enables them to understand who they are. Race is not easy to define. In the past, people believed that different races of people were somehow biologically different. It is almost impossible to define racial groups in terms of genetic differences or features to do with skin colour or physical appearance. People do classify themselves and are classified by others in terms of the social and cultural groups to which they belong. A person's culture, religion, style of dress, way of speaking, and so on may lead to classification in terms of ethnic group.

A key way in which people distinguish themselves is in terms of being black or white. Some people talk in terms of a black, white or Asian group. But there is no single black culture, and no single white culture.

A study of the British population by ethnic group is reported in *Social Trends* (2002). Details of the size of various ethnic groups are set out in the table below.

White	53 million people
Black Caribbean	0.5 million people
Black African	0.4 million people
Other black groups	0.3 million people
Indian	1.0 million people
Pakistani	0.7 million people
Bangladeshi	0.3 million people
Chinese	0.1 million people
None of the above groups	0.7 million people
All other groups – including people who refused to state ethnicity	0.8 million people

There has been law to prevent discrimination on the basis of race since 1965. The current Race Relations Act was passed in 1976 and amended (or updated) in 2000. The 1976 Act of Parliament set up the Commission for Racial Equality. This Commission seeks to investigate cases of discrimination based on racial and ethnic group membership.

Despite the law and the powers of the Commission, however, there is evidence of inequality between white and black groups in Britain. Black and Asian people are more likely to be victims of crime than are white people. The British crime survey in 2000 showed that black and Asian adults in England and Wales were roughly twice as worried about becoming victims of crime as white people. The table below shows the percentage of people in different ethnic groups who were worried about crime.

	White	Black	Asian
Theft of car	20	37	37
Theft from car	15	33	30
Burglary	18	37	41
Mugging	16	32	38
Physical attack	17	35	38
Rape	18	34	34

Source: The British Crime Survey published by the Home Office 2000

Unemployment rates vary between different black and white groups, but generally rates of unemployment are higher for black and Asian people than for white people. In 2001–2, 4 per cent of white people were unemployed. Among non-white groups, 21 per cent of Bangladeshi people, 16 per cent of Pakistani people, 14 per cent of black Africans, 12 per cent of black Caribbean people and 6 per cent of Chinese people were unemployed (*Social Trends* 2003).

More black and Asian families are likely to have a low income compared to white families. The table below shows the proportion of people from different ethnic groups who were in the bottom 20 per cent of the population for the amount of spending money that they have (spending money is called 'disposable income').

Ethnic group	Percentage of bottom 20 per cent of population
White	19
Black Caribbean	24
Black non-Caribbean	34
Indian	29
Pakistani / Bangladeshi	64

Source: Social Trends 2003

Many black and Asian people believe that they have poorer employment opportunities and are more likely to be victimised than white people.

Gender

It was only in 1928 that women were granted equal rights with men to vote in elections. Eighty years ago, women were considered to have a lower social status than men. Assumptions were made that women should look after children, do housework, cook and tidy and do light jobs. Men did the more valuable administrative, management and labouring jobs that women were not seen as being able to do.

Great changes have come about in the nature of work and the nature of family life since 1928. Women are now generally given equal opportunities in education and employment – the Sex Discrimination Act of 1975 made it illegal to discriminate against women in education or employment.

However, the government's Women's Unit (2003) reports that: 'women who work full-time are paid on average just 81 percent of men's hourly earnings. Women still hold fewer top jobs and seem to profit less from promotion. Women far outnumber men in jobs like nursing and primary school teaching – often, these jobs are not highly paid. Men often get the more highly paid jobs, such as becoming head teachers, even within areas of work dominated by women. When it comes to domestic work, men still generally do less of the child care, washing and cooking, although they may do more gardening and maintenance jobs'.

THINK IT THROUGH

Look at the table below. In general, it would appear that men and women still make assumptions about who should do what within the household.

Household task	Hours and minutes per week	
	Fathers	Mothers
Cooking/preparing meals	2:50	13:30
Cleaning	2:00	13:15
Washing and ironing clothes	0:55	9:05
Spending time with the children	5:05	8:45
Shopping	2:50	5:50
Washing up	2:00	3:40
Driving children to school	1:45	2:55
Gardening	3:00	2:00
Sewing/mending clothes	0:10	1:20
Other household tasks	2:25	1:40
All household tasks	23:0	62:00

Source: Social Trends 1997

How are tasks shared between men and women in households you know?

Age

Over 20 per cent (one in five) people are over the age of 60. In 1900, if you were over 60 you would generally have been considered old. In 1900 the average life expectancy of a newborn boy was 55, and the average life expectancy of a newborn girl was 57. Today a boy might expect to live to 73 and a girl to 79. Far fewer people die young, and far more people live to be old. People live longer because of better food, better housing, better public health and better medical care.

DID YOU KNOW?

An Age Concern survey asked people when old age began. The average suggestion of 16- to 24-year-olds' was 63 years. People aged over 75 suggested age 76, and were more hesitant to give an answer at all.

Most people want a long life, but people do not want to be old. In many black and Asian societies, being an elder is a very positive thing. As an old person you may not have the physical fitness you had when young, but you have developed wisdom instead. In Britain a large number of people seem to think that being old is a very bad thing.

| ASSESSMENT ACTIVITY |

Describe the ways in which people are different from each other.

1 Get together with a team of other students to design a quiz to test your knowledge of the ways in which people are different from each other. The quiz could consist of a series of cards with numbers and questions on one side. The answers to the questions could be kept on a separate sheet. Another team could design a similar quiz and both teams could 'play each other'. Use the sections on social class, financial viability, geographical location, family structure, ethnicity, gender, and age to help you make up this quiz.

2 Working with the people in your team, imagine two different teenagers. One of these people might live in a nuclear family, with professional parents, in a high-income neighbourhood. The other person might live with an unemployed single parent in a low-income neighbourhood. How do you think these people's lives might be different? How might being male or female, black, Asian or white affect the experiences of the two people? What values and beliefs would you expect the two people to have? Write a report which lists ways in which people are different because of the effects of social class, financial ability, geographical location, family structure, ethnicity, gender and age.

To achieve a **merit grade** you need to be able to explain the effects of employment, income, culture, values and family structures on individuals. At this level your report must explain some of the ways in which employment, income, culture, values and family structures influence people's lives. Use your discussions about the two different people to help you write this report.

Modern care services

The term 'Welfare State' was originally used to describe the provision of Health and Social Care services developed by Acts of Parliament in 1948. Before 1948 people had to pay money to see a doctor or get treatment. The development of the National Health Service and Social Services meant that people could get free treatment when they needed help, because the Welfare State services were funded by taxation.

Today, the National Health Service, Local Authority Social Services, and private and voluntary organisations provide health and care services. Details of these services are discussed in Unit 3. Since 1997 the government has set out to modernise health and care services. The main ideas behind modernisation are to provide a better quality of service and choice for people by:

■ defining national standards in order to be able to measure quality

■ encouraging a mixture of public, private and voluntary provision of services at a local level

■ encouraging economy so that local services are provided at 'Best Value'

- inspecting services in order to find out how they are performing in terms of meeting targets for quality and cost and to encourage continuous improvement.

Details of the modernisation principles for standards, flexible and diverse provision are set out on the Prime Minister's Office of Public Service Reform web site at www.pm.gov.uk.

The government created the **Care Standards Act 2000** in order to improve the quality of social care. This Act created a **National Institutional Framework for Quality in Social Care**. There are now five organisations in the National Institutional Framework which aim to improve quality in social care; these are outlined below.

- **The National Care Standards Commission (NCSC)** This organisation ensures that care services meet National Minimum Standards by publishing Standards for different services and by inspecting services, investigating complaints and taking action if services fail to meet the standards. In Wales the role of the NCSC is controlled by the National Assembly for Wales.

- **The General Social Care Council (GSCC)** This organisation seeks to promote high standards of practice and training; it is responsible for codes of practice, registering social care workers and improving training for social workers.

- **The Training Organisation for Social Care** (known as **TOPSS**) This organisation contributes to the development of training standards and planning for training development.

- **The Social Care Institute of Excellence (SCIE)** This organisation provides advice and reviews research on social care.

- **The Social Services Inspectorate (SSI)** This organisation inspects the quality of local authority services and checks how government policies are working in practice.

Both the NCSC and the SSI have powers to inspect care services. In the future the government plans to have only one organisation that inspects services; this organisation will be called the **Commission for Social Care Inspection (CSCI)**. In the future, health services will be inspected by a Health Inspectorate and all other care services will be inspected by the CSCI.

The National Health Service is being modernised through the **NHS Plan**. This plan is designed to 'replace an outdated system of health care provision'. The Plan aims to undertake the following:

- Provide greater choice for the public, even including the possibility of going abroad for treatment.

■ Provide standards and Local Targets for improved services, resulting in better cancer and heart care treatment, shorter waiting times for operations and improved services for older people and people with mental health needs.

■ Provide tough inspection of services involving the creation of a new inspectorate called the **Commission for Health Improvement**.

■ Provide support for NHS staff including the provision of more GPs, consultants, therapists, scientists, nurses, midwives and health visitors. More home care will be provided by Social Services working jointly with the NHS. Staff will also be supported through improved training and better equipment and facilities.

■ More money will be available to improve services. New systems will be developed to manage health budgets and to encourage the development of community and primary care services. Money will be used to encourage the development of private sector and voluntary providers of health care services in addition to NHS service provision.

The modernisation of health and social care services will mean that in future health and social care workers will be expected to meet high standards of professional conduct. Every service will have standards or targets that have to be met. Every service will be regularly inspected. In the future it is expected that health and social care workers will have to be registered and have appropriate qualifications to enable them to register as qualified workers. There will be defined codes of practice that define the conduct expected of registered workers.

Discrimination

Discrimination means telling things apart – knowing the difference between similar things. You can discriminate between, say, a sandwich filling that you don't like and one that you do. Telling things apart is a vital part of life – if we didn't do it we wouldn't be able to live independently.

Discriminating against people has a different meaning; it doesn't mean 'telling them apart'. It is important to realise that people are all different – with different life experiences. Discriminating against people means giving people an unequal service or treatment because of their differences.

If an employer did not want to appoint a woman to a job, because she might leave to have children, the employer would be illegally discriminating against her. The discrimination would not be simply that the employer realised she was female. The discrimination would be that she was treated differently from a man who might want to start a family. A man in the same situation would be appointed; the woman gets unequal treatment because the employer thinks she might leave the job or take maternity leave to have a baby.

Discrimination can take place against people who belong to any group. Common forms of discrimination are based on race and culture, gender, age, disability and sexuality.

How does discrimination come about?

People usually feel that they belong to certain types of group. We have friendship groups, families, and some teenagers belong to gangs or clubs. People get to feel that there are 'people like me who I belong with'. There are people who share the same views, who look similar to us, who think like us. But we all meet people who are different. There is a danger of seeing people who are not like us as being threatening, stupid or disgusting. Many people then divide their social world into us and them. 'Us' is the group we feel safe and OK with. 'Them' are the people who are different; people we don't like.

People who work in care have to be interested in learning about other people; interested in diversity and difference. Carers cannot divide people into 'types that I like' and 'types that I don't like'. Carers must never exclude people from receiving a good service because they belong to a different race, culture, religion, gender or age group, or because of their sexuality or abilities.

Seeing the world in terms of 'us and them' leads to certain kinds of thinking. Discrimination sometimes comes about because of assumptions that people make in their thinking. People will sometimes stereotype or label others.

Stereotyping

Life is very complicated for everyone. Sometimes people try to make it easier by seeing others as being 'all the same'. Perhaps a younger person meets an 80-year-old who has a problem with his or her memory. Perhaps the person

Figure 1.14 *An example of stereotyped thinking*

has seen someone like that on TV – it is then easy to think that 'all old people are forgetful'. This would be a stereotype. A stereotype is a fixed way of thinking about a group of people.

People may make assumptions based on stereotyped thinking. For example, a carer working with older people might say 'I'll just go in and wash and dress this next one – I won't ask what she would like me to do because she's old and old people don't remember – so it doesn't matter what I do'. Stereotyped thinking may cause us to discriminate against people.

When people say 'all women are ...' or 'all black people are ...' or 'all gay people are ...' they will probably go on to describe a stereotype of these groups. Skilled caring starts from being interested in people's individual differences. Stereotyping lumps people together as if they were all the same. Thinking in stereotypes usually stops a person from being a good carer.

Labelling

Another way in which discrimination can be shown is labelling. Labelling is similar to stereotyping, but labels are brief and simple. Instead of having a set of fixed opinions about a group to which a person may belong, the person is summed up in just one word or term.

THINK IT THROUGH

Some years ago there was a school for children with learning difficulties. When it came to meal times, the children had to sit down for their meal. The 'slow' children were allowed to start first because they took longer. Staff would label children 'slows'. The 'slows' knew who they were, and sat down when 'slows' were called for. Some children were not very skilled with holding plates, etc., and these were labelled 'clumsies'. Children would describe themselves as 'slows' or 'clumsies'.

I am a clumsy

Figure 1.15

What effect do you think describing herself as a 'slow' or a 'clumsy' would have on a child's development of self-esteem?

Labels can be words like:

- aggressive
- emotional
- disgusting.

These words might be used to describe ethnic groups, women or old people. Labels can be used to claim that a group of people are all the same. Labels may say that people are all only one thing, such as aggressive, emotional or disgusting. When individuals are labelled, it's almost as if they stop being people – labels take away people's dignity and individuality.

Prejudice

When people live in a world of 'us' and 'them,' it becomes easy to judge people who are different from us. People who are unemployed might be judged as lazy by people who have not experienced unemployment. People who do not follow healthy lifestyles might be seen as 'stupid' by people who can manage to do the right things. It can be easy to judge and label other people. Judging other people involves thinking that we are better or superior, our views are right and that people who do not meet our standards should be criticised or punished for failing to meet our expectations.

Prejudice comes from the term 'pre-judgement', and means judging other people without the knowledge to judge properly. No new information or understanding can alter such a judgement. If people believe stereotypes about groups, they may go on to make judgements about individuals. For instance, an employer who believes that 'women don't really care about work – they only care about their family', may develop a prejudice that women aren't suited for promotion to senior positions. Employers with such a prejudice might try to promote only men. Once people develop prejudices against groups of people they are likely to discriminate against them when in a position to make decisions.

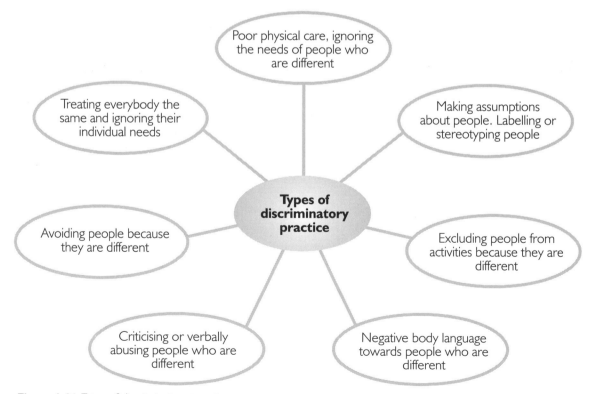

Figure 1.16 *Types of discriminatory practice*

The effects of discrimination

Carers have to make decisions about how to help others all the time they are working. If carers have prejudices or if they label or stereotype others, they may discriminate against some people in the way that they care. Some of the dangers of discrimination are listed in the diagram below.

Figure 1.17 *Effects of discrimination*

Sometimes people communicate in a way that does not show equal respect and value for others. A member of staff may not want to sit next to someone he or she has a prejudice about. People may use different body language when they have a prejudice towards someone.

Discrimination is not always obvious – very often carers simply make assumptions that everyone does, or should think like they do, and this can come out in conversation.

Service users' rights can often be ignored because of assumptions about people. For instance, the following interaction takes place at 7.30 am in a resident's bedroom in a care home.

Carer: Morning, Mabel, let's have you up, then – come on.
Resident: What time is it?
Carer: Seven thirty – time you were up and dressed for breakfast.
Resident: I want to stay in bed.
Carer: Now come on, don't give me a hard time. I have to get you up, just like everyone else. They'll say I'm not doing my job if you

stay here, and I'm not having that. (Lifts resident to side of the bed) Right now, what dress shall we have today? The blue one, that would look nice – let's help you into this.

Resident: What's for breakfast?

Carer: Bacon and egg, same as always – nice eh, I wish someone would wait on me and get my breakfast.

Resident: I don't eat bacon!

Carer: Well, you ought to be grateful – but you don't have to eat it, you know. Here, you're not one of those nutty ones who don't eat meat, are you? I hate all those moaners, never pleased whatever you do for them.

Resident: Nurr...

Carer: Right now, I'll wash your face and hands – it will be quicker, and I haven't got all day you know. After that, I'll put you on the loo while I help Rose downstairs. (Shouts down the corridor) I'm just putting this one on the loo, I won't be a minute, Rose.

This is not a pleasant way to wake up! The service user has no power – the carer does everything and decides everything. The service user's rights are not respected and the following problems arise.

1 Discrimination: The resident may not like bacon because of her ethnic customs, religious or moral beliefs. People who do not like meat are labelled 'nutty ones' by the carer. The carer is discriminating against people who do not think the way she does. The carer is also forcing opinions on a powerless service user.

2 Communication: The communication consists of orders from the carer and self-opinionated comments. It fails to value the service user and ignores what she thinks or wants. In the end, the service user is reduced to groaning 'Nurr...'.

3 Respect for others: There is no evidence of respect. The service user is accused of being 'nutty'. She is not allowed to stay in bed (although she may have been used to getting up late). The service user's routine is not respected. Finally, the service user is left on the toilet while the carer helps Rose. This must be a shock. The service user is treated like an object rather than a person.

4 Choice: The service user's rights are not respected, because she has no choice. She has no dignity, and is pulled out of bed against her wishes. The service user is not given any opportunity for independence and has to follow the carer's routine. The service user has no choice of what to wear or to eat for breakfast. Everyone gets bacon and egg.

5 Confidentiality: The service user has no right to privacy. The carer shouts down the corridor that 'this one' is being put on the toilet. Going to the

toilet is now a public event. If these problems were to go on happening through the day, the service user would have a very poor quality of life. Some people might even suggest that she would have little to live for. Non-discriminatory practice should look like this:

Carer:	Good morning, Mabel. How are you feeling this morning?
Resident:	What time is it?
Carer:	Half-past seven. Do you feel like getting up for breakfast yet?
Resident:	No, I want to say in bed a bit longer.
Carer:	That's all right. Shall I come back in half an hour?
Resident:	Mmmmm.
Carer:	See you later.
[Later]	Good morning, Mabel. It's 8 o'clock. Are you ready to get up now?
Resident:	All right.
Carer:	What would you like to wear? There's the blue dress or the white one – or the yellow top and skirt – what do you think?
Resident:	Don't know.
Carer:	Well, would the blue dress be good? It matches the colour of your eyes, you know.
Resident:	(Laughs) Come on then. What's for breakfast?
Carer:	Well, there is bacon and egg.
Resident:	I don't eat bacon.
Carer:	Oh, I'm sorry, I forgot you don't eat bacon. There are lots of things you can have – toast, cereal, or fruit, coffee, bread rolls and marmalade. What would you like?
Resident:	Don't know.
Carer:	Well, we'll go through the list when we get downstairs.
Resident:	Toast.
Carer:	OK, I'll make sure you get some toast. Would you like to wash now or later? Would you like me to help you? Do you use a flannel? Let me see if I can find it for you.

In this interaction the carer has time for the service user. Her needs are understood and she is not discriminated against. Communication is effective because the service user is respected, and she makes her own choices. There is no breaking of confidentiality.

Challenging discrimination – anti-discriminatory practice

It is very important to recognise how discrimination can happen and to make sure that we do not discriminate in our own professional practice. Professional carers also have a duty to challenge any discriminatory behaviour that they see. Anti-discrimination means taking action to stop other people being harmed or having their rights ignored.

The General Social Care Council (GSCC) code of practice for social care workers requires workers to tell their employer of any difficulties or bad practices that may lead to poor-quality care. The code also states (Section 3.2) that care workers must use 'established processes and procedures to challenge and report dangerous, abusive, discriminatory or exploitative behaviour and practice'. The code of practice for employers requires them to have policies and procedures that social care workers can use in order to report discriminatory or other dangerous practices. Employers are required to deal with these reports 'promptly, effectively and openly' (Section 4.2). The UK Central Council (UKCC) for nursing, midwifery and health visiting also has a code of professional conduct which requires that workers safeguard the well-being of patients and report unsafe practice.

Registration with the GSCC

The Care Standards Act 2000 requires that the GSCC set up a register of social workers and a register of social care workers. It is not yet known by what date all social care workers will need to be registered with the GSCC. At some point in the future all people wanting a career in care work will need to be registered. In order to register, social care workers will need to satisfy checks of criminal conviction, satisfy health checks, have appropriate qualifications and conform to the code of conduct.

Failure to meet the standards set out in the code of practice including the standards of non-discriminatory practice could result in a complaint to the GSCC. If a complaint is upheld the GSCC will have the power to caution a care worker, issue a conditional registration order (which will affect the employment of a worker), suspend the worker for a period of time, or remove the worker from the register. Suspension or removal would mean that the person would not be able to be employed by a care service.

All Health and Social Care employers will have policies and procedures that will enable discrimination to be challenged. People have specific rights to be free from discrimination established by law. The main Acts of Parliament that have established rights are:

- The Sex Discrimination Act 1975 (amended 1986)

- The Race Relations Act 1976 (amended 2000)

- Disability Discrimination Act 1995 and Disability Rights Commission Act 1999

- The Human Rights Act 1998.

Further details of this legislation and of the Commissions that people can complain to – if they believe they have been discriminated against – can be found in Unit 4.

ASSESSMENT ACTIVITY

Identify discriminatory practice, with particular reference to care settings.

1 Think about care settings you have visited or worked in; try to imagine examples of what might happen if everyone was treated the same. Then get together with other students and discuss the problems that you think might come about if:

- young children in a nursery were all treated the same

- adults with learning difficulty in a residential home were all treated the same

- old people in a care home were all treated the same.

What discriminatory assumptions might be made about ethnicity, gender and age if people are treated 'all the same'? Write a report which describes some examples of the discrimination that an individual service user could experience if staff were discriminatory.

2 While you are on placement, arrange an interview with a senior member of the care staff. Ask him or her about the organisation's policies and procedures for preventing discrimination and maintaining the rights and well-being of service users. Try to find out what a worker would be expected to do if he or she saw examples of discriminatory practice. Find out how managers in the organisation try to prevent discrimination and encourage high-quality care.

To achieve a **merit grade** you need to be able to explain the effects of discrimination on individuals in care settings. Your report must not only describe examples of discrimination but you must also explain how discrimination could harm service users. For each example of discrimination that you describe, go on to explain its effects on the well-being of the service user.

To achieve a **distinction grade** you need to explain how care settings can promote anti-discriminatory practice. Your report should include details of a care setting's policies and procedures for protecting the well-being of service users and preventing discrimination. You will need to explain how a person could go about challenging any discriminatory practice in this care setting. You should also explain how managers would support their staff in order to prevent discrimination.

The skills required of a care worker

The relationship between carer, service user and professional team members

Professionalism

A professional role is like being a character in a play. An actor has to do and say the things that their audience would expect them to do and say. Being a professional carer means that what you do and say has to fit the expectations of the people who have expectations of you.

THINK IT THROUGH

If you work as a carer, who will have expectations as to how you should behave? There may be a large range of people, but usually this will include the service users, managers, other staff, relatives and other professionals who work with service users.

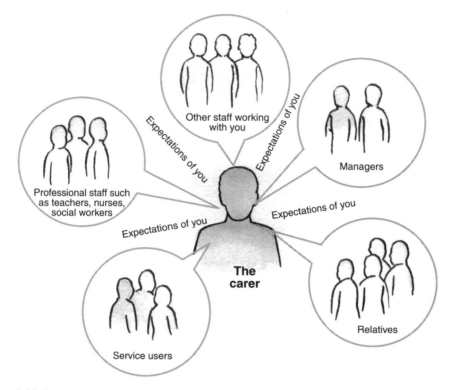

Figure 1.18 *As a carer, other people will expect you to behave as a professional*

Each care role may involve different expectations. Not everyone will expect exactly the same things. The following are some general expectations of professional behaviour.

- Carers must respect that people are different from each other or 'diverse'. Carers must be careful not to discriminate against people because of differences.

- Carers must maintain confidentiality.

- Carers must show respect for service users and their rights, including the right to control their own life and make choices.

- Carers should develop good communication skills and make appropriate relationships with service users.

- While at work, carers have to work to meet the needs of employers and service users rather than putting their own wishes first.

■ Carers should check and think about the work they do with people. Care work is not always easy and it involves lifelong learning.

Many care workers will have NVQ qualifications. The NVQ 'value base' unit defines some of the skills that care workers have to use. The key principles of the care value base are set out in the diagram below.

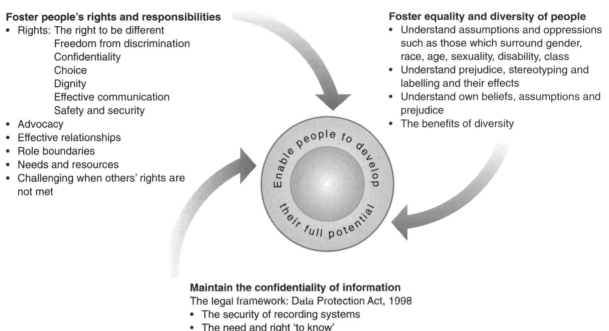

Foster people's rights and responsibilities
- Rights: The right to be different
  Freedom from discrimination
  Confidentiality
  Choice
  Dignity
  Effective communication
  Safety and security
- Advocacy
- Effective relationships
- Role boundaries
- Needs and resources
- Challenging when others' rights are not met

Foster equality and diversity of people
- Understand assumptions and oppressions such as those which surround gender, race, age, sexuality, disability, class
- Understand prejudice, stereotyping and labelling and their effects
- Understand own beliefs, assumptions and prejudice
- The benefits of diversity

Enable people to develop their full potential

Maintain the confidentiality of information
The legal framework: Data Protection Act, 1998
- The security of recording systems
- The need and right 'to know'
- Confidentiality can value and protect a client
- Policies, procedures and guidelines
- Boundaries and tensions in maintaining confidentiality

Figure 1.19 *The Care Value Base*

The care value base defines how qualified carers must behave. There are three main elements in this definition:

1 Foster equality and diversity: Carers must value the ways in which people are different. They must understand the prejudices, stereotypes and assumptions that can cause discrimination.

2 Foster people's rights and responsibilities: People have the right to their own beliefs and lifestyles. No one has the right to damage the quality of other people's lives.

3 Maintain the confidentiality of information: Confidentiality is a basic human right, but is so important that it has become a specific principle of the value base. The Data Protection Acts 1984 and 1998, the Access to Personal Files Act 1987 and the Access to Health Records Act 1990, made it a legal requirement that health and social care agencies keep service users' details confidential.

The General Social Care Council (GSCC) code of practice for social care workers

The GSCC has designed a list of statements that describe the standards of practice required of social care workers. This code is designed to apply to all social care workers in the UK. A summary table of the principles in this code is set out below.

You must:

. . . be accountable for the quality of your work and take responsibility for maintaining and improving your knowledge and skills. (Meet standards, maintain appropriate records and inform employers of personal difficulties. Seek assistance and co-operate with colleagues, recognise responsibility for delegated work, respect the roles of others, and undertake relevant training.)

. . . uphold public trust and confidence in social care services. (Not abuse, neglect, or exploit service users or colleagues or form inappropriate personal relationships. Not discriminate or condone discrimination, place self or others at unnecessary risk. Not behave in a way that raises suitability issues. Not abuse the trust of others in relation to confidentiality.)

. . . establish and maintain the trust and confidence of service users. (Maintain confidentiality, use effective communication, honour commitments and agreements, declare conflicts of interest and adhere to policies about accepting gifts.)

. . . protect the rights and promote the interests of service users and carers. (Respect individuality and support service users in controlling their own lives. Respect and maintain equal opportunities, diversity, dignity and privacy.)

. . . promote the independence of service users while protecting them from danger or harm. (Maintain rights, challenge and report dangerous, abusive, discriminatory, or exploitative behaviour. Follow safe practice, report resource problems, report unsafe practice of colleagues, follow health and safety regulations, help service users to make complaints and use power responsibly.)

. . . respect the rights of service users while seeking to ensure that their behaviour does not harm themselves or other people. (Recognise the right to take risks, follow risk assessment policies, minimise risks, ensure others are informed about risk assessments.)

Figure 1.20 *GSCC Standards of practice*

People who receive care services are usually vulnerable. Being vulnerable means to be at risk of being harmed. If people's needs are not met by carers then people may be harmed; or deprived of the quality of life they might otherwise have had. All people have the right to be cared for in a way that improves their quality of life.

Children

Young children are developing physically, intellectually, emotionally and socially all the time. In order to develop, children need to feel that they are physically and emotionally safe. Children need contact with loving and caring adults. They need to be able to form relationships with adults who care for them. They need to feel that they belong within a group of caring people. Children need to find interesting and mentally stimulating activities to assist with their intellectual development.

If young children receive quality care, they are likely to grow up with a sense of being worth something – a sense of self-worth. If children grow up in a caring setting, they should grow to like who they are, to be confident and to have self-esteem.

When children do not receive good care, they may fail to develop a sense of belonging, they may feel very negative about themselves, and they may lack a sense of being worth anything. Children are vulnerable – their sense of who they are can be strongly influenced by the type of care they receive.

The carer is intimately involved with the child – giving the child a sense of belonging, of being loved and important.

Figure 1.21 *Encouraging a child's social and emotional development*

THINK IT THROUGH

In Figure 1.21, how are the child's care needs being met?

The child's intellectual development can be helped by the exciting 'things to do' offered by the toy. The child's social and emotional development is encouraged by the carer who is using his relationship and communication skills with the child. Children who do not receive good care, may not develop so positively.

Figure 1.22 *Ignoring a child's needs*

THINK IT THROUGH

What is wrong in Figure 1.22?

The carer's attention is focused on the TV – not on the child. The child is strapped into her chair, even though she is not tired. There is little activity to support physical or intellectual development. There is no sense of love or belonging for the child. If this child is often treated in this way, she may not develop fully. Children's development is influenced by the quality of care that they receive – children are vulnerable people.

Adults with learning disabilities

Adults need a sense of who they are. This sense of self depends on a feeling that you belong with other people and that you have value and worth. It is important that adults develop a sense of self-esteem – a sense of liking who they are. A sense of who you are develops through making choices. Most adults choose what they want to eat, when they want to eat, what they want to wear, who they want to talk to and so on.

Children are often not trusted to make good decisions about food and clothes. Parents may say things like 'You have to eat your dinner before you can have sweets to eat.' 'You have to wear your coat to school – you will get cold if you don't.'

As people grow up they need to make their own choices and become independent. Adults usually feel angry and hurt if they get treated like children – it is hard to develop self-esteem if you are not allowed to make your own choices.

People with a learning disability will need advice and guidance to do things. There is a danger that carers can 'take over' and not treat them as adults. It can be easy to think 'these people need help and guidance – children also need help and guidance – so these people should be cared for as if they were children.'

Older people

Many, if not most, adults establish a sense of belonging, a sense of self-worth and self-esteem during their adult life. Most adults are used to organising their own lives; they may feel that their life has been important. People may take pride in their family or in their career, or in leisure activities that give a sense of achievement.

In later life there are many changes that can threaten to harm self-worth and self-esteem. When their children grow up and move away, some older people feel they are no longer important as parents. Sometimes when people retire, they lose the self-esteem that their job gave them. If people lose their partner, the loss can make them feel that they are no longer the valuable person they used to be. When people can no longer cope alone – when they need day or residential care – there can be a feeling of a loss of self-worth and self-esteem. Losing a home can be very damaging to a person's sense of who he or she is. A few older people become ill or develop disabilities. All these threats and losses can add up to make elderly people feel vulnerable, lose self-confidence and self-esteem, and feel worried and threatened about the future.

Carers working with older people need to understand the emotions they may have. Skilled care involves getting to know individuals and showing respect for their rights. Skilled relationship and conversation work can help people to a sense of worth and self-esteem, even though they are facing difficult challenges.

If service users are receiving care because they are vulnerable, one of the main purposes of care must be to prevent service users from suffering disadvantage or damage. Care workers have a responsibility to protect service users from physical harm and to ensure that basic physical and safety needs are met. If service users went without food or if they were injured it would be obvious that they were not cared for. But service users' rights go much further than safety and physical care. Caring includes the service users' needs for a sense of belonging and their needs for self-esteem and self-worth. The development and maintenance of the service users' sense of self lies at the heart of caring. Service users should be in control of their own lives, as much as possible. Service users should be given the power (empowered) to control their own lives as far as it is possible to do this.

Professionalism and the rights of service users

There are a range of rights that are set out in NVQ standards and the GSCC code of practice. **National Minimum Standards** have been produced for a range of care settings under the Care Standards Act 2000 and these standards define the quality of care that service users may expect. Local employers' policy documents will refer to the principles established by the National Care Standards Commission and the GSCC. Basic human needs can be described as shown in the pyramid below. Respecting people's rights will help to meet the needs that people have.

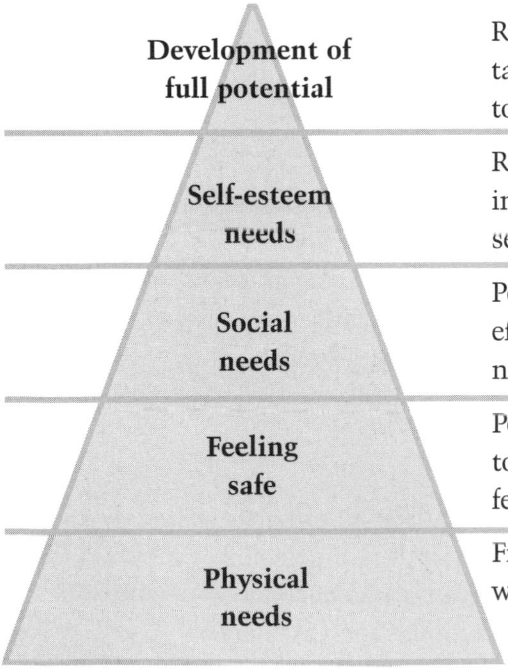

Development of full potential	Respect for individuality and support to help people take control of their own lives will often be necessary to help service users develop their full potential
Self-esteem needs	Respect for diversity, dignity and privacy will be very important in helping people to develop or maintain a sense of self-esteem
Social needs	People need to be able to trust their carers and receive effective communication in order to meet their social needs
Feeling safe	People need to be free from discrimination, have a right to confidentiality and be free from risks if they are to feel safe
Physical needs	Freedom from abuse and neglect will be important, as well as food and shelter in order to meet physical needs

Figure 1.23 *Human needs (based on Maslow's theory)*

Valuing diversity (the right to be different)

Care work involves supporting service users as they develop a clear sense of who they are and a feeling of self-worth. People are different from one another because of their age, gender, sexuality, where they live, their race, health, abilities and class, among other things. People have different values and beliefs based on their culture, political beliefs, religion and the social groups they belong to. People also have different personalities – they enjoy different things and develop different ways of understanding life. Two people can live in the same family, go to the same school, have similar life experiences and yet develop quite different attitudes and beliefs about themselves.

Care work involves celebrating the fact that people are different or 'diverse' – understanding and enjoying the fact that people have different beliefs and views. People should never be expected to be all the same, or to fit in with the views of a care worker. Carers need to avoid making assumptions or judgements about what is normal or what is the right way to live.

Freedom from discrimination

Receiving a worse service than others because of your age, gender, race, sexuality or ability would strike at the heart of a service user's sense of belonging, self-esteem and self-worth. When services or workers make assumptions about people, discrimination can easily follow. Architects in the 1960s designed buildings with steps and stairs – without lifts or ramps. Part of the reason they did this was that they thought 'everyone walks – like me and the people I know'. Architects didn't hate or want to discriminate against people in wheelchairs – they simply didn't think about it, so disabled people were discriminated against. Making assumptions that everyone eats the same food or everyone celebrates the same religious festivals results in people being excluded and discriminated against. Discrimination damages a sense of belonging and self-esteem.

It is important to find out about individuals and try to check that our own personal behaviour and the service we provide meets the needs of people. Where services do not provide equal quality to different groups of people it is important to challenge discrimination, first by raising the issue with managers. There should be a policy in every care setting to help prevent discrimination.

The right to confidentiality

Care services have to keep detailed information on service users in order to meet their needs. Care workers also have to find out a great deal of personal information about service users in order to ensure they can work effectively and not discriminate against people. It is vital that this information is shared only with people who have a genuine need to know it.

If care workers were to pass information on to friends, neighbours or members of the public, it could have the following effects:

- service users could feel that they didn't matter, and their sense of belonging and self-esteem could be damaged if they thought personal details could become public.

- service users could lose trust in a care worker if they thought their personal details were being discussed by others.

- service users could lose control over their lives if relatives or neighbours knew details of their medical conditions and made assumptions. For instance, if neighbours found out that a person had cancer, they might assume that he or she would go into hospital and perhaps die. It could be difficult for the service user to deal with this.

- service users' property and personal safety could be at risk if information became known to the wrong people about their savings and where they keep their money or valuables. If it becomes public knowledge that a service user keeps a door key under a flowerpot in the front garden, the service user could be burgled. If a service user is known to be forgetful, he or she could be exploited by criminals on the lookout for a potential victim.

The right to independence

A sense of self, a sense of belonging and self-esteem are often developed or maintained by involving service users in their own care as much as possible. Wherever possible, service users should be helped to take control of their own care. When people cannot do things for themselves they can still be asked to say how they would like care to be given. Wherever possible, service users should be given the power (empowered) to do things for themselves. Feeling independent may increase a person's self-esteem. Feeling out of control may threaten a service user, increase his or her vulnerability and reduce self-esteem.

If people are to be independent then they must be free to make choices. Part of being an adult is to make day-to-day choices about personal appearance, diet, and so on. Where people have serious disabilities or illnesses, or when they are very young, care workers sometimes limit what they are allowed to do, usually for health and safety reasons. Where service users are deliberately restricted there should be clear reasons for doing this, and normally those reasons should be recorded in writing so that they can be checked. Where service users have difficulty in expressing their wishes, care workers should try to find ways of helping them to choose what they want or need.

If a person feels that his or her wishes and needs are not being respected this is likely to damage that person's sense of belonging and self-esteem.

Dignity and privacy

For people to feel that they belong and that they are worth something, they need to receive respect. People may need assistance with very personal tasks in a care setting. They may need help with eating food, help to dress and wash, and help to use the toilet. With all these activities it isn't just a matter of getting the task done – the way the task is done matters very much.

Showing respect for other people involves understanding their feelings and wishes. Respect involves ensuring that service users have privacy when undressing, washing or going to the toilet. Respect involves not expressing negative attitudes towards difficulties that service users may have with eating, washing, dressing and toileting.

The right to effective communication

Respecting diversity, avoiding discrimination, showing respect for dignity and offering choices all depend on understanding the service users you work with. Before we can understand people, it is necessary to communicate with them. Communication is not just a matter of giving and receiving messages – it requires active listening as well as appropriate verbal and non-verbal skills. If service users do not feel that they are understood and listened to, they are unlikely to develop a sense of belonging.

The right to security and safety

If you are afraid or worried, you will not be developing a sense of belonging or self-esteem. If you feel in danger, the first thing you may want is to feel safe again! Service users have a right to feel that they are safe from risks of pain and abuse. They have a right to expect that they will not suffer accidents or harm whilst receiving care, and that their property is safe in care settings.

Rights and responsibilities

Rights of individuality, freedom from discrimination, confidentiality, choice, dignity, independence, effective communication and safety all protect individual well-being and encourage self-development and self-esteem.

Rights usually carry responsibilities with them – they are balanced with responsibilities because membership of a community involves both. Service users can expect respect, but they have a responsibility not to interfere with or damage other service users' rights. They have a right to be free from discrimination, but also a responsibility not to discriminate against others.

One way to understand this idea of rights and responsibilities is to think about the issue of smoking. Adults have a right to choose to smoke even though smoking usually damages health and might shorten a person's life. Smokers have a responsibility to make sure other people do not have to breathe in their

Figure 1.24

smoke. This means that in most places today, smoking is allowed only in specially set-aside areas.

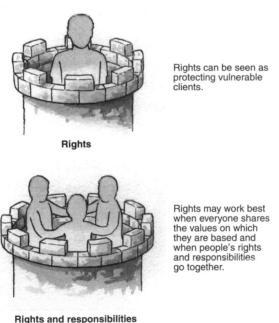

Rights can be seen as protecting vulnerable clients.

Rights

Rights may work best when everyone shares the values on which they are based and when people's rights and responsibilities go together.

Rights and responsibilities

Figure 1.25 *Rights and responsibilities go together*

Usually, little is said about service users' responsibilities because they have less power than staff and the managers of services. Service users are generally vulnerable, while care workers usually have a degree of control over their own lives. Just because a person is vulnerable, it doesn't mean they have a right to interfere with other people's rights, or for instance threaten people with racist or sexist behaviour.

It is a care worker's responsibility to respect service user rights, but in turn care workers should expect to enjoy similar rights in their place of work. It is a manager's responsibility to check that service users' rights are respected, but once again managers can expect to be treated with respect, not be discriminated against and to have a safe working environment.

Professional roles of a carer

Time management

Different people expect different things from you as a care worker. Service users will often want you to spend time and give your attention to them. Many service users feel special if you can spare time to listen and talk with them. Managers will expect that, as well as doing this, you will do all the tasks that are needed for all the other service users. Other professionals will want you to understand how busy they are and perhaps hope that you have the time to do things that they can't – like spending time talking to service users. Relatives will expect you to put their child, relative or parent first, perhaps before other service users.

People will all expect different things from you. Carers often have difficulty being able to please everyone!

1 Mrs Benson calls you over. 'Could you take me down the corridor in a wheelchair please?' 'Oh, but the nurse said that walking was good for your circulation,' you reply. 'Never mind all that – I'm 86 years old and it's just too much for me. It's my choice, and I want you to wheel me down!'

   Who do you please, the nurse or Mrs Benson?

2 You are working in a small hostel, and one of the residents comes to you looking sad. She holds your hand, hoping for attention, saying she is 'not well'. This means she is not feeling happy. Just at this moment another carer puts his head round the door and says 'Give us a hand with the shopping, can you?'

   Which do you put off for a moment, the service user or your colleague?

1 With Mrs Benson you have to balance her health needs – assessed by the nurse – for walking as exercise, against her wish to use the wheelchair. If she always uses the wheelchair she may lose her ability to walk. If she doesn't get her way and have the wheelchair, she will feel her rights have not

Figure 1.26 *Care roles involve balancing different people's expectations to get the best results*

been respected. She may lose self-esteem if her wishes are ignored. A balanced answer might be to agree her wishes now but offer to help her with walking on other occasions – or to ask her to discuss the issue with a manager and/or the nurse as soon as possible.

2 In this situation you could try to find out whether you can help with the shopping in 'just a minute'. Or you may be able to leave the service user and come back. You have to balance the service user's needs against the needs of your colleague.

It is important to manage your time so that you can work efficiently with a range of people. It is always possible to explain that you need to leave someone and be polite – perhaps offering to return at a later date.

Giving effective care means meeting people's needs (including needs outlined in their plan of care). Effective care always develops a sense of belonging and self-esteem. Giving effective care takes time. If you work with one child or adult all day, you would get to know each other really well. If you had only one person to work with, you might understand their needs in detail. You might find it easy to encourage the development of their self-esteem.

Many caring jobs involve working with a large number of people. Working efficiently means providing a service for everyone to an equal standard. Carers often have to achieve a balance between the efficiency of their work (giving everyone a service) and their effectiveness at meeting individual, social and emotional needs.

THINK IT THROUGH

Suppose you had to work in a residential setting and you had to assist ten people to get up, wash, dress and feed. Efficient care might mean achieving all this practical care in the least possible time,

An extreme form of efficiency might be to burst into residents' rooms and do everything for them without wasting time talking or asking questions. Residents could be left on the toilet while you worked with other people to save time. It might save time to feed residents rather than letting them do this for themselves. Such behaviour would save time, but it would be very uncaring and very ineffective. Residents might become angry or depressed, their rights to choice and dignity would be denied; they would not have self-esteem.

A very effective form of caring would be to sit with people, chat to them, gently support people to choose what to wear, how to wash and so on. This takes a lot of time. Caring usually has to balance the degree of effectiveness with the need to give a service to a number of people. Carers always have to respect the dignity and rights of service users, but at some points of the day it is not possible to restrict attention and care only to one person.

Carers have to think about the needs of all the people that they work with and plan to have enough time to provide an equal quality service for all service users. A carer working with children will need to make sure that he or she gives time and attention to all the children, not just the interesting or demanding children.

As well as balancing the pressures of time with the need to give effective care, carers have to be clear about the boundaries of their role.

Boundaries

A boundary is like a fence – it marks where your role ends. You can think of a boundary as the line between your caring role and your ordinary relationships.

> *A boundary is a line you go up to – but should not cross over.*

Boundaries of the care-worker role clarify what you should not be expected to do. Deciding on the boundaries of your role means that you need to decide the limits of what you can do and what you should refuse to do. If you are at work or on a placement, then understanding the boundaries of your care role may be an important task. Setting boundaries may help you to feel safe and comfortable with the pressures that the caring role might place on you.

Whether you work with children, people with learning disabilities, or other adults, there are some general boundary areas. You need to decide:

- how much time it is right for you to give service users

- how far you should become emotionally involved with service users' needs

- how far you should tell your service users about your own life history, lifestyle and feelings

- how much practical support you should provide for certain individuals.

Self-presentation

Carers need to behave appropriately in order to show respect for service users. Many people spend a great deal of time and money trying to look good – sometimes people want to attract attention, to shock others or to be different. It is important to celebrate differences in people and care workers will want to dress in a way that acknowledges their cultural and lifestyle differences. However, there is an important issue to consider as a member of a care team. Team members are employed to care for others, not to be the centre of attention themselves.

Clothing which is designed to shock, to make the wearer look sexually attractive or frightening, may be OK at a club or party, but within a care setting it can send the message: 'I'm the important person, I'm the one to look at – not you service users.' The way carers present themselves to service users and other staff should convey respect for their rights. In turn, others have a responsibility to respect cultural diversity.

Self-presentation includes personal hygiene, which means clean hair, teeth, hands and nails. Many service users or relatives may view body odour or a dirty appearance in a carer as a sign of not caring about others. Carers need to be sensitive to the messages that their appearance sends and need to consider health and safety.

- Flat shoes are necessary when lifting or physically supporting people. High-heeled shoes can increase the risk of falling or twisting an ankle.

- Long earrings could be dangerous – children could pull them or they could become caught in clothing.

- Necklaces and ties can get caught in service users' clothing or dangle into food.

- Some rings, especially those with stones, may provide an opportunity for bacteria to collect or might tear protective gloves.

- Long hair can brush over service users' faces and perhaps touch food – it may need to be tied back.

- Personal habits should include careful washing of hands to prevent the spread of infection. Lifestyle habits such as smoking need to be carefully thought through. Many parents may be concerned that their children may grow up to copy what they see adults around them doing. If you smoke in front of children, you may be sending a message that smoking is good. Parents may find this offensive.

- It is important to use skilled listening techniques based on an understanding of the communication cycle. Non-verbal body language should show respect for service users and colleagues. Further details of communication skills can be found in Unit 4.

As a care worker you need to check policies on self-presentation with senior staff. There can be variations in policies between different settings.

Reviewing own performance

Why reviewing own performance is important

Caring for vulnerable people is not a simple task. People have complex feelings and thoughts, and each person is unique. Because people can vary so much, and because people's needs are different, care work involves constant learning.

If people were not complicated – if they were all the same, then it would be necessary to learn only a few simple rules and procedures in order to do a good job. Because each person has individual needs, it is important to get to know them individually. In order to care for a person you have to learn about their situation, their needs and their life. The UKCC and the GSCC both have codes of practice that require care workers to undertake relevant training or professional up-dating as part of the professional duty of a carer.

Good caring involves constant learning. How do you learn about people?

■ Do you read about theories of needs and behaviour?

■ Do you sit in a comfortable chair and think about care work?

■ Do you get into discussion groups and talk about care work with others?

■ Do you work with service users – talk to them and listen to them?

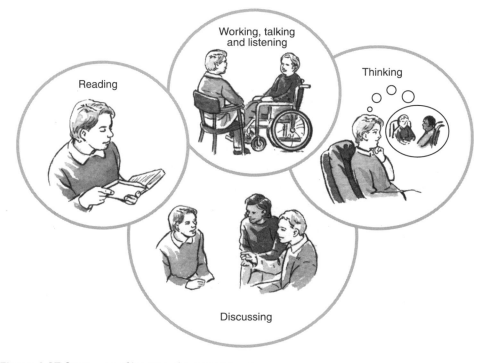

Figure 1.27 *Some ways of learning about service users*

All these ways of working could be useful. Many people would say that the best place to start would be to actually do the work – talk and listen to service users. But the very best way of learning about people's needs is to use all the ideas listed above.

Working with people gives you experience, lets you learn naturally by watching other people and copying the way they do things. If you listen to the people you work with, you may get some feedback on how good your practice is. Gradually, you can change what you do – until things seem to work well.

Working with people gives you 'know-how' on care work.

Sitting and thinking is useful because it is only by thinking things over that people realise what is going on. Sometimes difficulties can be sorted out if you think things over, and thinking things through often helps you to feel confident about your ideas. If you picture things you have done, you can work out why certain things happened, and it can help you to see things from other people's point of view. Thinking things through can help us to have new ideas.

Thinking about your work with others can help make sense of things and help you plan for the future.

Discussing care work is a great way of learning – when people work on their own, they are likely to develop assumptions. We can all develop stereotypes, label others and even become prejudiced if we never check our ideas with other people. Other people are not always cleverer or better than we are; it is just that discussing things often helps us to understand things better. There is an old saying: 'I know what I think when I hear what I say.'

Discussion is useful because it can help to make things clearer – it can help to check assumptions in our thinking.

Reading and going on courses is useful because books and teachers may have new ideas, information or ways of looking at things, all of which can help in understanding the situations or needs that carers work with.

Reading is useful because it can help give new ideas and understanding of care issues.

Emotions and working with people

The great thing about working with people is that they are all so different and each person provides a new learning situation, but having to find out about each child in a nursery, each adult in a day or residential centre, takes energy. It is always easier just to see people as being similar, and not to get too involved.

Not thinking about work, not discussing it, not reviewing your own performance saves emotional energy – but it can lead to a feeling that care work is boring. Once work seems boring, negative feelings about people and tasks take over. Emotions connected with boredom can make us want to give up and withdraw.

One reason for reviewing your own performance is so that you don't begin to see service users as 'all the same' and feel the boredom that can go with this.

Working with people creates a lot of emotions and feelings – some of them nice and some not so nice. Some people we work with will be good to us – they may praise us, and tell us that they like us. Working with interesting, attractive or kind people may make us feel good. But many people who receive care will be worried or even depressed or upset; these people may not always be rewarding to work with. Our first emotional reaction may be to want to avoid them. When we have to work with a difficult child it is only natural to feel 'I don't want to – I'd rather do something else'.

Figure 1.28 *Emotions and professional behaviour*

If we are to work in a professional way then we have to be sure that we don't follow the emotional urge to withdraw, but instead find ways of coping. Why does the child not want to do the activity? Is the child bored, frustrated? If we can think through some answers, we may be able to understand why the child is 'difficult'. If we can understand, we can cope with our emotions.

> *One reason for reviewing your own performance is to prevent negative emotions from blocking professional behaviour.*

Thinking a situation through can help us to solve problems. Why does a child throw his or her work on the floor? There could be many different reasons. Talking to other staff or to senior staff may help us to understand. Involving other people will probably help us to understand people we work with. Talking to the child may help us to understand. Observing what happens during the day may help. Thinking about our own behaviour – how good we are at talking or listening – may also help us to understand.

> *One reason for reviewing your own performance is to solve problems we face.*

You will have attitudes and beliefs and ways of understanding people based on your own life experience. It is possible that carers can make assumptions about other people – perhaps that they are bad or dangerous. Assumptions can turn into stereotypes and pre-judgements about other people. In the end there is a danger that service users can be judged, labelled and discriminated against because they are different.

One reason for reviewing your own performance is to recognise assumptions in your thinking and to prevent these assumptions turning into discrimination and pre-judgements.

It is very difficult to check our own thoughts alone. A good way to check our assumptions is to discuss practice with colleagues, tutors or workplace supervisors. Skilled supervisors may be able to help us question assumptions in our thinking.

How to review your own performance

It is often difficult to understand how we influence the people we care for. After we have been working with someone it is useful to stop and think about the work we have done. Sometimes discussing our work with supervisors, managers or other staff can be helpful to get new ideas. If we get new ideas they can be tried out in practice to see if they are right. When people have a problem to solve they sometimes go through a process like the one shown in Figure 1.29.

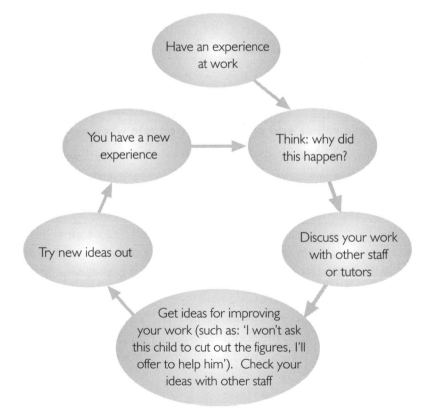

Figure 1.29 *A problem-solving process*

The important thing is to think about your experiences and learn from them. It is easy to forget our experiences and learn nothing from them if we don't think about them and discuss them. The main ways to review your own performance are to think about your work and discuss your work.

1 Think about the reactions you get from service users – try to imagine how they see you. What does service users' non-verbal behaviour towards you mean? What do service users say to you? How effective is your care work at meeting service users' needs, including needs to belong and needs for self-esteem?

2 Review your work by discussing your views of service users' needs and your work with them. You might discuss your practice with your work supervisor, a tutor or with colleagues.

When and where to review your work

Reviewing work is part of learning and developing care skills. Reviewing could take place at work, but you can think and discuss anywhere. College work should help you to review your practice, and the more you review practice, the more you may learn. Many work settings organise formal supervision or training sessions to help staff review their practice. Some work settings may use team meetings to discuss some practice issues. If months go by without any thinking about or any discussion of practice, then the risks of boredom, stress, negative behaviour towards service users, prejudice, discrimination and unmet care needs all increase.

Supervisors, managers, colleagues and tutors should be able to help you review your practice.

ASSESSMENT ACTIVITY

Describe the basic values and principles for people working in care.

1 Use the description of the NVQ Value Base, the GSCC Code of Practice and contents of this unit to make your own list of the values and principles that people working in care must follow. Share your list with other students in order to check that you have included all the important issues.

2 Think of a vulnerable service user you have met on placement. Use your list of values and principles to think about the needs of this service user. Were this person's social and emotional needs met by the way they were treated in care? What might have

happened to this person if the staff had not behaved according to the values and principles on your list? Discuss your ideas with other students, and with tutors and placement supervisors if possible, so that you can check that you have not missed important ideas. Remember to keep details of the service user confidential.

3 Visit several different care settings and find out about their policies and procedures for providing quality care. Try to arrange to talk to staff about the values and principles of caring. You might ask about policies to

prevent discrimination, policies on staff meetings, record keeping and staff training, supervision and feedback to staff on their performance. If appropriate, ask about the GSCC Code of Practice and how this code is being implemented and monitored. Some care services may have a booklet or a leaflet which can be given to service users which explains the entitlements that service users may expect. Compare the different information that you can get from different care settings.

Using the list you made for activity 1, write a report that describes the basic values and principles for people working in care. Use the work you did for activity 2 so that your report can go on to explain how the values and principles of care settings can affect service users. Use the work you did for activity 3 to further develop your report, so that it compares ways in which different care settings promote the values and principles of care practice.

To achieve a **merit grade** you must identify the ways in which the values and principles of care settings affect individuals.

To achieve a **distinction grade** you must compare ways in which different care settings promote the values and principles of care practice.

Responsibilities of the individual carer

As well as forming professional relationships with service users, it is important to form them with the team of people with whom you work. Even if you work in the community providing care in service users' own homes, you will probably have a team that you belong to.

Being in a team

Teams are important in care work because it is hard to provide good-quality care on your own – support and help from others is needed to provide constant, effective care. Good teams share values and understandings about the purpose of care.

THINK IT THROUGH

Story one: Placement heaven

You arrive for your first day in a small residential centre, and you are greeted by your supervisor. She is very friendly and has time to spare – she gets you a cup of coffee and sits down with you. She tells you about the home and explains who the residents are and how the home tries to respect their rights and meet their needs. She talks about the importance of understanding individual needs and the importance of confidentiality. You are invited to sit in on a team meeting. The meeting includes some administrative issues but also a discussion of some of the residents' needs. Each member of staff looks interested. The staff don't necessarily agree, but they all listen to each other. You can tell from the smiles and eye contact that the staff all care about each other's feelings. They also care about how you feel, and are concerned that you should feel included in their group, even though you don't know much about the home. The manager seems to get on well with the staff, and there is some humour in the group. At the end of the meeting you feel welcome – you feel good about working with these people.

Story two: Placement hell

You arrive for your first day in a small residential centre, and no one knows who you are or why you're there. One staff member says: 'You want to work in care – you must be mad. Anyway, you can come with me, and I'll show you how it's done – I could do with some help, because they leave all the work to me and Iris, you know, the other lot. I came in this morning, and they hadn't even got that end one up – not by 8.30 – I had to do it all. They spend their time jawing away – don't know what work is. Are you on one of those college courses, then? All a lot of nonsense, you know – there's no time here, you've just got to get 'em all up, wash 'em, feed 'em, clean 'em up when it comes out the other end (you know what I mean) and put 'em to bed again. Topping and tailing them, that's what I call it. Yes, it would be lovely to sit round all day talking about it, but who does all the work then!'

In story one there is a team:

■ the team shows respect for individuals

■ the team values equality

■ the team respects self-esteem needs

■ the team has good communication skills

■ the team believes that to give good-quality care you have to benefit from a caring approach by others

■ the team believes that service users have rights, staff have rights, and managers have rights.

Because the staff in story one care for each other, they also care effectively for the residents – they share professional values about skilled caring.

In story two the carer thinks care is about physical needs only, and there is no team:

■ the staff do not trust each other

■ the staff do not share the same values about rights and responsibilities

■ the staff member quoted sees working with people as 'topping and tailing them' – like fish in a canning factory

■ the staff do not feel that they belong

- the staff do not feel a sense of self-esteem

- in this situation the staff are unlikely to care about the self-esteem of people working on placement.

Because it is important for team members to work together, it is important for each carer to be committed to professional conduct and values. To become a member of a team you will need to understand the values of that team.

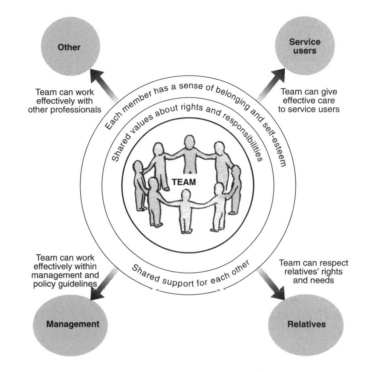

Figure 1.30 *Teams need to share values and support each other*

Team values and expectations

Teams in care settings should value:

- the diversity and equality of people

- anti-discriminatory practice (being prepared to challenge discrimination)

- the rights of service users – especially to self-esteem and independence

- confidentiality.

Together with these values, most teams will expect members to:

- present themselves in a way that shows respect for service users, relatives and other staff, and in a way that shows an understanding of safety issues

- maintain health and safety for all

- be reliable, punctual and show commitment to the team, including attending meetings

- maintain the security of service users and property that belongs to both service users and the service

- join in both the practical work and the administrative work that the team has to do

- understand and work within care plan guidance

- understand their own role and be able to prioritise what is important in the job (time management) and show flexibility where necessary

- be able to review their own skills, recognise limitations and ask for help from others when necessary

- be willing to listen and communicate effectively with others, including being able to report and record events.

Being reliable and showing commitment

Most teams of staff have a heavy workload. If you turn up late or not at all, or if you don't let people know where you are, this leaves other people to do work that they were expecting you to do. Even if other people can cover for you, it sends a message: 'I don't care about the team – I don't want to be with you anyway.' It is not always possible to be punctual, and sometimes transport problems prevent people from getting to work or meetings on time. It is always important to apologise and offer a brief explanation for lateness – sending the message: 'I do care about colleagues.' If you are ill, you should always telephone to explain and let people know the situation, so that they can plan ahead. This also lets people know that you care about belonging with them. It is unprofessional not to let colleagues know when they expect you and you can't keep your appointment.

Joining in administrative work

Being a member of a team means sharing the practical and administrative work of the team. If care work is right for you, you will enjoy building relationships with people and probably enjoy a lot of the practical work and activities. But not everyone enjoys the necessary report-writing and record-keeping.

Reports and records can be very important, however. Records of how children behave, what people with learning difficulties can do, the needs of older people, and so on, help staff to know if care and care plans are meeting objectives. When staff change over on work shifts, it is important that they know what has happened while you were caring for a service user. Written records provide evidence that procedures were correctly followed. It is necessary to record details of all accidents and incidents in care that may need to be investigated.

Report-writing and record-keeping are skills. When you explain something in speech, other people can always ask you questions if they are not sure what you mean, and when you speak your non-verbal messages often give the listener a good idea of what you mean.

THINK IT THROUGH

Perhaps you are working with children and you say: 'Sam had a bad temper this afternoon – he hit me!' The listener could ask questions like: 'Did he hit you hard?' and your non-verbal behaviour would also help to explain how serious the incident was. If you were smiling while you spoke you would send a message saying: 'It's OK – it wasn't a real problem.'

When you have to write reports it is much harder to be sure other people will understand what you mean. Suppose you wrote a report including the comment 'Sam had a bad temper and hit me'. When someone else reads these words later, they will not know exactly what happened – were you hurt, did he become violent and threaten the other children, or did he accidentally touch you when he was feeling angry or frustrated?

The problem with written language is that people have to imagine what words mean when they read them. People often form a mental picture in their heads, based on what they read. Somebody having a bad temper can mean different things. Writing that someone is confused, demented or angry, does not give a clear message, because words like 'confused' can mean different things. A confused person could be a bit forgetful, or seriously physically ill, or very distressed, crying and shouting out. Different people build different pictures in their minds.

When writing reports about people's behaviour, you should:

- say what you saw
- say what you heard
- be as clear as possible
- not put your own interpretation into your report.

Going back to the example above about Sam, the report writer should write a description like this: 'Sam threw his pencils on the floor and slapped my arm gently. When I asked him why he did this, he just looked at me and then looked away.'

Care plans

Under the National Health Service and Community Care Act (1990), service users are entitled to have their needs assessed. Needs include physical, social, financial, transport, mental health, accommodation, education and cultural needs. Needs are assessed by social workers and other professional staff who decide which services need to be purchased for an individual.

This first assessment results in a 'care plan' to buy in certain services. If you are just starting a career in caring, you are unlikely to be directly involved with the purchase of services.

National Minimum Standards require that service users needs are assessed and a care plan is produced before people receive a service. Standard 3 in the National Minimum Standards for Care Homes for Older People requires that a 'needs assessment' is carried out if people come into care without going through the 'care planning system'. National Minimum Standards require that people have an individual plan for their care, which may be drawn up by providers of care. This individual plan will be based on an assessment of an individual's needs and may help staff to assess the effectiveness of care. Standard 7 (Care Homes for Older People) states that homes must provide 'a **service user plan of care** generated from a comprehensive assessment (which) is drawn up with each service user and provides the basis for the care to be delivered'.

When you work with adult or older service users there should be a written plan that explains many of the most important needs for which care aims to provide. You may need to discuss each individual's care needs with the team and with supervisors and managers.

Sometimes, individual care needs change and then it is important to discuss new issues with managers. Managers can arrange for a review of a service user's care needs where things have changed. You might be providing home care – giving help with shopping and housework – when you notice that your service user is become increasingly forgetful and upset. Although the care plan outlines your basic tasks, you will need to report the service user's increasing difficulties, and a new assessment of need may be required.

Health and safety

Under the Health and Safety at Work Act of 1974, all employees must take reasonable care for their own safety and that of others. As a team member you will be expected to watch out for risks to your own and service users' safety. This will include looking out for hazards such as wet floors, things you could trip over like boxes on the floor, loose rugs or carpets, trailing leads, overloaded electric points and so on. You must make sure you do not create any hazards, and report any problems that you are not sure about. As well as preventing or reporting hazards, you must understand and follow safety procedures while at work or on placement. Unless you have had formal training you should not lift people or heavy objects. You must follow safety procedures when using equipment or cleaning, and also when dealing with body fluids, like blood and urine. Health and safety issues are discussed in Unit 3.

Maintaining security

Carers have a responsibility to protect themselves and their service users from safety and security risks. You will probably be aware of newspaper stories involving crimes in hospital or social care settings. It is important that you know who visitors to your setting are. You should ask if you can 'be of assistance' to any strangers who enter the building. Many care settings ask visitors to sign in and state who they are visiting or why they are there.

Maintaining security is a role that links with confidentiality. Before giving any information away about a service user, you must check who is asking and that they have a need to know. If a telephone caller claims to be a social worker who needs to check on a service user, you should ask to call back before giving any information. By calling back you can check that the caller is of the address that he or she claims to be. Your work setting may have a policy about giving information on the telephone – you may be forbidden to give information to mobile phone users.

When contractors enter premises, they will usually carry identification, invoices or order forms proving that they are who they say they are. When relatives arrive it is not usually necessary to ask for identification – instead, you can offer to lead them to the person they are visiting. They should recognise each other or give some sign that all is well.

THINK IT THROUGH

You enter the lounge of a residential home to find a stranger unplugging the video recorder. He says: 'It's OK, I'm just taking it for servicing.' You know nothing about this! Do you:

a   Stand in the way to prevent him from leaving and call for help?

b   Shrug your shoulders and say: 'Nothing to do with me'?

c   Ask him if he would leave the machine for a minute and come to the office to check details of the service contract with the manager?

Answer:

a   This could be hazardous if your assumption is correct that the person is stealing the video – they may attack you in order to escape. You could be injured – you should not place yourself at risk in this way.

b   This is wrong – how do you know what he says is true? You should try to protect the home's property, although your own personal safety is more important.

c   This is the best answer. If the stranger is a thief, perhaps he will run off without the video. If he is servicing the machine he might congratulate you on your care – after all, you have been polite and have not jumped to conclusions.

ASSESSMENT ACTIVITY

Identify the qualities and skills needed to be a care worker.

Use the diagram set out below to record some of your ideas about the skills and qualities that a care worker needs. Check your ideas by looking at the summary of the GSCC Code of Practice or discuss your ideas with a colleague or a member of staff on placement. When you have collected enough ideas in note form, write a list of the skills and qualities that care workers need and say why they are important.

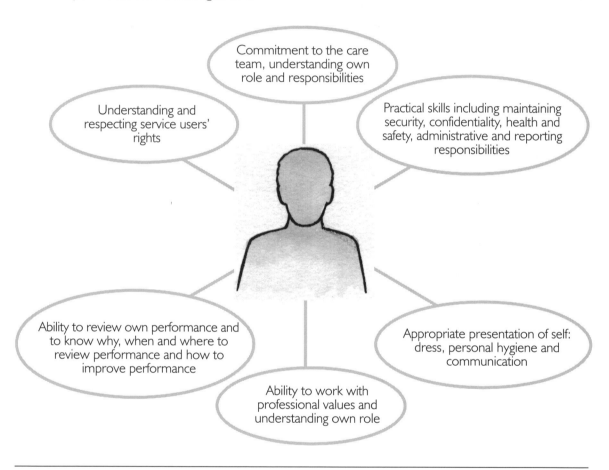

Commitment to the care team, understanding own role and responsibilities

Understanding and respecting service users' rights

Practical skills including maintaining security, confidentiality, health and safety, administrative and reporting responsibilities

Ability to review own performance and to know why, when and where to review performance and how to improve performance

Appropriate presentation of self: dress, personal hygiene and communication

Ability to work with professional values and understanding own role

LIFESPAN DEVELOPMENT AND CARE NEEDS

This unit explores the physical, intellectual, emotional and social changes associated with life stages such as infancy, childhood, adolescence, adulthood and old age. The concepts of disability, impairment, socialisation, and self-concept are studied. The impact of life events represents a major focus for this unit.

The unit builds on Unit 1 with an exploration of care needs at different life stages.

This unit is internally assessed and ideas for evidencing the grading criteria are presented.

In this unit you will learn about:

- changes associated with different life stages
- positive and negative influences on individuals at different life stages
- care needs at different life stages

Life stages

Principles of physical growth and development

People do not all grow and develop at exactly the same rate. Many things can influence how an individual develops. Each person is born with a pattern formed by their genes – a 'genetic pattern'. Genes control the sequence of human development, so that many abilities like walking and talking seem to 'unfold from within' a growing child. This unfolding process is often called 'maturation'.

Maturation is not just an unfolding genetic process, however – the environment a person grows up in always influences it. Genetics provide a plan for the building or physical development of a human being, and the environment provides the building materials – and influences what actually happens.

The baby in the womb grows according to a genetic pattern, but this can be influenced by the diet and habits of the mother. For example, alcohol can damage the development of the baby's nervous system. If a mother smokes it can harm her unborn baby, and the mother's diet is important too. After a child is born, he or she will be affected by experiences. A child will not develop language if nobody speaks to him or her. A child will not learn to walk if he or she is prevented from standing. The kind of support and encouragement a child receives will influence the development of skills and abilities.

Diet, illnesses and infections can have a major influence on physical growth. For instance, too little protein in a diet may limit the height to which a child grows. Too much fat in an adult's diet may increase the risk of heart disease.

The environment can influence the delicate hormone balance within the body that influences growth. Our genes will influence the type of physical impairments we are likely to develop as we grow old, but a good diet, for example, may help to prevent heart disease, and exercise may help to stop bones from becoming brittle.

Although we all grow up following a similar pattern, we do not all grow exactly the same. There is a pattern to human life stages, but each person will have a different experience of maturation caused by the interaction of his or her genetic plan for development and influences in the environment.

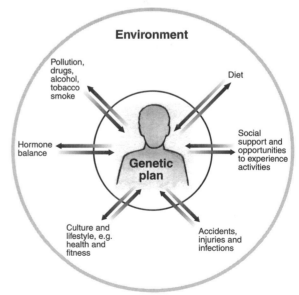

Figure 2.1 *Some factors that influence physical growth and development*

Ways of understanding life stages

Human beings grow from a tiny fertilised egg to a baby in nine months. From birth to adulthood takes 18 years. The average life expectancy at birth is now 74.2 years for boys and 79.6 years for girls, although some people live well beyond 100 years.

DID YOU KNOW?

On average, men live for 74.2 years, but the average man is expected to have only 59.2 years of healthy life. An average man may expect 15 years of illness at the end of his life. On average women may expect to live for 79.6 years of life, but the average woman may only expect 62.2 years of healthy life. An average woman may expect 17.4 years of illness at the end of her life.

Source: Our Healthier Nation 1998

A person's lifespan could be compared to the face of a clock. We grow rapidly in the phases called infancy, childhood and adolescence. We become fully developed adults in the first quarter of the lifespan. Adult life involves very gradual changes, and eventually ageing becomes apparent and a person's life completes its cycle.

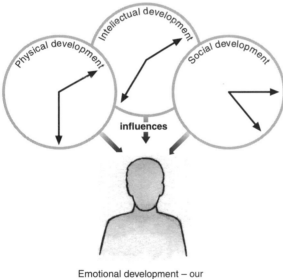

Figure 2.2 *Our understanding of who we are is influenced by our social, physical and intellectual development*

Society has different expectations of people at different stages of the life cycle. Social development can also be seen as a clock, with different social roles becoming appropriate at different stages. Infants are dependent on their carers. As children grow older so they become more independent, although adolescents are not allowed the responsibility of driving a car until they are 17 and people are not allowed to vote before 18 years of age. Establishing a career, marriage and parenthood are events that are expected in the first half of the life cycle. Retirement might be expected in the third or fourth section of the clock face.

Although we seem to go through an unfolding, physical ageing process, and although society has expectations of us, neither of these clocks makes us who we are. Our physical and social development provides the setting in which our life story is acted out. Our social, physical and intellectual development all influence the development of our self-awareness.

Development of self

Each life story can be seen as being like a journey. When we start our lives we have little sense of who we are, and we react to others 'instinctively'. The first sense of being an individual may not come until we are about two years of age. A child may not develop a general sense of self-worth until eight years of age. Young people often begin to compare themselves with other young people between the ages of 10 and 12, and sometimes after 15 or 16 years of age young adults can explain their sense of who they are, a self-concept. The full development of this sense of self then becomes the goal of adult life. Happy, successful people may have a sense of 'becoming the person they want to be'. This journey of growth and development does not have to end until an individual dies. Some writers feel that the way a person faces his or her own death is in itself a developmental task.

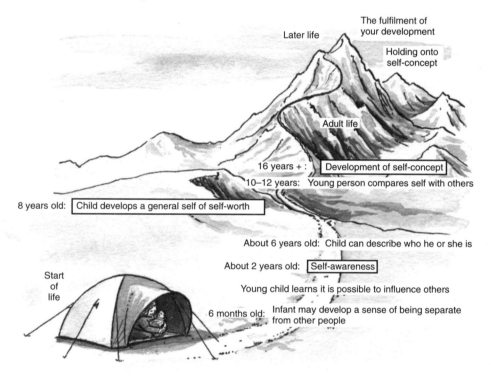

Figure 2.3 *Self-awareness, self-worth and self-concept are all stages on life's journey*

Conception

Human life begins with conception. A fertile woman usually produces one egg cell each month, roughly two weeks after the last menstrual period. The egg cell travels from the ovary, along a tube (known as the fallopian tube) towards the uterus. If sexual intercourse takes place while the egg is in the fallopian tube, then there is a possibility that a new life will be started. Millions of sperm are ejaculated by a man during orgasm. Just one sperm may fertilise the

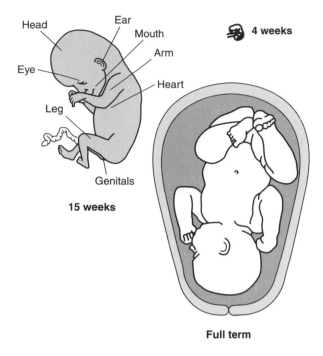

Head
Ear
Mouth
Arm
Eye
Heart
Leg
Genitals

4 weeks

15 weeks

Full term

Figure 2.4 *The growth of a baby in the womb*

egg. Fertilisation means that the genetic material in the sperm joins with the genetic material in the egg to form a genetic plan for a new human being.

Normally, each sperm and each egg contains 23 chromosomes. Chromosomes contain the genes that control our physical development. Human cells are made from 46 chromosomes, so each egg and sperm contain half the genetic material needed to make the 'plan' for a human being.

Only about half of all fertilised eggs develop to become babies. Many eggs are lost without the woman knowing that fertilisation ever happened. One to one-and-a-half days after conception, the single egg cell begins to divide. After two or three days there are enough new cells to make the fertilised egg the size of a pin head. This collection of cells travels to the wall of the uterus, where it attaches itself to the wall. The developing collection of cells is now called an embryo. Once the embryo is attached to the uterus wall, a chemical signal stops the woman from having another menstrual period. After eight weeks, the embryo may have grown to between 3 and 4 cm, has a recognisable heartbeat and the beginnings of eyes, ears, mouth, legs and arms. At this stage the growing organism is called a foetus.

During the remaining seven months before birth, all the organs continue to develop. By 20 weeks, the foetus will have reached about half the length of the baby at birth. By 32 weeks, the foetus will be about half its birth weight.

Birth

At about nine months after conception the baby will be born.

Infancy (0–2 years)

Physical development

The newborn baby (or neonate) has to take easily digestible food such as mother's milk in order to grow. A newborn baby does not have a fully developed brain but can usually hear sounds, tell differences in the way things taste, and identify the smell of his or her own mother or carer. Infants are born with various reflexes.

- A newborn baby will turn his or her head toward any touch on the cheek. This reflex is called the rooting reflex, and helps the baby to get the nipple into his or her mouth to feed.

- If you place your finger in the palm of a baby's hand, he or she will grasp your finger tightly. This reflex is called the grasp reflex.

- If a baby is startled – perhaps by a loud noise – he or she will throw hands and arms outwards, arching the back and straightening the legs. This is called the startle reflex.

- If a newborn baby is held upright with the feet touching the ground, he or she will make movements as if trying to walk.

Infants have the physical ability to recognise and interact with people. Babies prefer the sound of human voices to other sounds, and soon learn to recognise their mother's voice. Within a few weeks babies show interest in human faces. It is as if babies come into the world ready to make relationships with their carers.

Babies are helpless when it comes to muscle co-ordination and control. Babies can't hold up their head, roll over, sit up or use their hands to move objects deliberately. The average age for some types of control over the body are shown in the table below:

Ability to lift head slightly	0–1 months
Ability to pass an object from one hand to another	6 months
Ability to roll over	6 months
Ability to crawl	9–10 months
Ability to stand alone	12 months

Intellectual development

The first year and a half or two years of life was described as the sensorimotor stage of development by a famous psychologist called Piaget (1896–1980). Infants have to learn to co-ordinate their senses and their muscle behaviour (the term 'motor' in the word 'sensorimotor' means control of muscles).

To begin with, a baby will rely on inbuilt patterns for behaviour such as sucking, crawling and watching. A baby will adapt this behaviour in order to explore a wider range of objects. Babies explore by sucking toys, fingers, clothes and so on. In this way they are slowly able to develop an understanding of objects. According to Piaget, thinking is at first limited to memories of actions. The infant will remember grasping a toy. If given the toy, it may repeat the action. Piaget believed that very young infants would not be able to remember objects they could not see.

Stage	Age	Key issue
Sensorimotor stage of development	1–2 years	Children don't understand how objects exist
Pre-operational stage (pre-logical stage)	1–7 years	Children don't think in a logical way
Concrete operational stage	7–11 years	Children can understand logic only if they can see the issue
Formal operational stage	11 years on	People can understand logical arguments

Piaget also believed that infants could not understand that objects existed on their own. For instance if an infant's mother left the room, the infant would be afraid that she had gone for ever. Piaget thought that an infant would not be able to understand that the mother still existed, if he or she could not see, hear, smell or touch the mother. At the end of the sensorimotor period, Piaget thought that infants could at last understand that objects and people continue to exist, even if you can't sense them. Modern research suggests, however, that many eight-month-old infants can understand that people and objects still exist, even when you can't see or hear them. Infants are more able than many people used to think!

Social development

Infants soon learn to recognise their mother's voice and smell, and can probably recognise their mother's face by two months of age. Infants try to attract attention. Many infants will smile and make noises to attract adults.

Infants will often respond to the speech and smiles of their carers, and both infants and carers seem to have an inbuilt desire to make an emotional bond that ties them together.

At about 12 months of age infants often develop a fear of strangers, and will protest if they are separated from their parents. After the first year of life infants feel safe with familiar family members if they have formed the necessary social bonds.

Some psychologists believe that this process of bonding is vital for future mental health and well-being. Infants who are rejected or who fail to make relationships during the first few years of life may face great difficulty in coping with relationships in later life. Infants who make safe and secure ties with their carers have a good foundation for future social development.

Figure 2.5 *Young infants attract their carers to bond with them*

Emotional development

Young infants probably do not have a sense of being an individual person. Five- to six-month-old infants do seem to recognise emotions in their carers. As infants grow, they gradually learn that they can influence their carers. Infants may develop the idea that they are persons with a fixed gender at about two years of age. This idea of being a person is called self-awareness.

Childhood (2–12 years)

The word 'childhood' doesn't have a fixed meaning in terms of age. Here, the word is used to cover two to twelve years of age, although exactly where childhood ends and adolescence begins is difficult to say.

Physical development

Children grow steadily at this time but less rapidly than during infancy. By the age of six a child's head will be almost adult size – even though the body still has a lot of growing to do.

Children's practical abilities continue to develop; at two years of age children may be able to run and to climb stairs one step at a time. By four, children may be able to kick and throw a large ball. By six or seven, a child may be able to skip and ride a bicycle.

Puberty often starts for girls between the ages of 11 and 13, although some girls may begin earlier. (See the section on adolescence for more about puberty.)

Intellectual development

By the age of two, children generally start to talk. By the age of six, children can often use language as well as some adults. Language develops very rapidly between two and six years of age.

Between the age of two and seven years, most children learn to count and to explain how much things weigh. Young children don't always fully understand the logic involved in counting and weighing things, however.

Piaget called the period from two to seven years of age the 'pre-operational' period. Pre-operational means 'pre-logical'. Young children make decisions based on what things look like rather than the logic of counting – for example, they will say that there are more sweets in a long line than in a small heap, even though they can count the same number in each.

Older children don't make the mistakes that younger children do. But children aged seven to 12 can often understand logical problems only if they can see what's involved. For example, you could ask a nine-year-old: 'Tanya is taller than Stephen, but Tanya is smaller than Tolu, so who is the smallest out of these three people?' Obviously Stephen is the smallest. A nine-year-old might not be able to work this out without looking at pictures of the people.

Piaget called the period from seven to 12 the 'concrete operational period', because children can work out logical problems only if they can see 'concrete' examples to help them.

Social development

Young children still depend very much on their carers to look after them. They need secure emotional ties with their family. As children develop they become more and more independent, but the family provides safety and a setting in which to learn social roles. Young children use imagination to play-act social roles. Children learn how to behave socially through the process of socialisation in the family (see the section on socialisation in this unit).

Emotional development

As children develop language skills they can understand and explain who they are in greater detail.

Children develop from being aware of themselves at two years of age to being able to describe their feelings by 12. Children need to develop a sense of being worth something to their friends and family. This sense of self-worth forms a basis for an effective concept of self to develop during adolescence (see the section on self-concept for further details).

THINK IT THROUGH

Try the 'I am' test. Ask children to describe who they are, and six-year-olds will probably just say their name and where they live. They may be able to tell you other factual things like who their brothers and sisters are. Eight- or nine-year-olds may be able to tell you about things they are good at or things they like – they can explain who they are in more depth. By 12, children may be able to compare themselves with others and say things like 'I'm quite good at sport, but not as good as Nisha – she's faster than me.' By 12, children may begin to work out how they fit in with others. Try asking children of different ages and see what kind of answers you get.

Adolescence (12–18 years)

The word 'adolescence' is used here to cover ages 12 to 18 – 18 is the age when people are first allowed to vote and take on adult responsibilities.

Physical development

Girls generally start puberty before 13, but for boys this comes between 13 and 15. Puberty is a development stage which prepares the body for sexual reproduction. It is set off by the action of hormones that control sexual development. Both boys and girls may experience a 'growth spurt', where they grow taller at a faster rate than before.

Girls' sexual development during puberty includes the enlargement of breasts, the development of pubic hair, increased fat layers under the skin, and the start of menstrual periods. Boys will experience the enlargement of their testes and penis, the development of pubic and facial hair, and increased muscle strength. Boys' voices also 'break' and become deeper in tone. These major changes mean that adolescents look and behave very differently from children.

Intellectual development

An adolescent may be able to imagine and think about things he or she has never seen or done. By adolescence, people can often imagine their future and how to achieve things. Children are unlikely to plan and think ahead in the same way. Piaget believed that adolescents have the ability to solve problems in an adult way, using formal logic. He called development after about 12 years of age the 'formal operational' (or formal logical) period. Although adolescents may reason in an adult way, many adolescents do not know enough to make good decisions. People continue to improve their decision-making skills during adulthood.

Social development

Adolescents become increasingly independent of their family, and friendship groups can become more important than family for the development of social skills. This phase of development is called secondary socialisation.

Between 13 and 18 years of age, most adolescents will begin to explore relationships with possible sexual partners. Towards late adolescence, people will begin to think about, plan or take on job responsibilities.

The five years between 13 and 18 can involve major changes in social behaviour, as people learn to take on adult roles and adult independence. Some adolescents experience conflict with their parents during this period of change.

Figure 2.6 *Adolescent social development*

Emotional development

Adolescence can involve major emotional stresses as people go through rapid social and physical change. Some adolescents feel a loss of self-esteem as they transfer from school to work. Becoming independent from parents can involve conflict and stress. The search for love and affection from a sexual partner may not be stress free.

The famous psychologist Eric Erikson (1902–1994) believed that a successful adult life depended on people developing a secure sense of self or self-concept. During adolescence people have to work out a self-concept that will guide them through leaving home, perhaps setting up home with a sexual partner, and getting work.

Adulthood (18 onwards)

In Britain the right to vote is granted at 18, and 18 years of age might be taken as the beginning of the social category of adulthood.

Physical development

Young adults are often at their peak of physical performance between 18 and 28 years of age. Most champions of highly active sports are aged between 16 and 30 years. Professional footballers and athletes usually have to retire and move into management roles during their 30s. Older adults generally tend to lose some strength and speed with age, although outside competitive sport these changes can be so gradual as to go unnoticed.

Exercise can help develop physical fitness and athletic skills. An older adult could easily achieve a personal peak of fitness at 40 or 50 years of age if he or she takes up exercise late in life.

There are a number of age-related changes that slowly become apparent as we grow older. Many people develop a need to wear glasses to help with reading during their 40s. Some people cannot hear high-pitched sounds so well during late adulthood. Many adults show a thinning of hair in their 50s, with hair loss being common for men.

Women are most able to conceive children in their late teens and early 20s. The risk of miscarriages and complications rises with age. Usually between 45 and 55 years of age women stop being able to have children when the menopause begins. Older adults in Britain often put on weight. This middle-age spread may be caused because adults still eat the same amount of food that they did when they were younger, but they have become much less active.

The risk of disease and disability rises with age. Older adults are more likely to develop health problems than younger adults.

Intellectual development

Intellectual skills and abilities may increase during adulthood if they are exercised. Older adults may have slightly slower reaction times, but increased knowledge may compensate for this in many intellectual tasks.

Older adults may be more skilled than adolescents and young adults when it comes to making complex decisions. Some adults may develop increased wisdom as they become older.

Social development

Early adulthood is often a time when people continue to develop their network of personal friends. Most young adults establish sexual relationships and partnerships. Marriage and parenthood are important social life events that are often associated with early adulthood. The pressure to obtain paid employment and hold down jobs is also a major social issue for adults.

Many adults experience a degree of stress in trying to cope with the demands of being a parent, a partner and a worker. Nowadays, many individuals work long hours or even take more than one job in order to achieve a high standard of living. If a person has to go to work and maintain a family home, this can create social and emotional problems. Adult life can often involve trying to balance the need to earn money, with the needs of partners and other family members.

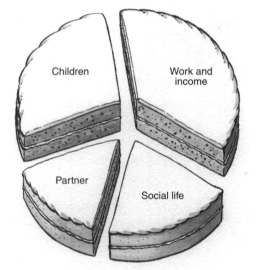

Figure 2.7 *Adults have to work out how to divide up their time in order to meet different needs*

Older adults may find that as well as coping with work pressures, they have to provide support for their parents and their children. Some older adults may feel that they are torn between different demands on their time. When children leave home some pressures may be taken off parents. But some may feel that they have lost part of their social purpose when children no longer need their support.

Many people now retire from full-time paid employment in their 50s, and most people retire by their mid-60s. Retirement is seen as a positive release from pressures by some people, and as an end to usefulness by others.

Emotional development

An individual's sense of self and self-esteem will continue to develop throughout adulthood. During early adulthood, many individuals may struggle to develop the confidence to share life with a partner. Some individuals may prefer to live alone, or may feel that partnership relationships are too demanding. A person's previous family experience may strongly influence his or her expectations of a partner.

Some research suggests that adults often feel more confident and satisfied with their lives in their 30s and 40s than they did in their 20s. It may be that many young adults experience some stress in establishing a satisfying lifestyle.

One theory suggests that older adults may struggle to stay interested and involved with other people after their own family grows up. Some adults may get into 'a rut' and withdraw from active, social involvement as they get older. Successful ageing means remaining emotionally involved with other people.

Old age (65 onwards)

Most people retire by the age of 65 and the period of life after the age of 65 is generally regarded as old age. Most 65-year-olds do not see themselves as 'old', however. Some writers distinguish between the 'young-old' (65 to 80) and the 'old-old' (80-plus). But many 80-year-olds still claim that they are not old!

Physical changes

The period of life after 65 usually involves some reduction in the efficiency of the body:

- the heart, breathing and circulation become weaker

- muscles may become weaker and skin becomes less 'elastic'

- muscles, skin, joints and bones become less flexible and this can mean that people become less mobile, more at risk of fractured bones and more likely to develop wrinkled skin

- blood capillaries in the skin are more likely to burst, meaning that bruising can happen more easily

- most organs in the body, such as the liver and kidneys, work less efficiently

- many people develop problems with arthritis

- there may be a loss of hearing ability

- the risks of impairments and disability rise with increasing age

- reaction times and speed of thinking slow down.

Physical health varies from person to person. Where people have poor health, their ability to remember and think things through can sometimes be affected. Life after 65 involves a general slowing down of physical activity. People can still go jogging, dancing, mountain climbing and so on, but the body becomes less flexible and less able to cope with exertion – limiting the extremes to which people can perform.

Intellectual development

Some people seem to become less able to solve problems and cope with difficult, intellectual challenges in later life. To some extent mental abilities are influenced by physical health. If people develop problems with blood circulation, this can involve the brain and lead to difficulty with mental activities such as problem-solving.

Other people who enjoy good health, and who exercise their minds, often keep their mental abilities and continue to develop their store of knowledge. Some older people seem to develop their ability to make wise decisions and judgements. Even if thinking slows down, the opportunity to develop wisdom may increase with age.

The risk of developing dementia or Alzheimer's disease seems to increase with age; but dementia is not a part of normal ageing. Most old people never develop conditions such as dementia or Alzheimer's disease. There are different types of dementia, but in general dementia can cause a range of disabilities including:

- a loss of ability to control emotion
- difficulty in understanding other people
- difficulties in communicating and expressing thoughts
- loss of memory
- difficulties in recognising people, places and things
- problems with making sense of where they are and what is happening
- problems with daily living activities like getting dressed.

The reasons for dementia are not fully understood, but bad health habits like heavy drinking and smoking may increase the risk of dementia for some people. Other people may inherit a risk factor for dementia with their genetic pattern.

Social development

Older people lead varied and different lives. Many retired people have a greater opportunity for meeting and making new friends than they did while they were working. A network of family and friends can provide vital practical and emotional support. Health problems and impairments can sometimes create difficulties for older people, which might result in social isolation (see case study of Mrs Baddock, page 81).

Emotional development

People continue to develop their sense of self as life progresses. Some theorists suggest that the main challenge of old age is to keep a strong sense of self-esteem, despite the problems that can arise. Older people may not only develop health problems but they can be stereotyped by other people who assume they are less able. Some older people may be at risk of losing their self-confidence and self-esteem because of the way others treat them.

Decline and death

Physical processes

There are different theories to explain why we age and die. One theory is that the cells that make up our body have to continually renew themselves, but they can do this only a limited number of times. Eventually, body cells start to go wrong as they try to renew, and other cells die out, causing problems.

> ### THINK IT THROUGH
>
> *One way of understanding ageing is to look at what happens when you make photocopies. Imagine you copied a photograph of a face on a photocopier, and then copied your copy rather than the original page. If you keep copying your copies rather than the original, the copies will gradually fade and start to look wrong. You can copy only a limited number of times before you can no longer see the picture clearly.*
>
> *Some people think that as our cells have to copy themselves, like the photocopier they can manage the task efficiently only a limited number of times. We change as our cells copy and renew themselves. Eventually we lose vital parts of our pattern – and then we die.*

Social issues

People think about death and dying in many different ways. Some people fear death and do not like to think about it. Other people have strong religious or personal beliefs which protect them from worry. In general, older people often have less fear of dying than young adults. It may be that some older people feel ready to let go of life at a certain stage of physical decline. Some older people may prepare for their own death by thinking over their lives and the things they have achieved.

Some people who face death want to see family, friends and relatives and need social support to help them cope with dying. Other people may prefer to die alone. Each individual will have his or her own social and emotional needs.

Death as the final stage of growth

Elisabeth Kübler-Ross wrote a book with the title *Death – the Final Stage of Growth*. In this book she explained how people who were dying might go through a process of:

- denying that they were dying
- trying to bargain or sort things out
- acceptance of being ready to die.

- feeling angry
- depression

Being ready to die, not angry, afraid or depressed, might represent the final achievement that a person makes in the journey of emotional development.

The human life cycle – why does it matter?

The genetic material in a sperm and an egg fuse together to create a plan for a new person. This plan is then influenced by the person's environment. If the plan and the environment are good, the person will grow and develop well. We don't just grow physically, we also develop our social and emotional behaviour. Most people develop a sense of self – an idea about who and what they are. Our bodies are not designed to last for ever, and at some age our physical abilities start to decline. The sense of self that we develop never needs to be 'finished' before we die. Our lives influence others, and leave their mark on the history of the world. The world would not be exactly the same if you or I had never existed.

Many of the world's great religions believe that the self we have created (or soul) is 'kept on record', and that God will re-create this self in heaven or in some sort of afterlife.

Quality care depends on workers valuing and caring about other people's sense of who they are. If people do not have a sense of self-worth, they may see little point in living. If we have our basic needs met and a sense of self-esteem, we can go on to enjoy the whole of our lifespan.

ASSESSMENT ACTIVITY

Describe the physical, intellectual, emotional and social growth characteristics of each life stage.

Design a series of posters with one poster for each life stage. Each poster should describe the physical, intellectual, emotional and social characteristics associated with each life stage. Use your own imagination to design each poster but an outline idea is shown opposite:

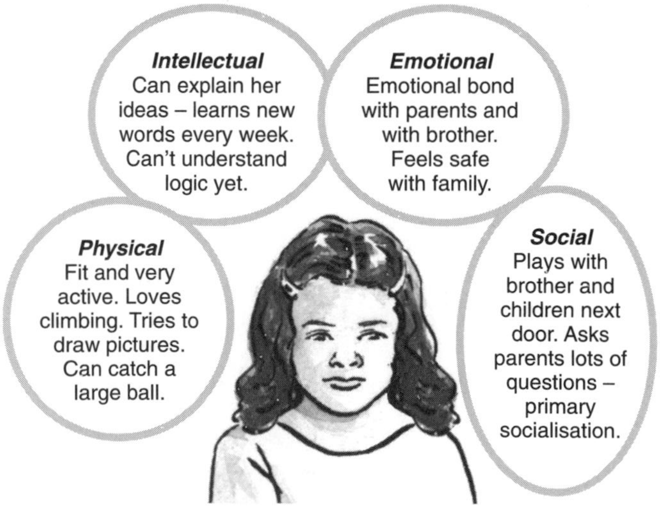

Intellectual
Can explain her ideas – learns new words every week. Can't understand logic yet.

Emotional
Emotional bond with parents and with brother. Feels safe with family.

Physical
Fit and very active. Loves climbing. Tries to draw pictures. Can catch a large ball.

Social
Plays with brother and children next door. Asks parents lots of questions – primary socialisation.

Figure 2.8 *Key issues for four-year-old Yemi*

Disability and impairment

The Disability Discrimination Act defines a disability as 'a physical or mental impairment which has a substantial and long-term adverse effect on a person's ability to carry out normal day-to-day activities'.

Physical impairment

A physical impairment results from a part of the body being damaged, lost, or not working as it should. Impairments cause disabilities.

For instance, if you develop cataracts on the lens of the eye, you have a physical impairment which will mean you cannot see clearly. This could lead on to a disability if you can no longer read books or magazines. However, if you had the right computer equipment you could have books and magazine articles scanned and translated into speech that you could hear. The computer could remove the disability of not being able to know what was written down but the impairment would still be there.

Mental impairment

A mental impairment can result from damage to the nervous system or from the experiences that a person has in life. Mental impairments can also come about from a combination of experiences and damage. The cause of some mental impairments is not fully understood.

For instance, a person might have a disability due to slight brain damage at birth. This might involve problems with reading, writing and spelling. If a person's work doesn't involve reading and writing, people may not know that the person has a disability. If the person uses a computer to help with grammar and spelling, the disability isn't there any more.

DID YOU KNOW?

Over six million people in Britain have a disability, but only 200,000 people use wheelchairs. Wheelchair users are a small proportion of disabled people.

Developmental delay

Young children are expected to show abilities such as talking and walking around certain ages. If a child does not show new abilities within the expected age range then the child may be regarded as experiencing 'developmental delay'. The term developmental delay is usually used only to describe problems with development in children under the age of five.

Developmental delay can be caused by physical impairments such as brain damage, or damage to the eyes, ears or other organs of the body.

Developmental delay can also be caused by poor quality of food or starvation, and by poor interaction between an infant and his or her carer. Some causes of developmental delay are not fully understood.

Child development is checked when children are taken to a baby or well-child clinic. Parents may also contact a health visitor or family doctor if they think that their child is not developing new skills at the same age as other children.

Delayed development and impairments can result in a disability. Carers will be aware of the disability although they may not fully understand the causes of impairment or delayed development.

Types of disability

There may be as many types of disability as there are disabled people – no one person's disability is the same as another person's. Equipment and adaptations that are useful for certain people are not useful for other people. It is very important not to see disability as some sort of label for people who are different. Disabled people are not 'all the same'.

For instance, people who use wheelchairs may need open, flat spaces where there are no steps. If they have to go up or down levels, ramps are important. People who are partially sighted often like stairs to have a hand rail that they can follow. People who use a wheelchair may need low-level kitchen worktops and sinks, yet people who have arthritis in the back might find it painful and difficult to cope with low-level kitchens. People with disabilities all need different types of support. The most important thing to remember about disability is that people have disabilities – but people *are* not disabilities.

Disabilities can be classified as **sensory**, **physical** or **intellectual** disabilities. All disabilities can interfere with a person's ability to cope with daily living activities. Daily living activities include being able to prepare and eat food, bath or shower, dress, use the toilet, clean, go shopping, read, write, do laundry, use transport, and manage money.

Sensory disabilities

Disabilities of the senses include those of sight and hearing. Many people lose their sense of taste and smell as they get older, but in Western society this impairment rarely results in a disability. People who cannot taste food very well usually have few problems with social life or work – who would know how good your sense of taste was?

People who have impaired vision or hearing usually do have a disability, however. There is no single condition of blindness or deafness. Many people who are 'registered blind' can sense differences between light and dark – they can tell where the window in a room is, because they can sense the light. Others may have tunnel vision, where they can see only a small area, as if they were looking at things at the end of a tunnel. Others may have blurred vision, or be able to see only the outside area of what they look at. So it can be possible for a 'blind' person to see a coin on the floor and pick it up!

People can also have many different types of hearing impairment. As they grow older, many people lose the ability to hear high-pitched sounds. Nearly a fifth of people over the age of 75 wear a hearing aid. Many people can hear the speech of people they are used to hearing, because they know their voices and speech patterns. People can sometimes have difficulty understanding strangers, and those with a different accent. Some people with a hearing impairment can make sense of speech if they can see a person's lips – many people can 'lip-read' a little. So a person with hearing impairment might say 'I can't hear you – I need to put my glasses on'.

People are sometimes born with impairments to hearing or vision. Some people develop impairments due to injuries or accidents and other people develop impairments as they grow older.

THINK IT THROUGH

How can visual or hearing disabilities influence work, meeting people, mobility, shopping and so on?

Disability can be reduced if a person's needs are understood and the right kind of support is provided. People who are born with a serious hearing impairment may never be able to hear spoken language, but many people who are born 'deaf' in Britain may learn British sign language. BSL is a complete language system, and it reduces the disability that having to learn English might create.

TV programmes are now often subtitled or signed, so that people who have a hearing impairment need not be excluded from enjoying TV. If a deaf person has a signer or interpreter, he or she may be able to engage in the same study, recreational and work activities as hearing people.

People with visual impairment may also be helped by a range of equipment and services that can reduce the restrictions their disability might otherwise create.

Physical disabilities

One of the major causes of physical disability is arthritis. Arthritis can limit people's ability to cope with daily living activities and reduce their mobility. Other causes of physical disability include heart and circulation disorders, which can limit people's ability to undertake any activity requiring physical effort. Some illnesses cause temporary or permanent disability – ME, for example, is an illness that can leave a person weak and unable to cope with work or daily activities. A range of illnesses and injuries can cause mobility problems, where people lose the use of hands, arms or legs.

The disability of not being able to walk to shops or board a bus can be overcome if a person can use an electric wheelchair or an adapted car and continue with his or her activities. Even if a person cannot use an adapted car, a home carer might be able to assist with shopping and domestic needs. The impairment need not result in a wide range of disability.

Intellectual disability

About 2 per cent of Britain's population has a learning disability. This means that a person may not learn things as quickly or as easily as most people do. People with a serious learning disability may not be able to lead fully independent lives as adults. Some people with a learning disability may not be able to manage money or plan daily activities like cooking or shopping without help.

Various impairments can result in a learning disability. People may be born with genetic abnormalities (Down's syndrome) or with damage to the nervous system due to infection or injury before or during birth. Infection, injury and poor environment (such as poor diet, poor social contact and poor opportunities for learning) can create a learning disability during infancy or childhood.

In the past, people with learning disability were often thought of as being too different to mix with other people. People with serious disabilities lived in long-stay hospitals or other isolated settings away from other people. Over the past 30 years there has been growing concern to protect the rights of people with learning disabilities and to provide opportunities for individuals to live independently in the community. Most services for people with learning disability now try to support individuals to live as independently as possible and make choices. Many people with a learning disability can develop and lead an independent life with the right help and support.

Intellectual disability can include problems other than a learning disability. There are differences in the way people's brains work, and some people have difficulty understanding how sounds link to written words. This can be due to a condition called dyslexia, which involves a difficulty in learning to read and to spell, but is not usually classified as a learning disability. People with dyslexia may be good at learning generally.

Illness and injury can cause impairments that lead to particular disabilities. For example, aphasia is a disability that leads to difficulty with speaking. Agnosia is a disability caused by not being able to make sense of what you see.

Case Study – Mrs Baddock

Mrs Baddock is 84, and lives on her own in a terraced house. Her husband died five years ago and her daughter lives 20 miles away. Mrs Baddock used to do her own housework and shopping, and used to go out to meet friends and to a local club.

Mrs Baddock has a sensory impairment to her vision due to cataracts and long-sightedness, and a physical impairment of the use of her hands and body due to arthritis.

Mrs Baddock has a disability relating to housework and shopping. She has lost her confidence about going out because she cannot read signs and notices clearly. She has some pain when she walks and she cannot carry shopping. Mrs Baddock has difficulty with housework – even making a cup of tea or a sandwich is a serious problem because her two impairments create a lot of small disabilities. When Mrs Baddock tries to make a sandwich, she often drops food on the floor, or spills food on the kitchen work surfaces. Trying to prepare food is painful, stressful and sometimes unsuccessful. Mrs Baddock used to be able to look after her own needs, and she feels depressed that she now has so much difficulty. When Mrs Baddock's care needs are assessed, she says 'I can't cope any more – I can't cook, I don't get out, I can't do anything any more'.

THINK IT THROUGH

Imagine you have poor eyesight, pain in movement, and difficulty using your hands. What disabilities would you develop? You could try this experiment: Find some old glasses, safety glasses or sunglasses, and paste some thin tissue over most of the lens area. Use masking tape to tie your fingers together and restrict the movement of your thumb. Now try making a sandwich! It may be more fun (and safer) to try this experiment with a friend or in a small group.

Mrs Baddock has the disabilities shown in Figure 2.9. New routines and new equipment could prevent the arthritis and poor eyesight from causing Mrs Baddock major problems. Her disability could be reduced if the right assessment and the right help were available. For instance, a wide handle on cutlery could make it easier to use. Changing the kitchen layout might make it easier for her to find things. For jars, labels that can be understood by touch might help. Non-slip mats may help prevent things from falling on the floor. Some ideas to limit disability are shown at the edges of Figure 2.9.

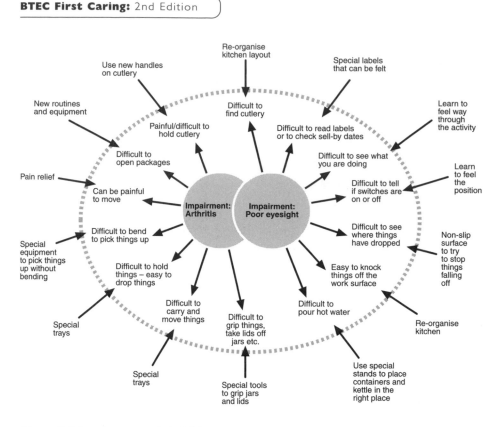

Use new handles
on cutlery

Re-organise
kitchen layout

Special labels
that can be felt

New routines
and equipment

Difficult to
find cutlery

Painful/difficult to
hold cutlery

Difficult to read labels
or to check sell-by dates

Learn to
feel way
through
the activity

Difficult to
open packages

Difficult to see what
you are doing

Pain relief

Can be painful
to move

Impairment:
Arthritis

Impairment:
Poor eyesight

Difficult to tell
if switches are
on or off

Learn
to feel
the
position

Difficult to bend
to pick things up

Difficult to see
where things
have dropped

Special
equipment
to pick things
up without
bending

Difficult to hold
things – easy to
drop things

Easy to knock
things off the
work surface

Non-slip
surface
to try
to stop
things
falling
off

Special
trays

Difficult to
carry and
move things

Difficult to
grip things,
take lids off
jars etc.

Difficult to
pour hot water

Re-organise
kitchen

Special
trays

Special tools
to grip jars
and lids

Use special
stands to place
containers and
kettle in the
right place

Figure 2.9 *Impairments and disabilities*

ASSESSMENT ACTIVITY

Describe the effects of impaired or delayed development.

Impairments or delayed development can result in a disability. During your placements you will have met a range of people who experience a disability. You may have worked with people who have a disability associated with an impairment of their sight or hearing. You may have worked with people who have impairments to their joints caused by arthritis. You may have worked with people with a learning disability.

Think of two people you have worked with and write a detailed description of the nature of each person's disability. If appropriate, you might be able to discuss a person's disability and the problems that they face in their everyday life with them. This discussion will help you to write a description of the effects of impairment. You may also be able to discuss a service user's care

needs with senior members of staff. Remember to ask the individual person for permission to use their information, and remember not to use any details which might identify the people you have worked with (keep all personal details confidential).

To achieve a **merit grade** you need to explain how care needs are affected by delayed or impaired development by using examples of two different individuals. Your description of disability must also discuss the way in which impairment influences the care needs of two service users. Care needs will be identified in the individual care plan (or needs assessment) that has been negotiated for each service user. However, you may be able to identify additional needs in your conversations with service users or with staff.

Positive and negative influences

Life events

Buddhists teach that, apart from birth and death, the only certainty in life is that there will be change. Since you were born you will have experienced many life events that have changed you. As you grow older you will experience many more changes. Everyone has a different life, and some life events seem insignificant to some people; for example, a new job may be something that you just drift into, but for other people their first job may change their lives for ever. Going to school, getting a job, leaving home, marriage, parenthood, retirement, ageing and bereavement are all common events that involve change. Many people will not experience all of these events; and other events such as divorce or changing jobs may be far more important for some people.

Change

Some life events change us for ever. Life events that change us involve some stress, because change can cause:

■ a sense of **loss** for the way things used to be

■ a feeling of **uncertainty** about what the future will be like

■ a need to **spend time** and/or money and/or emotional energy sorting things out

■ a need to **learn** new things.

Going to school

Some children are taught at home because of travelling problems or personal needs, but most go to school and many people will remember their first day.

Starting school can involve a sense of loss. This might be the first morning your mother and family have left you to cope with other people on your own. You might cry because you miss them. You also might feel uncertain. Where are the toilets? Who should you speak to? What will happen if you don't eat the food?

Starting school can also be stimulating and positive. Some children feel that it is exciting to meet new people. They might find school interesting and be proud that they are 'grown up' enough to start school activities. Starting school can be a positive experience, involving increasing independence – it all depends on how each child is helped to cope with the change.

THINK IT THROUGH

How positive or negative was your experience of your first day at secondary school? Do you have relatives who started infant school recently? How positive or negative was their first day? Rate experiences on the scale below:

1	2	3	4	5
Stressful	Not good	OK	Good	Great

Think of the reasons why you have rated things this way.

Getting a job

Starting a first job is a different experience for everyone. Many people have part-time jobs, perhaps in a shop, before they start their first full-time job. Part-time work might help you to be prepared for the changes that going out to work involve. Some people get only temporary work and suffer periods of unemployment. Other people have several jobs in order to earn enough money. Some people work for their own family business and don't have to get a job with people they don't know. Many people have to search hard for a full-time job and are anxious to do well when they find one.

Getting and starting a job can involve a feeling of loss – it would be nicer not to have to bother, and to stay at home! Getting and starting a job involves lots of uncertainty: 'Will I like the people there?', 'Will they like me?', 'Can I do the job?' Getting a job and getting started takes a lot of time and energy. Starting a new job involves a lot of new learning; who is who, where things are, what you have to do, and so on.

For some people, getting and starting a new job is frightening and unpleasant. Some people feel that they are forced to work at things they don't really want to do, or are being paid low wages to do. For these people, starting work is a negative experience. Other people experience getting a job as exciting, and as a chance to develop and improve skills. Some people see going out to work as a sign of freedom and independence, and for these people, starting work is a positive experience.

Leaving home

Moving out of the family home can be a major life event. Sometimes, leaving happens gradually. A person might go away to study or work but return home at weekends or at the end of term. Sometimes people may leave home to marry, and the major life event is getting married. Some people leave home after a dispute with parents – they may 'run away' rather than leave. Some people do not leave their family home during their early life.

Leaving home is a great change for some people, who miss their family and feel a loss of company. Some people will feel uncertain about their future and how to cope with a new house or flat. Those who leave home will need to spend a lot of time and energy sorting their new home out. There is much to learn about paying bills, buying food and doing your own housework. Many people will find that the change is a positive experience, but people who feel that they have been forced to leave, perhaps to find work, or because of arguments, might see the change as a negative life event. For many people, however, 'having your own place' is the final thing you need to be an independent adult.

Leaving home can be a big step to independent life if it is planned carefully. If there are problems with money or with people you share accommodation with, then it can become a negative event.

Marriage

In Britain, marriage is the legal union of one man to one woman. Gay and lesbian couples cannot currently be registered as married (although this may change). Some other cultures permit a husband to have more than one wife or a wife to have more than one husband, but the legal definition of marriage in Britain restricts marriage to one man and one woman.

Many heterosexual couples live together without marrying – some go on to marry after living together for some years, but about half of all couples who live together do not go on to marry each other. Current trends suggest that perhaps one in five people will never be married during their lives.

Marriage involves a commitment to live with a partner permanently. It ties financial resources and the networks of family relationships together. Marriage is a big change in life, and it can involve moving house and leaving your family. This may cause a sense of loss. Many people feel some anxiety about getting married; are they marrying the right person, will they get on well together, what will living together for ever be like? Learning to cope with married life takes a lot of time, money and energy. Living with a partner involves learning about his or her needs and ways. For some people marriage is the most positive change that can happen in life. Other people regard it as involving a loss of freedom, or even as entering a relationship where one person dominates or exploits another.

THINK IT THROUGH

How positively or negatively do you and your friends see marriage? What rating would you give it on a five-point scale from one (very negative) to five (very positive)

Divorce

At present, one in three marriages is likely to end in divorce. In the 1950s many people stayed married despite being unhappy with their partners – in the past, it was often difficult to get a divorce and there were likely to be serious problems over money and finding somewhere to live following divorce, particularly for women.

Divorce is much more common nowadays, but many people who divorce go on to re-marry. Each year, over a third of marriages are likely to be re-marriages. Nearly a quarter of children in Britain may expect their parents to divorce before they are 16 years old.

Although many people experience divorce as a negative experience, it may often be better than living in a stressful situation. Sometimes people develop a deeper sense of self following divorce. Agencies such as Relate provide counselling services to help people to understand the emotions involved in partnerships. Counselling may help some people to decide whether it is best to divorce or not.

Case Study – Marriage

Davinder is 21 years old and is about to complete her studies for a university degree. Davinder is a Sikh, and she has lived in a Sikh community in the UK all her life. Davinder has thought about marriage a lot during the past few years. Many times, she has discussed the possibilities and whom she might marry with her family. Davinder's family are concerned that she should make a good marriage with someone of an equal educational status.

Davinder has met Sohan and thinks he is attractive and intelligent. Davinder's family know Sohan's family and have agreed that they would make a good couple. Sohan has visited Davinder's family and an 'engagement' ceremony has taken place at their local Gurdwara (or temple). Davinder has been given a gold ring by Sohan's mother.

Davinder is now looking forward to her wedding day. She is extremely happy and excited. She will be the centre of attention, and she will go through a ceremony that will mark a major change in her life. Everything about this change is welcome. Davinder will wear red and gold, lucky colours. After the ceremony she will live with her husband, and not with her family. There have been many gifts exchanged between the families. Davinder feels a mixture of joy and anticipation. After the wedding she will be different, she will have her own house, and she will have a husband to care for, although she will not be with her own family. All the changes involved almost make Davinder feel a bit 'giddy'.

Figure 2.10 *A Sikh bride*

Davinder will find marriage positive because she wants to be married. She has had a great deal of support from her family and feels that she has some idea of how to cope with her new role. Marriage is a major change that Davinder has looked forward to for a long time, and she is sure that Sohan will be a good husband.

Parenthood

Becoming a parent involves a major change in life. Many parents experience their relationship with their child as an intense and new emotional experience. There may be strong feelings of love and a powerful desire to protect the child. But becoming a parent also involves losses – parents can lose sleep because the baby wakes them up, and they may find that they can't go out very easily – so that they lose touch with friends and social life. Parents can lose money because they have either to pay for child care or give up full-time work to care for their child. Parents can lose career opportunities if they stay out of full-time work to bring up a family. These losses can sometimes place a relationship or marriage under stress – sometimes a parent can even become jealous of the love and attention that a child receives from the other parent.

Becoming a parent can involve some anxiety about the new role of being a parent. 'Will the baby be healthy?' 'Is the baby safe?', 'Am I being a good mother/father?' New parents usually seek advice from family, friends, doctors and health visitors. Parenthood involves a lot of pressure on time, money and energy. A new infant will need nappies, clothes and toys, food, cot, high chair, car seat and so on. An infant needs a lot of attention. Carers will need time and emotional energy to care for the child. Parents often need advice on caring skills – there is new learning involved in being a good parent and always a lot to learn about the child as a new relationship develops.

Retirement

The nature of work is changing rapidly. Many people will work as self-employed or temporary workers in the future, and retirement may become very flexible with some people effectively retiring in their 40s and others continuing to take on work in their late 60s and 70s. Retirement can represent a major change for people who have worked in a demanding, full-time job and then completely stop working. A sudden break from full-time work might cause a feeling of loss. Work roles influence self-concept, so a person's self-concept and self-esteem can change following retirement. People may lose their routine and perhaps their work friends when they retire, and some people may not be prepared for the leisure time they have and be unsure what to do with their time each day. Some people say that retirement makes them feel useless – they are no longer of use to anyone. People who have to live on the state pension alone may experience a loss of income. Some older people live below the 'poverty line'.

On the positive side, people with private pensions and savings often have the time and money to travel, study or take up hobbies and thoroughly enjoy themselves. Some people see retirement as a time of self-fulfilment, when they harvest the rewards of a lifetime's work. Retirement can lead to greater freedom and the opportunity to spend more time with family, relatives and friends.

THINK IT THROUGH

Retirement provides a mixture of positive and negative possibilities. If you were to talk to people who have been through retirement, what would they say were the main problems and the main advantages? How positively or negatively would they rate retirement?

Death of a loved one (bereavement)

People can lose their partners at any stage of life, but as couples grow older the chances that one person will die increase. Bereavement means losing someone you loved, and it causes a major change in people's lives. There is a very strong sense of loss – you might lose the main person you talked to, the main person who helped you, your sexual partner, a person you shared life with and a person who made you feel good. Living without a partner can involve great uncertainty. Your partner may have helped with household bills or with shopping or housework – now you have to do it all yourself. Bereavement can mean you have to learn to live a new life as a single person again. Learning to cope on your own can take a lot of time and energy.

People who try to cope with a major loss often experience the following feelings:

- not being able to believe that the person is dead

- sadness and depression

- anger or guilt

- stress because they have to learn to cope with a different lifestyle.

Few people describe bereavement as a positive life event, but the final outcome need not only be sadness and grief. Over time, people can take a positive outlook on life again.

Ageing

Most people hope to grow old and many people enjoy a high quality of life in old age. Many cultures honour older people as 'elders', people who have wisdom and who deserve respect. Whether ageing is mainly positive or negative is greatly influenced by a person's level of self-esteem, and the resources and support that person has. If you feel proud of your life, that you have lived a worthwhile life, this will help to make ageing a positive experience. If you enjoy your lifestyle, and you have enough money to meet your needs, this will help to make ageing positive. If you have friends, family and a partner to support you, this will also help to make ageing a positive experience.

Ageing can involve bereavement, but high self-esteem, friends and enough money can all help people to cope with loss. Low self-esteem, poverty and social isolation (no friends or family) can make it harder to cope.

Ageing can involve the development of illnesses and physical or sensory disabilities, for some people. Again, high self-esteem, friends and enough money can all help a person to cope. A lack of self-esteem, money or support can increase the problems caused by a disability.

Some older people live below the 'poverty line' and some lose contact with friends and family. These problems are social problems – they are not caused just because people have lived a long time.

THINK IT THROUGH

Look at the case study of Mrs Baddock on page 81. What are the positive and negative issues involved in ageing here?

Kinship groups and family

There are many different types of families and relationships within families, but most children are born into some sort of social group. Many children will have brothers and sisters, parents or step-parents, aunts and uncles. Children grow up surrounded by other people and are influenced by the people in their family or kinship group.

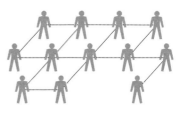

Figure 2.11 *A kinship group is like a web or network of contacts*

A kinship group means all the people you know who are related to you. This includes the family you might live with and other people and families that are related to you. A kinship group can be like a web or network of contacts – people who can offer advice and help.

Kinship and family groups are very important because they are usually the people who first influence our lives. Infants and young children copy what they see. As we grow up, we may copy what the adults and other children in our kinship network do. We learn from the reactions of parents, brothers, sisters and other relatives towards us.

Socialisation

Kinship and family groups usually provide the first experience of socialisation for children. Socialisation means to become social – children learn to fit in with and be part of a social group. When children grow up within a family group, they will usually learn a wide range of ideas about how to behave. For instance, at mealtimes, some families will have strict rules that everyone must sit down at the table and it is considered 'rude' if one person starts to eat before the others. Other families may not even have set mealtimes – people may just prepare food for themselves when they feel like it.

In the evenings, some families might sit round the TV as a social group, while other families might all sit in different rooms doing different activities. Some families are very concerned that people take their outdoor shoes off before coming into the house, and others have no rules about shoes.

THINK IT THROUGH

Are, or were, any of the following 'norms' important in your family?

- *to say 'thank you' or 'thank you for having me' to the head of a household you visited?*
- *to give thanks in prayer before a meal?*
- *not to eat hot food with your fingers?*
- *to go to bed at a fixed time – unless there is a special event or festival?*
- *never to interrupt when an older member of the family is speaking?*
- *that children have set tasks to help adults with the housework?*
- *that male members of the household are responsible for decorating and repairing the house?*
- *that female members of the household are responsible for all the washing and ironing?*

You could compare your list with others in your group.

Families and similar social groups develop attitudes about what is 'normal' or right to do. Sociologists call these beliefs 'norms'. Each family will have 'norms' that cover how people should behave.

By the age of two, children usually understand that they are male or female. During the socialisation process, children learn how to act in masculine or feminine ways. Boys may copy the behaviour of other male members of the family, and girls may copy the behaviour of other female members. Sociologists call this learning a gender (male or female) role. Learning a role means learning to act as a male or female person.

During childhood, children learn ideas about what is right or wrong. They learn the customs of their culture and family, they learn to play gender and adult roles, and they learn what is expected of them and what they should expect from others. Socialisation teaches children ways of thinking, and these ways of thinking may stay with a person for life.

Primary socialisation

Not everything that a child learns during first (or primary) socialisation within the family group is learned by copying adults. Children also spend time watching TV, listening to radio and playing computer games. Children will be influenced by the things they see and hear over the media as well as their experiences within the home.

THINK IT THROUGH

Look at the picture of a breakfast scene in Figure 2.12. Think carefully – how many influences on the children can you spot?

Figure 2.12 *Breakfast time in a family home – how many things to do with socialisation can you spot?*

Did you notice the media influence in this home? The radio sends messages about love and relationships in the songs that are playing. The TV sends messages about news and opinions. The newspaper invites the reader to share its views on current events. Even the cereal packet has an advert encouraging the family to get money and spend it!

Did you notice the gender roles in this home? Who is preparing the children's breakfast, and who is being waited on? What differences are there in the way the two children are playing – what toys have they chosen?

Does playing with dolls or playing with toy cars influence children's expectations in life? Note the length of hair for males and females and their clothes.

Thinking about this scene, what do you think the children might be learning? Will the daughter tend to copy the mother's behaviour as she grows up – will she see her role as 'looking after people'? Will the son copy the father's role and expect to be waited on at mealtimes. What expectations might people develop just from being with each other? How far does the media influence people's expectations of their lives? Do you think violence on TV could influence these people in any way?

Secondary socialisation

As children grow older they go to school and learn to read and use computers. The range of influences on them grows larger. Even though children make friends and learn new ideas at school, however, the main group experience for most children will still be with their family and kinship group. Children's need for love and affection and the need to belong to a group will usually be met by the family. If a child is rejected or neglected by the family, he or she will be at risk of developing a low sense of self-worth and poor self-esteem.

During adolescence the importance of the family group begins to change. Between 11 and 15 years of age adolescents become very involved with their own group of friends. Most adolescents have a group of friends who influence what they think and believe, usually people of the same age. This is the second influential group to which people belong, and it creates a second type of socialisation, that sociologists call secondary socialisation.

After the age of 12 or 13, a person's sense of self-worth is likely to depend more on the reactions of others of the same age than on what parents say. During adolescence it is important to be accepted and to belong with friends. Adolescents tend to copy the way other adolescents behave.

THINK IT THROUGH

Try to remember when you were 14 or 15 years old. Can you recall what you and others in your class at school thought about the following topics? What sort of beliefs and values did your parents have at that time? Which beliefs are closest to your beliefs now?

- *It is important to get a good job.*
- *It is bad and dangerous to use drugs.*
- *It is important to go out and have a good time.*
- *Wearing the right clothes to look good is a priority.*
- *Saving money is a priority.*

Socialisation does not finish with secondary socialisation. People continue to change and learn to fit in with new groups when they go out to work and when they start new families.

Primary socialisation = First socialisation within a family or care group.
Secondary socialisation = Later socialisation with friends and peer groups.

The value of kinship groups

Kinship groups are often important during the whole of a person's lifetime. Kinship groups not only provide the setting for first (or primary) socialisation, but they can also provide a buffer against stress. A buffer is a shock-absorbing barrier that gives protection from an impact. Buffers are used to protect trains at railway stations. Partners, family and friends can act as 'shock absorbers' to protect us from the knocks that we take in life. When we change jobs, move home, get married, become ill or unemployed, partners or relatives might help us to cope with the stress of change.

Talking to family members can help you to feel that you matter to them. Family and relatives might help you with practical jobs if you are ill or too busy to do them. They might help you with shopping, arrange for doctors to visit, sort out bills. Relatives may be able to give you advice or know people who can advise you. A number of studies in both Britain and the USA have found that people with good partnerships, marriages, family and friends are generally happier and healthier than people who do not have these relationships.

Kinship networks can help us with difficult life events, but they can also cause stress. We hope that we would get support, help and advice from our family, so it is only fair that they expect us to help them. Being part of a kinship network means that we have to spend time supporting other people, and often giving practical help. We may have to visit older relatives and listen to them to help them keep a sense of self-worth. Kinship networks involve giving as well as receiving. At some stages in life, such as childhood, we may mainly receive help; at other times during adult life we may have to give more help than we get back.

Kinship relationships can also be stressful when people fail to cope with each other. A third of marriages end in divorce, and a quarter of all children might experience the divorce of their parents before they are 16. Kinship relationships can be very good for us – but very difficult when they break down.

Self-concept

Self-concept means the way we think about ourselves (see Figure 2.13).

Figure 2.13 *Self-concept*

A simple way of understanding self-concept is to see ourselves as having a physical self-concept, an intellectual self, an emotional and a social self. Using this idea you can fill in the questionnaire on self-concept below.

The self-concept questionnaire

Thinking about yourself in relation to other people that you know, how would you rate yourself on the questions below? Give yourself a mark out of five: 1 for a low opinion, 5 for a high opinion.

Your physical self

■ How attractive are you?

■ How healthy are you?

- How fit are you?
- How good are you generally at sport and physical activity?

Your intellectual self

- How good are you at maths and number work?
- How good are you at communication and English?
- How good are you at scientific thinking?
- How good are you at art, music, and general academic work?

Your emotional self

- How good are you at guessing what other people are feeling?
- How good are you at understanding your own feelings?
- How good are you at getting on with other people, including people who are sad or angry?
- How good are you at making yourself concentrate on work that you know you have to do?

Your social self

- How good are your relationships with members of your own family?
- How easy do you find it to mix and make friends with new people?
- How good and satisfying are your close friendships?
- How good are your relationships with other students or colleagues?

When you have shaded in all your scores on the chart below, your 'self-concept pattern' will be shown. Compare your pattern with others. Can you work out why there might be differences or similarities between you?

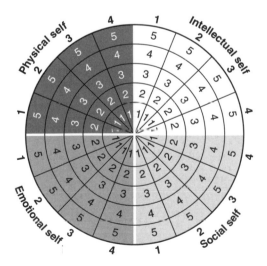

Fig 2.14 *Scoring the self-concept questionnaire*

Each person develops his or her own special view of him or herself. This is because of the experiences that people have as they grow and develop across their life-span.

Why is self-concept important?

Some psychologists have seen our concept of self as being the most important thing in life. Developing and keeping a clear sense of self has been described as 'the goal of living at any age.'

Our view of ourselves is important because it can:

- motivate us to do things or stop us from doing things, for example, doing well at school or at sport

- create a feeling of social confidence or cause us to feel anxious with other people

- mean that we experience happiness or unhappiness from life experiences

- help us lead a successful and enjoyable life or it can lead us into trouble and difficulties in coping with life.

If we think we are good at school or work we will probably enjoy going to school or work. Our concept of ourselves will lead us to want to be there. If we think that we are not good at school or work, we may not want to go there. The way we think about ourselves influences what we do and how we feel.

Can you change your self-concept?

Yes – because our knowledge of ourselves changes as we go through life. But we cannot change our confidence or our motivation just by wishing to be different. Our self-concept develops and changes because of the experiences we have. New life experiences can lead to a changed self-concept.

How does self-concept develop?

Figure 2.15 *The way we see ourselves can influence how we choose to behave*

When we are born we do not understand anything about the world we are born into; we do not know that we are each an individual person. The beginnings of self-awareness may start when an infant can recognise his or her own face in a mirror. This usually happens before the age of 2, when an infant begins to demonstrate that he or she is different from other people.

From this point on, children begin to form ideas about themselves. Children are influenced by the environment and culture they grow up in; they are also influenced by the relationships they have with their family and friends. As a child's ability to use language develops this will also affect how they can talk and explain things about themselves.

People develop an increasingly detailed understanding of their selves as they grow older. A general outline of the development of self-concept is given in the table overleaf:

$1\frac{1}{2}$–2 years	Self-awareness develops; children may start to recognise themselves in a mirror.
$2\frac{1}{2}$ years	Children can say whether they are a boy or a girl.
3–5 years	When asked to say what they are like, children can describe themselves in terms of categories such as big or small, tall or short, light or heavy.
5–8 years	If you ask children who they are, they can often describe themselves in detail. Children will tell you their hair colour, eye colour, the family and school to which they belong.
8–10 years	Children start to show a general sense of 'self-worth' such as describing how happy they are in general, how good life is for them, what is good about their family life, school and friends.
10–12 years	Children start to analyse how they compare with others. When asked about their life, children may explain without prompting how they compare with others, for example: 'I'm not as good as Zoe at running, but I'm better than Ali'.
12–16 years	Adolescents may develop a sense of self in terms of beliefs and belonging to groups, e.g. being a vegetarian, believing in God, believing certain things are right or wrong.
16–25	People may develop an adult self-concept that helps them to feel confident in a work role and in social and sexual relationships.
25 onwards	People's sense of self will be influenced by the things that happen in their lives. Some people may change their self-concept a great deal as they grow older.
65 onwards	In later life it is important to be able to keep a clear sense of self. People may become withdrawn and depressed without a clear self-concept.

The self-concept we have when we are very young is influenced by our family or carers. Primary school age children are influenced by the adults that they live with. As we grow older the friends we mix with gradually take over and influence what we think. As adolescents we often compare ourselves with others and choose a particular set of friends to belong with.

Our self-concept does not usually settle down until we are ready to go out to work full-time or until we plan to leave home and live with a sexual partner. Until this time of life it may be that we experiment with ideas of what we may be like and what we may be good at. Adult commitments may force us into making decisions about ourselves. For this reason some people may not be able to explain their self-concept clearly until they are in their early twenties.

Adults usually develop the power to think about themselves using logic. For instance an 8-year-old girl might look in the mirror and think: 'that's me'. That might be all she thinks. But a 16-year-old might look in the mirror and think to herself: 'so that's me. I'd like to be more like my friend; shorter hair, thinner, different clothes'. The 16-year-old person will be able to plan how to change her looks, how to lose weight and so on. This ability to think about self may be partly due to intellectual development.

A clear sense of what you think your personality is like and what you think you are good at may be necessary if you are to be happy, confident and successful at work and in love.

Age	Expression of self-concept
Young children	Self-concept limited to a few descriptions, for example, boy or girl, size, some skills
Older children	Self-concept can be described in a range of 'factual categories', such as hair colour, name, details or address, etc.
Adolescents	Self-concept starts to be explained in terms of chosen beliefs, likes, dislikes, relationships with others
Adults	Many adults may be able to explain the quality of their lives and their personality in greater depth and detail than when they were adolescents
Older adults	Some older adults may have more self-knowledge than during early adult life. Some people may show 'wisdom' in the way they explain their self-concept

Figure 2.16 *The differences in self-concept between various age groups*

ASSESSMENT ACTIVITY

Identify positive and negative influences on growth and development.

I   Use the table below to help you think about some of the influences on people's development during the different life stages. Using the table as a focus for discussion, work with a small group of other students in order to identify examples of positive and negative influences that can affect each life stage.

Life stage	Life events such as getting a job, leaving home, parenthood, bereavement	Economic factors	Socialisation including family and peer groups	Physical health and ability	The influence of self-concept
Birth					
Infancy					
Childhood					
Adolescence					
Adulthood					
Old age					
Facing death					

After thinking about and discussing development, write a report that identifies some positive and negative influences on development.

2 Arrange to interview a member of care staff while you are on placement. Discuss with them how life events might influence the lives of service users. Following your discussion, imagine two different individuals and explain how their lives might be altered by the impact of life events such as marriage, retirement or bereavement.

To achieve a **merit grade** you need to explain how growth and development at each life stage can be influenced positively and negatively. Your report must cover each life stage, explaining how development at each stage can be influenced positively or negatively.

To achieve a **distinction grade** you need to use examples from your work experience to analyse the effects of life events on two different individuals. You should use activity 2 in order to develop your report to include an analysis of the possible effects of life events on two individuals. Remember that if you use real-life experiences you must obtain permission to use this material from the individuals concerned and you should also disguise their identity so as to preserve confidentiality.

Care needs

People can have four main types of needs.

Physical care needs involve help with tasks like getting meals, help with mobility, help with washing and going to the toilet.

Safety and security needs mean that people have a need to know what to expect, and they need to feel safe from abuse and pain, and from major changes that may alter their lives.

A need to belong involves the feeling of being included – people need to feel that they have a relationship with those who care for them. Young children have a need to build a loving attachment with their carers. Adults need to feel that they fit in with a care setting and that their culture and life experience are respected.

A need for self-esteem is important – most adults have a need to be given respect, a need for dignity, and a need to be treated as a person who is worth something. People receiving care may have a fear of being 'talked down to', or of being seen as a problem rather than as a person.

Caring for people is about meeting all the needs people have. A carer might see his or her task as moving an old person down the corridor so that he can have lunch. Moving the person to the dining room will meet his physical needs. But if this small task is all that is done, the person's other needs may be ignored. Skilled caring is not just doing things to people. A skilled carer would not just take a person to the dining room – he or she would smile, talk to the person, show respect and check that the person was ready to go. A skilled carer would always think about the service user's safety and security needs.

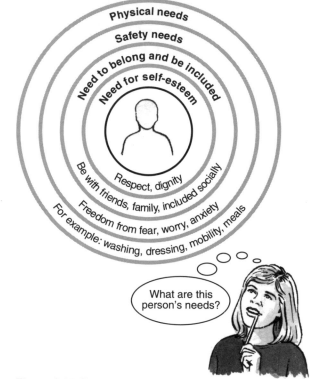

Figure 2.17 *Four circles of need*

If you are sitting in a wheelchair and it suddenly moves off without warning, you cannot feel safe. You can't guess what might happen next in a place where people just do things to you – you might get frightened if you were cared for like this. If you are sitting in a wheelchair and your carer says, 'Right, I'm taking you for lunch now', at least you know what is happening, but you couldn't feel that your feelings mattered or that you were equal to the carer. The carer makes the decision.

The way your carer talks to you is very important. As well as offering you a choice, you will need to feel that your carer values you, and that you are respected by other people. If you don't get respect then you will find it hard to value yourself – your self-esteem needs will not be met.

Case Study – Mrs Markovitz

Mrs Markovitz is 84 and lives alone in an old terraced house. Her husband died five years ago, and since then she has been supported by her daughter and son-in-law who make regular visits to her. Mrs Markovitz has home help three times a week to collect shopping and help her with housework. Recently, Mrs Markovitz has been increasingly forgetful and has left her front door open at night. Her daughter and son-in-law want to go abroad for a month or so and have arranged with Mrs Markovitz that she should go into a residential care home for a short period.

What kind of care needs will Mrs Markovitz have?

Physical needs	Mrs Markovitz will need a warm, comfortable room. She will need regular meals and clean toilet and washing facilities.
Safety and security needs	Mrs Markovitz will need to be sure that her personal possessions will not be lost or stolen. She will need to feel confident that staff will not abuse her, that she will not fall over or suffer pain if staff use hoists to lift her.
Sense of belonging	Mrs Markovitz is used to her own personal diet. She is hoping that she will not be offered food she doesn't like or that doesn't fit in with her culture. Mrs Markovitz will not know anyone in the home, and she hasn't even left her house for five years. She will need to build a relationship with care staff before she will feel that it is OK to be in the home.
Sense of self-esteem	Mrs Markovitz is very proud of her daughter and of her own life. Now that she has gone into care, Mrs Markovitz feels that her life is over – 'I'm no use to anyone now, I'm just a burden'. She might recover her feeling of self-worth if her relationships with carers and other residents make her feel worthwhile again.

Nearly all care settings would cater for Mrs Markovitz's physical needs. Care homes are inspected to ensure they provide reasonable standards of care, and all care settings will try to provide a safe setting. How Mrs Markovitz gets on in terms of her social and emotional needs will depend on the skills of the care staff.

Maslow's hierarchy of needs

Abraham Maslow (1908–1970) was a psychologist who became famous for his theory of human needs. Young children have an inbuilt need to learn to walk, to learn to talk and to make social relationships, but Maslow believed that humans have a natural need to learn, grow and develop for the whole of their lives – not just during childhood.

Although humans have a tendency to want to learn and to grow and develop emotionally, not everyone does this. Some people get stuck – they stop developing emotionally. Maslow explained why some people grow and others get stuck, in terms of a theory of human needs.

Maslow believed that there were different levels of human need. If your needs are not met at one level, it becomes difficult to develop yourself beyond that level. The levels are shown in the diagram in Figure 2.18, which is called Maslow's hierarchy of needs. A hierarchy is a system with different levels; some needs are higher up in the hierarchy.

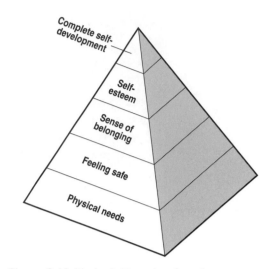

Figure 2.18 *Maslow's hierarchy of needs*

At the bottom are physical needs. Physical needs include the need for food, water, air, freedom from pain, sleep and sex.

Physical needs

If a person is constantly hungry and can never find enough to eat, that person will not care so much about general safety, and will not be concerned about relationships or what other people think of him or her. If you think you might die of hunger no other needs matter, so all your thoughts will focus on getting food. When people feel that their physical needs are met, they can concern themselves with the next level in the hierarchy – safety needs.

Safety needs

If we have enough food and are free from pain and so on, we will think about our safety needs. People generally need a stable, predictable setting in which to live and work, but many people feel anxious about losing their health, jobs, money, or relationships. Other people are anxious simply because they cannot predict the future – they don't know what might happen to them. Anxious people will try to make their lives more predictable, stable and safe. They will not worry about love and affection until they feel safe.

Belonging and love

The third level of human need is the need for affection, the need to be with other people, and the need to be accepted. People need to be loved and to love others, but loneliness may become a worry only when you are safe and your basic needs are met.

Self-esteem

Self-esteem means thinking well of yourself, having self-confidence and believing that you have the respect and recognition of others. A high level of self-esteem will mean that you feel good about your performance at work and your relationships with others. Self-esteem is built up from the way other people speak to you and the degree of respect you receive.

When people feel safe, when they have their basic physical needs met, and when they feel they belong with others, they will be concerned about what other people think of them. Life has to be fairly good before people worry too much about being praised or criticised. People who are hungry may steal to get food, because they wouldn't worry what people thought. If your more basic needs are met, however, you will care about the degree of respect you are shown by others.

Self-actualisation

Maslow believed that some people spend most of their lives struggling to feel safe and to find love and affection, but a reasonable number of people do develop good levels of self-esteem in their lives. The goal of living should not be just to get respect from others, however – Maslow thought people should try to develop their abilities and talents to the fullest extent possible. His name for this complete development was 'self-actualisation'. 'Self-actualisation' means achieving everything that you have the potential to achieve. Self-actualisation brings a high level of happiness and contentment to life. Maslow thought that most people never reach this stage, as they become stuck with more basic social and emotional needs.

Upbringing and health

Most people want to live a long and healthy life – but not everybody does so. Why do some people live to their 90s, or to be over 100, and yet others die young? Why do some people have many health problems and others very little illness?

A general explanation for health differences is that we are influenced by:

- our genetic make-up
- our behaviour, our diet, our lifestyle, our activities
- our attitudes and beliefs about health
- our socialisation or upbringing
- the wider environment we live in.

Genetics

People are born with different genetic patterns, and these patterns can make a person likely to develop certain illnesses or more resistant to particular diseases. Usually an individual might be at risk of one illness, such as cancer, but at less risk of another illness – perhaps heart disease.

Your genetic make-up reacts with the things you do. Steve Jones, a professor of genetics, thinks that as many as one person in every ten has resistance to lung cancer caused by smoking. Some other people may be at great risk from cancer if they ever smoke. At present, we don't know who is at high risk and who is at low risk, so the best advice to everyone is not to smoke.

The same is probably true when it comes to the risks involved in drinking alcohol, not taking exercise or having a high-fat diet. Some people can get away with some unhealthy behaviours, but many people can't. Your genes can influence how much damage a particularly risky behaviour might do to you.

Behaviour

There are a range of risks to health that can be prevented. Health advisers are careful to warn people of the dangers of unsafe sex and of taking non-prescribed drugs.

DID YOU KNOW?

The two main diseases that kill people are heart disease and cancer. In the mid 1990s, 46 per cent of all deaths were caused by heart or circulatory disease. Currently, one in three people is expected to develop a cancer during his or her lifetime and roughly one in four people in Britain dies of cancer.

Is there anything people can do to prevent cancer or heart disease? The main recommendations are as follows.

- do not smoke
- eat a healthy diet – low in fat, high in fibre, fruit and vegetables
- take regular exercise
- if you drink alcohol, carefully limit the amount you drink.

If people followed this advice, the amount of cancer and heart disease in the population would be reduced. People can choose to reduce the degree of risk in their lives.

Attitudes and beliefs about health

Advice on how to stay healthy is freely available, but not everyone believes it or takes it seriously.

When people believe there is nothing they can do, or that health is all a matter of luck, they will not try to follow advice on staying healthy. Other people will ignore health advice because they think that having fun or making money is more important. If you worry only about germs, you might not worry about smoking, diet, exercise or sensible drinking. Only people who take their health seriously and who believe that they can influence their own health are likely to make healthy choices and follow health advice.

THINK IT THROUGH

How far do you agree with the following attitudes? Score 1 for totally agree, 2 for partly agree, and 3 for disagree.

a *How healthy you are is all a matter of luck – how you live doesn't matter.*

b *How healthy you are is all up to you – if you live your life the right way, you will stay healthy.*

c *There is no point in thinking about health. Other things are more important – like enjoying yourself.*

d *Disease is caused by germs, genetics and pollution – you need to do what you can to protect yourself.*

e *Whatever is going to happen to you will happen anyway – you can't change it.*

f *You can't guarantee your health, but you can reduce the health risks you face in life.*

Researchers have found that different people agree with each of these statements. People have different attitudes towards their health.

Socialisation

Why do people have different attitudes and beliefs about health? Primary socialisation within a family group and secondary socialisation within an adolescent's age group can influence what people think. Children copy the views and behaviour of their parents. If a child is socialised into a group that does not make healthy choices, he or she may copy negative attitudes and

behaviour. If children are brought up to see a high-fat diet, smoking and excessive drinking as normal, they may continue with this behaviour later in life. They may say, 'It must be OK – everybody does it'.

Later on, young people are influenced by their own age group. Sometimes people ignore their health – take up smoking, take drugs, or drink too much – in order to fit in with what other people do. People often want to look good, and some think that taking drugs or smoking makes them special, or that it brings

Figure 2.19 *Children may learn to copy the lifestyle they see*

them more attention and respect. Once you take up an enjoyable but dangerous habit, it can be hard to change the habit later. Other people mix with friends who think that healthy behaviour is important – that smoking or drug-taking is stupid. These people will copy this attitude and perhaps avoid smoking for the rest of their lives.

Sometimes people make choices for complicated reasons. In one study, girls who took up smoking explained that they knew it was unhealthy, but they thought it helped them to stay slim. Being slim was more valuable than health.

The environment

Why do some families and some social groups value health, whereas some don't? Economic and environmental differences may influence people's health directly, but they may also influence group attitudes.

During the 1970s and 1980s many studies showed a link between social class and health. Children born to working-class parents were more likely to be stillborn, more likely to die in childhood and more likely to die during adulthood than children born to middle-class parents. Working-class people had more illness during adulthood, and took more time off work. There appeared to be a health divide, with middle-class people having much better health.

More recent research suggests that poverty causes ill-health. Money may not make people healthy, but a lack of it seems to be linked with disease and illness. Reasons why poverty may contribute to poor health include the following.

- Low-income families may live in stressful housing conditions, including overcrowding, noisy neighbours, and property that is poorly maintained or poorly heated and ventilated.

- Low-income families may live in more polluted neighbourhoods.

- Low-income families may find it more difficult to purchase and prepare healthy foods compared with wealthier people.

- Having a low income may create stress and worry about debts, bills and coping with life.

- People who are stressed may have poorer social relationships with family and friends.

- Over-eating, smoking and drinking alcohol may offer simple and relaxing pastimes to stressed people.

- People on a low income and who are stressed may have low self-esteem and may not feel that their future health matters – getting money may seem more important.

■ People living in a stressful neighbourhood with little money may feel that health advice about diet, exercise, smoking and drinking only adds to their stress – so they may choose not to believe it.

Care needs at different life stages

Infancy

Newborn babies are helpless, and completely dependent on parents or carers to provide for their needs. Infants' physical needs have to be met by others – they have to be fed, washed, clothed and kept warm by parents or carers.

Infants learn to recognise their mother by voice and smell during the first week of life. Infants can usually recognise familiar faces by six months and may cry if separated from carers after this age. Infants need to make a safe and stable relationship with carers during the first year of life, and there is a need to make an emotional bond with carers. Infants will smile and make sounds to attract attention from carers. Relationships are important right from the beginning of life, but infants do not have self-esteem needs because they have not yet developed an understanding of 'self'. The first three levels of Maslow's pyramid are those that are important in infancy.

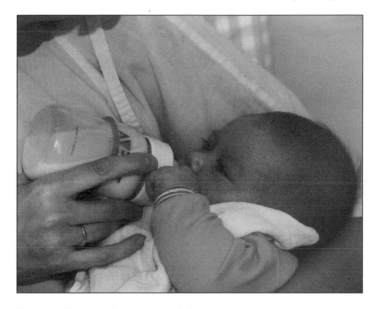

Figure 2.20 *Infants' physical needs have to be met by others*

Childhood

As children grow they learn an ever-increasing range of skills, like running, climbing, skipping, riding a bicycle, and reading. As they gain new skills, children enjoy doing things for themselves and being more independent. Children are still dependent on adult carers to provide a stable, loving home for them, and although children will explore and experiment, carers often need to guide and supervise what they do. Adult carers will need to provide for children's physical needs and create a physically and emotionally safe environment for them. During primary socialisation, children should feel they belong to a family or group; they will have a need to feel loved and wanted.

Children will need to feel approved of and included in care activities. They may often be able to be independent in meeting physical care needs but adults will need to advise on things like diet.

Adolescence

Young people develop an increasing level of skill and understanding as they grow towards adulthood. The need to belong to a family or care group may still be important, but adolescents will be increasingly concerned to fit in with groups of their own age. Around 13 to 15 years of age, young people often copy each other's style of clothing and appearance. Young people learn to become gradually more independent of their parents or carers. Adolescents may be able to make independent choices about physical needs, choose their own friendship groups and lifestyle. When carers work with adolescents they need to encourage and show respect for their developing sense of self.

Adults

People often need practical help and assistance, and they may receive care because they cannot live completely independent lives. Carers may need to provide a range of physical and practical care such as assisting with mobility, cooking, making arrangements for visitors, offering guidance on daily living activities, and so on. Service users will also need to feel safe, to feel included, and to feel respected. Carers will need good communication skills in order to meet all four levels of need.

Older adults

Older people should have the same rights to autonomy, choice and independence that all adults have. Some older people can suffer a range of losses, including a loss of health, of income, of friends and partners. Some older people feel threatened by the changes that can happen. Some older people are stereotyped or labelled as being useless, or a burden. Needs for respect and to be treated as a person with social as well as physical needs may be critically important. Carers will need to pay attention to all four areas of need.

The final stages of life

When people are dying they will often have complex physical needs for comfort, pain relief, keeping the mouth moist, and so on. All the levels of Maslow's pyramid will also be relevant.

People will often be anxious, and will need emotional support. They will often want to see friends and relatives – the need to belong is important. People sometimes need to make sense of their lives and some need a life review or counselling to enable them to cope with the end of life. Self-esteem – the need to feel that life has had value – may be a major factor in enabling people to cope emotionally with the end of life. People who have fulfilled their potential may be able to face the end of life with a sense of inner peace. Self-actualisation links with spiritual needs.

The conversation and communication skills that carers develop may be of great importance for meeting the social, self-esteem, and anxiety needs that people may have in the final stages of their lives.

Different care needs

Some writers have used the word autonomy to sum up service users' rights in care. Autonomy means having freedom and independence to choose what you do – within limits. Most adults are free to choose how they live, but choice is always limited – you can only choose things you can afford and that don't cause serious problems for other people. There are always boundaries to what we can or should choose.

Therefore money may limit some choices and service users must respect other service users' and carers' rights, but carers should encourage independence and choice wherever possible. Carers should be careful not to hurry service users by making choices for them and taking independence away.

ASSESSMENT ACTIVITY

Investigate and describe the care needs of individuals at different life stages.

1   Use the table below to help you identify the care needs of people at different life stages. Using your placement experience, think about how well individual care needs were met for three people of different ages and a write a report that records your ideas.

Life stage	Physical needs, e.g. washing, dressing, mobility and meals	Safety needs, e.g. freedom from fear, worry and anxiety	Belonging needs, e.g. being with friends and family, being included socially	Self-esteem needs, e.g. respect for individuality, independence and dignity
Infancy				
Childhood				
Adolescence				
Adulthood				
Old age				
Facing death				

2 Thinking about the three people you have identified, work out how life events such as starting school, starting work, leaving home, marriage, divorce, parenthood, retirement and bereavement might have influenced these people. Develop your report so that it explains how major changes in life, such as these life events, might alter the physical, safety, belonging and self-esteem needs of the people you have identified.

3 It may be possible for you to get permission from service users so that you can interview them about their life history. Some people may be happy to share their experiences of life events and the way this has changed them. You may also be able to interview care staff about the ways in which workers can meet needs and have a positive influence on the lives of service users.

Reading may also help you to understand the theory of care needs.

To achieve a **merit grade** you need to investigate and explain how life events can influence development and care needs of individuals. Use activity 2 above to help you achieve this level.

To achieve a **distinction grade** you must use a range of sources of information to suggest ways in which professional care workers can meet care needs and have a positive influence on growth and development.

If you can use a range of sources such as those suggested in activity 3 above, you may be able to develop your report so that it uses a range of sources to suggest ways in which professional care workers can meet care needs and influence development.

UNIT THREE

CARE PRACTICE FOUNDATIONS

During your placement or work experience you will find that you need to use many of the skills you will learn about in this unit, regardless of the service user group you work with – some basic requirements are the same. On the other hand, each service user group will also have its own particular needs and it is important that you learn to recognise the requirements of different groups.

You will need to know how to work safely in a care environment for your own protection, for the safety of work colleagues and especially for the people for whom you are providing care. It is also important that you understand the different types of services that are available to meet the different needs of the many people who require care. This unit will introduce you to the way in which caring and health services are provided.

In this unit you will learn about:

- skills required to be an effective care worker
- health and safety principles
- health and social care services.

Skills required to be an effective care worker

In previous units you have learned about the physical, intellectual, emotional and social needs that people have. It is easy to remember this as PIES, but never forget that you must think about the whole pie, and not just one slice! This is called the holistic approach to care and to be a good care worker you must make sure that you are meeting all of the needs a person has. It is not enough simply to meet their physical requirements – providing them with food and warmth and making sure they are clean and cared for is not enough if you neglect their emotional or social needs.

It is often easy to concentrate on one area of caring and forget about some of the other important aspects. This could mean that while you provided meals and clean clothing for people in your care, you neglected to talk to them, to ensure that they had plenty of interests, that they were able to meet with their friends and people who were important to them, and that they were able to take part in physical activity.

Figure 3.1 *Remember PIES, but think about all four slices!*

Individuals

To work well in care you need not only to recognise that people have needs in many areas, but to value each person you deal with as an individual. Everyone you meet is interesting, and all human beings have their own fascinating set of experiences, life history and personality. You must never make the mistake of making assumptions about what people want or what they need.

Service user groups

Your work in care may well be defined by the group of service users you work with – for instance you may be working with 'the elderly' or 'children' or 'younger people'. Alternatively you could find yourself working with 'people with disabilities', 'people with learning difficulties' or 'people with mental health problems'. These are examples of how people can be put into categories or groups according to age or a particular problem or difficulty they may have.

It can seem natural if you are working in a particular setting to assume that all of the people for whom you provide care will need the same type of care and the same response from you. But look at these three examples:

Case Study – Three Service Users

Mr S is 70 years old and has just come out of hospital following a stroke. He can get around slowly, but because he has very little use in his right limbs, he will have problems in cooking or cleaning for himself. As Mr S lives alone, and has no nearby relatives to help, it has been decided that he should come into residential care for a few weeks until he is able to do a little more for himself and feels more confident about returning home.

Joel is 3 years old and attends a day nursery each day. His mother has a full-time job, and his father is a shift worker, so it is often his father who brings and collects Joel. Joel is a lively little boy, who has met all his milestones and is progressing well. He is inquisitive and often asks questions. Joel can tend to be boisterous, and can sometimes hurt other children if he becomes over-excited. It is important that he is given plenty of stimulation as he gets into mischief when he is bored.

F is 17 years old and has multiple disabilities. She has severe physical disabilities and learning difficulties as a result of brain damage at birth. F is in a wheelchair and cannot do anything for herself. She has been in residential care since she was a year old, and has regular visits from her parents, who are not able to manage her at home although they do go away on holidays arranged by the residential home. F is doubly incontinent, is unable to walk or use her arms, and her movements are jerky and uncontrolled. She needs to be dressed, fed and bathed and all personal care must be provided. Although she has no speech she does laugh at things and has a beautiful smile. F is very affectionate and likes to be hugged.

In small groups discuss the different needs these three service users may have and what specific care and activities you could help to provide for them.

THINK IT THROUGH

Look at the people in your class or tutor group and think about the different ways that you can categorise them. You could start with all the people with brown hair, and all the people with fair hair. Or you could have all the people taller than 5 feet 2 inches and all the people who are 5 feet 2 inches or shorter, and so on.

Choose three different ways of putting people into groups – it does not matter which three you choose. After you have split up your class or group, look at the people who have fallen into each group. You will realise that even though they may all have one factor in common (they are all tall, or short, or they are all wearing navy blue) they are still all very different people. This is clear because you know them. Remember, when you are working in care, that all people are different, despite having some factors and some aspects of their lives in common.

Treating all people as individuals

Not only do you need to recognise that each person is an individual, but you need to treat people with respect and dignity. Treating people with respect is about more than just being polite to them – it is also about respecting their rights to privacy and confidentiality, and their right to have their views taken into account. There are many ways in which this respect for the people you are working with can show itself in the day-to-day tasks you carry out, and the care you give.

Good practice: showing respect for people

- Always ask people's permission before you perform any service for them or carry out any activity that affects them in any way. For example, ask, 'Mrs Smith – is it OK with you if I take you to the bathroom now so that you can have your bath?'

- Always offer people a choice wherever possible. For example, ask, 'Mr Jones, would you like to have your tea in your room or in the dining room at the table?'

- Avoid discussing anything that goes on in your place of work outside.

- Avoid discussing individual service users with each other.

- Ensure that service users always have privacy for personal matters like using the toilet, dressing and undressing, sleeping.

- Provide privacy for people when they are upset.

Communicating well with people

Another important principle of good practice in care is to make sure that you communicate well with all service users and their families. As Unit 4 explains, there is much more to being a good communicator than simply talking. You will need to make sure that you are also a good listener and use all the listening and communication skills you have learned.

Good communication is the key to providing a good level of service for any service user group, regardless of age, disability or need. The communication skills needed, for example, to deal with children and elderly people may be quite different, but the principles remain the same.

The diagram in Figure 3.2 will show you some of the aspects of communication you need to consider.

Some aspects of good communication may be more important with one service user group than with another. For example, the need for non-verbal communication may be greater where people have difficulties in hearing, or where there are language differences. On the other hand if you were dealing with a service user who has visual difficulties, your verbal communication and touch may be the most important of your range of skills.

Figure 3.2 *Aspects of communication*

Communicating well with the people you are caring for is a vital part of working effectively. There is little value in providing a good level of physical care unless you also practise good communication so that people do not feel isolated, uncertain and unhappy. Research has shown that human beings need to communicate in order to be happy and to feel confident in their environment. Where people are deprived of communication with others they become disturbed, withdrawn and depressed.

Meeting basic needs

In Unit 2 you learned about Maslow's Hierarchy of Needs, which identifies the basic human needs – physical, safety, belonging and self-esteem. We all have these needs across the life span, although there will be different reasons why people may need help to meet some or all of their needs. These may depend on the life stage that they are in or the amount of support or help they need in one area of their life.

What basic needs may different service user groups have?

Service user group	Needs
Baby	**Regular feeding,** either breast or bottle, prepared hygienically and regularly
	Warmth, both clothing and the surrounding environment
	Cleanliness, bathing, washing and nappy changing
	Emotional needs, stimulation by talking, playing, touching and looking – affection, cuddles, love and care
	Mobility, equipment to carry babies and in which to sleep
Toddler/pre-school child	**Regular, nutritious meals** giving a balanced diet with not too much sugar and fat and plenty of protein, prepared safely and hygienically
	Warmth, good clothing for outdoors and an even temperature indoors
	Personal hygiene, teaching children to use the toilet independently and care for their hair and teeth
	Mobility, space to play, equipment to encourage physical development
	Social contacts, meeting other children and learning to play with others
	Intellectual stimulation, activities to help develop the ability to think and learn
	Love and affection, so that toddlers know they are loved and feel secure
Child	**Regular, nutritious meals** still need to be prepared for them but children become less dependent as they move towards adulthood
	Warmth is still important, but children become better able to regulate their own body temperature
	Personal hygiene, encouragement to follow personal cleanliness routines
	Social contacts with others and support in making friends
	Physical activity, exercise and movement to encourage physical development
	Intellectual stimulation, learning and developing understanding
	Love and affection is essential so that children feel loved, safe and secure
Older person	**Food and warmth** are still vital, meals may be smaller as appetite decreases, need for warmth may increase. May need help with preparing and eating food, for example someone with a stroke may need special cutlery or food that does not need to be chewed
	Personal hygiene – if a person becomes ill or infirm, he or she may need assistance to use the toilet or bathe
	Social contacts are still important to maintain a social life, but this can often decrease as friends die or relatives move away. Assistance may be needed to meet new people

Service user group	Needs
	Intellectual stimulation, since older people should not lose their interests, even if physical abilities decline. Interests may need to be adapted if physical and/or mental abilities change. For example, someone who was previously a footballer might start watching football on TV
	Love and affection – since the close emotional relationship with a partner may be lost, it is even more important that other contacts with friends and family are maintained
People with disabilities	**Food** may be a special diet, or food may need to be prepared in a particular way, with assistance to prepare or eat food
	Warmth may be an increased need if movement is limited
	Personal hygiene may require assistance. There may be special requirements if appliances are worn, for example incontinence pads
	Social contacts are important, both with other people with disabilities and able-bodied people. May need help with practical arrangements like transport and access
	Intellectual stimulation and interests are the same as for able-bodied people at the same life stage. May have to overcome the assumption that physical disabilities mean that people are less intelligent
	Love and affection and emotional needs are the same as for anyone at the same life stage. People with disabilities give and receive love and affection in the same way as everyone else
People suffering from illness	**Food** needs will depend on the illness, but there may be a special diet or special preparations. Otherwise good nutritious meals are important to assist recovery
	Warmth can be a greater need during illness as people are less mobile
	Personal care may, depending on the illness, require help
	Intellectual needs depend on the illness – some people may be too ill to be able to sustain much interest, but stimulation is always important, and everyone should be talked to, even unconscious people. For people who are getting better, or have been ill for a long time, intellectual activity can be very important
	Social and emotional needs – most people especially need to know that they are cared about when they are ill
People with emotional needs	**Physical needs** are likely to be similar to others at the same life stage, but people who have specific mental health problems may need specialist **emotional** support to meet their needs

Specific help and support needed by service users

After considering the type of help that people may need you should think carefully about the skills you would need in order to offer that help. Make sure you know what practical help you can provide that will support people to maintain their personal hygiene and prepare, serve and consume food and drink.

Some service users also need help to move around, either assistance with walking or using aids to do so, or moving around in bed or in a wheelchair. Where service users are suffering pain or discomfort you need to know the most effective ways of helping them to be more comfortable and to rest. Like all other caring skills, the practical skills vary depending upon the service user group. You may need to offer help with preparing a meal for a person recovering from an illness or an injury, but you will always have to prepare food yourself for babies, toddlers and young children. If you are working with people who are fit and healthy but have learning difficulties, you may simply need to provide some element of supervision while they prepare their meals and feed themselves. They would require no help at all when it comes to mobility.

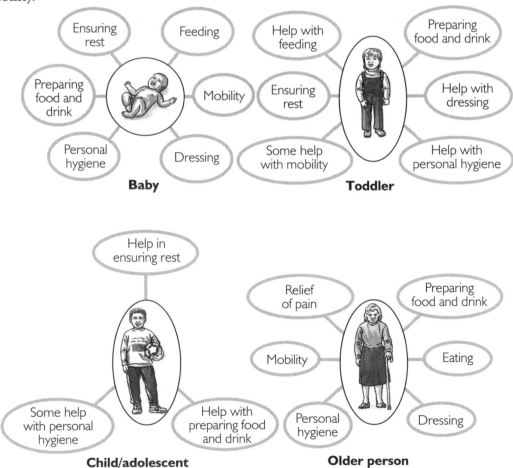

Figure 3.3 The help needed by different service users

These are a few examples of the different kinds of skills that you may need in different situations. You may like to look at Unit 5 for detailed information on helping service users to eat and drink, maintain personal hygiene and improve mobility. You will learn about the skills in detail in Unit 5, but the most important are shown in Figure 3.3.

Good practice: providing specific support

Enabling service users to eat and drink

Helping people to eat and drink includes:

- storing and preparing food hygienically
- knowing how to provide a balanced diet and how to present food and drink attractively
- knowing how to use special utensils to assist people with particular problems
- knowing how to assist both adults and children to eat and drink.

Maintaining personal hygiene

Assisting with personal hygiene includes:

- washing and bathing babies and children
- establishing routines for teeth cleaning
- nappy changing and toilet training
- hair washing and grooming
- nail and eye care
- choosing clothes and helping to get dressed or undressed
- help with using the lavatory.

Helping with mobility

Assisting with mobility includes:

- ensuring safe areas and providing supervision for babies and children to move and play
- using equipment and play to encourage movement
- assisting with movement
- ensuring the correct use of mobility equipment
- providing support and encouragement to take exercise.

For further information about providing assistance to eat and drink, maintaining personal hygiene and mobility, see Unit 5.

Factors affecting service users' need for care and support

Life stage

As you will already have seen from the table on pages 116–117, people may need help and support to meet their basic needs at different life stages. For example, babies will need a lot of care and support as they will be too young to meet those needs for themselves. Children will be developing independence but will still need support and help until they are old enough to care fully for themselves. Adults may have experienced particular events or problems that will mean they might need some extra help after suffering a fall, an accident or an illness. A reduction in mobility or an illness may affect elderly people, or they may suffer from hearing or sight loss and this might make it difficult for them to care for themselves.

Motivation to care for oneself

It is important to remember that meeting basic needs does not necessarily mean helping someone to wash or dress. It may also mean providing emotional support if a client has experienced a distressing event such as the death of a close family member or friend. If a client is distressed or depressed he or she may find it difficult to motivate themselves to undertake the activities of daily living and may need support and encouragement to do so. People suffering from an illness or disability that leaves them in pain or discomfort may not feel motivated to care for themselves and will also need help and support. It may be necessary to call on the services of other health and social care workers to help to provide this.

ASSESSMENT ACTIVITY

Describe the practical skills required to provide care for service users in your chosen setting.

1   During your time at work placement, you will be helping to provide care and observing care workers providing care for clients. Keep a diary of the care provided for service users, by you and by others (over three days). Describe the practical skills that you and they used to provide good-quality care.

2   Get together with three or four other people in your group who are undertaking work experience with different service users from yours. For example, if you are working in a residential home for the elderly form a small group with students who are working with adults with learning disabilities and children in a nursery. Discuss the different factors that affect the provision of care for the different groups. Make notes on your discussion and write up a clear explanation of what these factors are, and how they can be affected by the needs of different service user groups.

To achieve a **merit grade** you will need to explain the factors that affect the different skills that care workers require for different service user groups.

To achieve a **distinction grade** you will need to analyse the ways in which service users benefit from the practical skills of care workers. You will need to include in your report the benefits that service users gain from the practical skills of care workers. You need to think about the particular needs of the service users and the skills that are needed to meet those needs. What benefits will the service users gain? Think about physical, intellectual, emotional and social needs, and the feelings that service users will have if these needs have been met by care workers who have developed good practical skills.

Health and safety principles

Health and safety is very important in all care settings, because the service users you deal with are very vulnerable and you need to be sure that they are protected from risks. It is also essential that you, as a worker in the care setting, are not putting yourself at risk. The whole area of care is covered by comprehensive laws that lay down what can and cannot be done in a care setting.

The main Act of Parliament that affects all care settings is the Health and Safety at Work Act 1974 (HASAWA). This law is like an umbrella under which are many other regulations designed to cover particular areas of risk.

The Act broadly identifies which areas are the responsibility of the employer and which are the responsibility of the employee. The employer and employee

Figure 3.4 *The Health and Safety at Work Act is like an umbrella*

are jointly responsible for safeguarding the health and safety of anyone who uses the premises – this includes both service users and visitors. The employer is responsible for providing a safe place to work, but the employee also has to show reasonable care for his or her own safety.

The Health and Safety at Work Act requires all workplaces where there are five workers or more to have a written health and safety policy.

Employers' duties	Employees' duties
Employers must ensure that their employees know about the following: ■ carrying out the job without risk and in a safe way ■ any risks that may affect the employee ■ how risks have been minimised ■ how to get first aid treatment ■ action to be taken. In an emergency employers must provide the following free of charge: ■ protective clothing and equipment ■ safety training.	Employees must: ■ protect themselves as much as possible ■ use equipment provided for its intended purpose ■ carry out tasks with proper training in a safe manner ■ report any safety hazards ■ co-operate with employers on safety issues ■ inform someone if an accident occurs.

In a care setting the Act would apply to:

■ infection control

■ correct lifting techniques

■ good hygiene in food preparation areas

■ observations and measurements

■ disposal of clinical waste

■ proper heating, lighting and ventilation.

Case Study – Treetops and The Beeches

Read the following case studies and, as a class, brainstorm what each care setting must do to comply with the Health and Safety at Work Act.

Treetops Day Nursery is registered to take 30 children from birth to five years of age. The nursery is privately owned and managed, and it is mainly used by children whose parents work in the nearby hospital and local college. Under the Health and Safety at Work Act, some of the steps which the owner of the nursery is obliged to take are:

■ make sure that the entrance and approach to the nursery are safe for parents and children

■ ensure that the inside of the premises is safe with no dangerous wiring (e.g. exposed wires or wrongly fused plugs), plumbing (e.g. scalding hot water where children could reach, or with no warning sign)

■ check that all dangerous substances are properly stored and labelled, and are out of reach of the children

■ ensure play equipment is regularly checked and repair it or replace it if it is worn or faulty

■ make sure that the building is secure and that children are not able to wander off from inside or outside

■ develop a system for checking visitors and making sure that no unauthorised people have access to the children.

The Beeches is a large residential home for 40 elderly residents. It is owned and run by the Social Services department. Some of the things the Social Services department must do in order to comply with the Health and Safety at Work Act are:

■ ensure the access to and grounds of the home are safe for staff, residents and visitors.

■ check that there are no dangers inside the home such as wet floors, trailing flexes, frayed carpets, etc.

■ ensure that all dangerous substances are safely stored and properly labelled

■ carry out a risk assessment for all residents who require assistance to move

■ ensure that equipment such as hoists, slides and slings are supplied for use where necessary

■ make sure that all equipment is regularly checked and replaced if faulty or worn

■ arrange for staff to receive training in how to move and handle people

■ ensure that there is system in place for checking visitors to the premises.

Food handling

If you are involved in handling and preparing food in your workplace, this too is governed by health and safety regulations, and you must be careful that you observe all the regulations to ensure a safe place for people to eat and drink. The regulations cover such areas as storage and refrigeration of food and personal hygiene.

The regulations cover both the individual handling the food and the area in which food is prepared. There are regulations about the cooking of food and which foods can be served raw. All care settings are required to follow hygiene rules and also to ensure that they observe the use-by dates on food they offer to service users. Somebody in your workplace will be responsible for ordering food and for regularly checking that food is being stored safely and is within the recommended time limits for safe use. If you do handle food for service users, you may be required to hold a basic food hygiene certificate to show that you know and understand how to handle and prepare food safely.

Risk assessment

One of the requirements of employers under the Health and Safety at Work Act is that they must carry out an assessment of risk involved with any work activity. This covers all activities in the workplace, not just those directly concerned with providing care to service users. Activities such as cleaning and working in kitchens, are included, as are risks from visitors to the workplace or from service users' behaviour.

Reducing risks

After employers have carried out an assessment of risk, they have to ensure that they reduce the risk as far as possible by taking whatever steps may be necessary. This could mean:

- providing hoists and slings to lift and move people
- installing a security system
- employing extra staff to ensure that employees are not exposed to risks from violent service users
- providing additional training or further guidelines as to how to deal with particular risks.

The responsibility of the employee is to use any equipment provided and to make use of any additional training or to follow any guidelines or advice supplied by the employer.

Manual Handling Operations Regulations (1993)

The Manual Handling Operations Regulations (1993) require employers to avoid all manual handling where there is any risk of injury, so far as it is reasonably practical.

Handling and moving service users should always be undertaken using appropriate equipment. Manual lifting is never safe – there is no such thing as a safe lift, and it should never be undertaken in a care setting. The only places where lifting can safely be carried out is on maternity units where babies are being moved around.

As part of a care plan, any moving required for a service user (even a child) should be assessed to find out what equipment is needed. The assessment has to be carried out by the employer and should take into account factors such as:

- the extent to which the person to be lifted can help himself or herself
- weight
- risk of injury
- likelihood of pain and discomfort
- height and distance of lift or move
- special circumstances such as skin problems.

A risk assessment should also be done before moving large or heavy equipment.

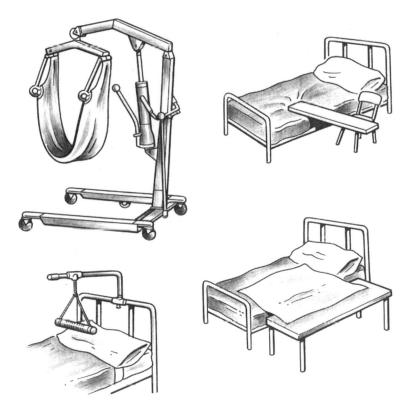

Figure 3.5 *Equipment for moving and handling*

Many serious injuries have been caused to workers in care settings in the past by lifting and moving people without using equipment. You may find that some workers in care settings still believe that it is quicker and easier to carry out a lift or move manually than to use a hoist, a sling or other appropriate equipment. *This is not true.*

Not only care workers can be severely injured by attempting to move and lift people manually – service users can also be injured by a lift carried out without proper equipment. It is never worth the risk – always use the proper equipment.

Control of Substances Hazardous to Health (2003) (COSHH)

The COSHH regulations cover all the substances you may use in your workplace. This includes everything from cleaning fluids to dangerous drugs. The regulations apply to any caustic or corrosive substances in your workplace and also gases or substances that could potentially release dangerous fumes.

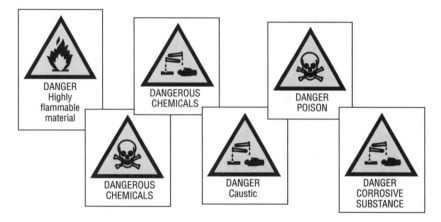

Figure 3.6 *These symbols, which warn you of hazardous substances, are always yellow*

An employer must meet basic requirements for hazardous substances in a workplace. There must be a COSHH file listing all of the hazardous substances in any workplace, and it has to:

- identify what they are
- say where each is kept
- say what the labels are
- describe the effects of the substances
- state the maximum amount of time it is safe to be exposed to them
- describe how to deal with an emergency.

What to do with a COSHH file

Once you have read the information in the COSHH file in your workplace, you must make sure you follow the advice for working with any particular hazardous substances. The advice could be to wear gloves or protective goggles, or may involve limiting the time you are exposed to the substance. The file will also tell you how the substances must be stored and you must make sure you follow those instructions.

■ It is always essential that the correct containers are used and that they are properly labelled.

■ You must never use the container of one substance for storing another, and you must *never* change the labels.

Handling bodily fluids safely

One of the things that you will have to learn to deal with if you are going to work in care is handling the fluids produced by all human beings. These are:

■ blood
■ urine

■ vomit
■ faeces

■ saliva
■ mucus.

■ sweat

Regardless of the age range or service user group you work with, you will deal with some or all of these fluids at some point. There are important reasons why they must be handled safely and in particular ways. The broad principles which apply are shown below.

Good practice: handling body fluids

■ Always wear gloves and a plastic apron when you are coming into contact with any type of body fluid. This will minimise the risk of cross-infection if there is any harmful agent present in the bodily fluid. Cross-infection occurs where harmful and infectious bacteria are spread from one person to another.

■ Make sure that body fluids are disposed of safely so that they cannot present a risk to others in the care setting.

■ Always wash your hands and put on clean gloves and apron between service users.

Your workplace

All care settings have their own procedures for dealing with disposal of body waste such as urine, faeces and vomit. Normally this will mean disposing of it in a toilet or a sluice – which is designed to dispose of waste hygienically and looks a bit like a sink but flushes like a toilet. However, sometimes waste may need to be retained for measuring or further testing.

There will also be arrangements for disposing of blood, mucus or any other fluids, and these should be listed in the safety procedures in your workplace.

Spills and splashes

If body fluids have been spilt, the area must be thoroughly cleaned and disinfected to minimise the risk of infection. Make sure you wear gloves and an apron while cleaning up any spill.

Soiled linen or clothing should be handled with care. Wear an apron and gloves, and do not place linen or clothes on the floor but put them directly into the container for soiled linen.

ASSESSMENT ACTIVITY

Investigate and provide a basic description of the main principles of health and safety legislation and guidelines as they apply in your chosen setting.

1 Discuss with your workplace supervisor the health and safety legislation, policies and guidelines that apply in your setting. Find out where the information for staff is kept. Is it available to everyone, and is there a policy book?

2 When you have gained all the information that you need from your work placement, explain the reasons why the relevant health and safety

legislation is used. Remember that some of the legislation will not only be in place to protect your service users, but also to protect you, your colleagues and visitors to the setting.

To achieve a **merit grade** you must explain the reasons for the main principles of health and safety legislation that you have described.

Health and social care services

Health and social care services cover a vast area of need, ranging from acute medical care to care in the home, from providing advice and support to providing care and education. The range is enormous and the services are provided in several different ways.

Public provision

The first and largest area of provision is made by the government. This is called **public provision** and is known as the **public** or the **state sector**. This includes the National Health Service, Local Authority Social Services departments, and Local Education Authorities.

It is called the public sector because the funding for the services provided in this sector comes from the government, and is raised from the taxes and National Insurance contributions of the public.

Voluntary sector

The voluntary sector consists of charities and similar organisations who either directly provide services for a particular service user group, or offer advice and support, and direct service users towards services that are appropriate for them. The sector includes organisations like the Salvation Army, Barnardo's, SCOPE, Citizens' Advice Bureaux and the NSPCC.

Figure 3.7 *A charity shop*

It is called the voluntary sector because it is funded through voluntary contributions made by the general public. A great many charitable bodies also receive grants, either from central or local government or sometimes from other charitable organisations known as foundations, who provide money for worthy causes. Many organisations in the voluntary sector rely very heavily on fund raising, often arranged by local volunteers.

Private sector

The private sector includes those organisations that provide services in health and care for a profit – these are businesses and are run as such. The profit may go to an individual business owner, or alternatively it may be put back into the services provided, as in many private hospitals owned by organisations such as BUPA. This sector is referred to as the private sector because it is funded by people making private payments for the services they receive. If people want to receive medical treatment on a private basis they may pay to do so, either directly to a hospital or through taking out an insurance policy. Many people pay privately for child care and for nursery provision. It is also quite common to find people paying for the care of older people in nursing homes or residential homes in the private sector.

Services provided by the voluntary sector

The services provided by the voluntary sector in many ways mirror those provided by Social Services. They range from residential accommodation to day care and child care facilities, and also include advice, guidance and support services. Usually, however, the service is provided to reflect a particular service user group, which is the interest of that particular voluntary organisation. For example, the NSPCC provides services for children, whereas SCOPE provides services for people with cerebral palsy, and Age Concern provides day care and advice services for older people. You will find this kind of specific service provision throughout the voluntary sector. All services provided by the voluntary sector must meet with the same requirements as those provided by the public sector. They are bound by health and safety regulations, and must provide services to the same standards.

Services provided by the private sector

In the same way as the voluntary sector, the private sector will provide services in all of those areas covered by social service provision. It also provides health care services. No element of public funding is involved in private health and care provision and all of the funding comes from direct payment for the services provided. This payment is either from individuals, insurance companies, or Social Services departments paying for services for particular service users.

Structure of the public sector

The public sector is by far the largest service provider for health and social care. If you think about the number of hospitals, health centres and Social Services departments there are, you will see that this huge service requires a massive amount of public funding to maintain standards and services. The National Health Service is constantly in the news, as public funding levels are always a matter for political debate and discussion. The present structure of the health service looks like the diagram in Figure 3.8.

The health service is ultimately the responsibility of the Secretary of State for Health, but the Secretary of State has a great many responsibilities, so the particular body within the Department of Health responsible for the health service is the National Health Service Executive.

The National Health Service Executive works with the National Health Service Trusts, GPs and Health Authorities. Health Authorities have the

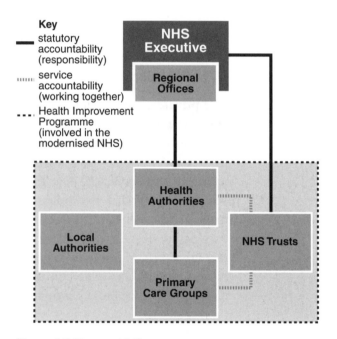

Figure 3.8 *The new NHS*

responsibility to look at overall plans for health in their area and to examine the needs there may be among their local population. For example, because of the risk associated with a particular industry in one area, there may be a greater need for one type of health care; an area may have a particularly large number of older people. Commissioning health and care services comes from Primary Care Groups where GPs, community nurses and midwives work together in a group to look at the level of service needed from their local NHS Trust.

Local Social Services are also part of the process, where decisions are made at a local level about what services are needed. This system is different in Northern Ireland and Wales.

On 1 April 2003, the health system changed in Wales. Health Authorities and local health groups have been replaced by 22 Local Health Boards, which are managed by three Regional Offices across the country. The LHBs work in partnership with their local authorities to improve the health of the local people and to provide primary, community and secondary health care services for the local area.

Two other bodies have also been established – the National Public Health Service and Health Commission Wales (Specialist Services). The National Public Health Service is responsible for all public health in Wales and will provide expert help and information to LHBs and local authorities, which will include health promotion, prevention and control of disease and child protection.

Health Commission Wales (Specialist Services) has been set up to provide some specialist services nationally. These include cardiac surgery, emergency ambulance services and some children's services. This has been done to ensure better planning for these services across the country.

Further information is available at www.wales.nhs.uk

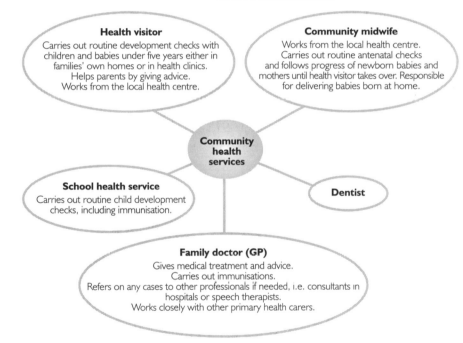

Figure 3.9 *Community health services*

Social Services

Social Services departments are part of local government. This means that they are run by the local council from the local town hall, county hall or council buildings. They usually have a range of local area offices and also a wide range of establishments such as nurseries, children's homes, elderly persons' homes, and resource centres. Social Services departments have a responsibility to provide services for children, people with disabilities, people with mental health problems, people with learning difficulties and older people. The services they provide may be residential, or they may be provided in service users' own homes. Social Services also have a responsibility under the Care in the Community Act to use both private and public sector facilities in order to provide the most appropriate care for any individual for whom they are responsible.

Social Services departments are just one of the many departments in most local councils. They are funded through the local authority annual budget, which in turn receives money from central government and from taxes raised locally. This is called the Council Tax, and everybody who lives in a particular local authority's area must pay Council Tax for the provision of services.

The Social Services department has its allocation of funding alongside other council departments like Education, Leisure, and Environmental Health. Each Social Services department is headed by a Director of Social Services, who works with a committee of local councillors who must decide how the budget is to be spent and which services will be provided. Some services must be provided by law. These are called statutory services and includes such things as provision to protect children from abuse, provision of accommodation for elderly people, provision of aids and adaptations for people with disabilities, and provision of a service for those who have mental health problems.

Look at the following examples of how service users might use the health and social services.

Case Study – Mrs J

Mrs J is 83 years old and lives with her daughter and son-in-law. Although she is mentally alert, she is physically frail and her eyesight is poor. Her daughter and son-in-law both go out to work and Mrs J has had a few falls. She also began to feel lonely and isolated in the house all day as she became unable to get out to the shops or the park. Her family contacted Social Services to discuss the help that could be offered. Following an assessment by a social worker, Mrs J now attends a day centre three days each week. She is collected and returned home by the transport service. On the remaining days, she has a visit from a local community group who 'pop in' to make sure she is well.

Which of the services used by Mrs J are provided by:

a the public sector?

b the private sector?

c the voluntary sector?

Case Study – Ellen

Ellen is 10 years old, and she has Down's Syndrome which means that she has some learning difficulties. She is a loving and cheerful little girl who laughs a lot and has a mischievous sense of humour. Ellen attends a local special school, and she is picked up by the school transport service each day. She loves school and has lots of friends. She is looking forward to the next school holiday because her social worker has arranged for her to go away on a week's holiday organised by a local community group.

One evening each week, Ellen goes to a club in the local community centre where she has the chance to play games and sports. Most of her friends from school go too. Ellen has a heart condition and has to attend for regular check-ups at the hospital, and she is also regularly seen by the school nurse and her own doctor. Her eyesight is poor and she wears glasses, but she did not like the frames she was offered this time because they were not trendy enough! So her mother bought her some fashionable ones.

Which of the services used by Ellen are likely to be provided by:

a the public sector?

b the private sector?

c the voluntary sector?

Range of care settings and how they provide for different needs

It is important that you know about the different types of service offered by health and care service providers. You may need to advise service users which services would be of value to them according to the particular needs they may have.

Early years settings

Services for young children can be provided by the local authority or the voluntary or private sectors, and they include day nurseries (where full-time day care is provided for children from babies to school age), play groups, nursery education, childminders (who care for children at home) and nannies (who look after children in the child's home).

Services a child may need include:

- full-time care while parents are working
- part-time care while parents are working
- the chance to meet other children
- the opportunity to start learning
- special services to meet special needs.

Play groups are usually provided by the voluntary sector where children (usually between the age of two and school age) can attend for a short period, normally two to three hours each day. As the name suggests, the major activity is the chance for children to play with others in a safe, supervised setting.

Childminders are normally part of the private sector, but regulated by the local authority. Childminders may care for one or more children in their own home, but there is usually a maximum of three or four. Their homes have to be inspected by OFSTED (the school inspectors). The charges are usually paid by the child's parents.

Nannies work in a child's home and can provide full- or part-time care. They are almost always employed by the private sector. Most parents insist on qualifications for the nanny they employ, but there are no legal requirements for them to be qualified. Nannies are not subject to any inspections or regulations.

Schools

These are provided by the local education authority, but can also be part of the private or voluntary sector. They provide education, sometimes with boarding accommodation. Most schools have nursery classes where children can begin to attend school as they reach their fourth birthday. All schools are inspected by OFSTED (the schools inspectors) and have to reach certain standards.

Hospitals

Hospitals provide both for acute care in emergencies and also for any health care needs where medical treatment is necessary. They also provide outpatient services where people can go for follow-up treatment and where service users can receive services such as physiotherapy, occupational therapy and chiropody.

Health Centres are situated in local communities and provide general practitioners, community nurses, community midwives, and health visitors.

Residential homes

Residential accommodation can be provided for a wide range of service user groups and can also be provided by any of the three sectors. The majority of residential accommodation is for older people, and can be used either to provide a permanent home for people who are unable to care for themselves or as a 'respite' break for people being looked after at home.

Special schools

If children have special needs, they may attend a particular type of school with special facilities, for example special physiotherapy and hydrotherapy equipment in a school for people with physical disabilities, or lessons using braille or voice-recognition technology for visually impaired people.

Day centres

Day centres offer contact, support and stimulation to a range of service user groups. This can be people with mental health problems, people with disabilities, those with learning difficulties or older people. They can be provided by the public or voluntary sectors. Service users attend each day, or on set days each week. Day centres are often important for people who are cared for at home by a relative.

Access to health and social care services

Although many people have access to health and social care services, there are some who experience difficulty in getting the help that they require. There may be several reasons for this, which include the following.

Lack of information

Many people are not aware of the services that are available and do not know who to ask to get the information. This may be because they are housebound and have little contact with health or social services departments. Others often feel that they do not want to be a nuisance and will not ask for the information that they need. People who have difficulty in reading or writing may have access to the information but cannot make sense of it unless they have help to read it. This may also be the case for people who have hearing or sight difficulties – the information may be easily available to them but again they require assistance to use it.

Lack of mobility

People may be aware of what is available but they not be able to access services because they are not able to get to them. Difficulty in using public transport may be the problem or the service that they require may not be easy to get to by public transport. As a carer, you may be able to let them know of services such as volunteer transport services or the ambulance transport service that may be able to help them.

Financial constraints

Although health and social care is free at the point of delivery, there may be a charge for certain services. Sometimes these will be means tested, which means that the amount of money a person has will determine whether they have to pay for the service, and how much. People on low incomes or pensions may find difficulty in paying for public transport to reach the services they require.

Health authorities and social services departments are given a budget to spend on providing services in their area. They have to decide what services are most needed and will fund them accordingly. As a result, some people may have a need that is not or cannot be funded and so is not available in their area.

The role of regulatory bodies in ensuring the quality of care provision

In recent years there has been a drive to modernise health and social services and this includes putting in place the National Institutional Framework. This is a national system to monitor the quality of care provision for different service user groups. There are five national bodies that contribute to the quality of social care services.

Commission for Health Improvement

This Commission has been set up to improve the quality of patient care within the National Health Service. The CHI highlights best practice and advises on improvement where it is required to make sure that service users get the best possible treatment.

The Commission works on behalf of patients to ensure that they get the best-quality care and treatment. This includes making sure that patients and carers have a say in care, treatment and planning local health care.

The General Social Care Council

This is the first regulatory body for the social care profession and was launched on 1 October 2001. It was set up under the Care Standards Act 2000 and its role is to improve public protection and raise professional standards in social care. Among its objectives are:

- to establish a register of social care workers
- to enforce professional standards of conduct and practice
- to ensure high-quality training and education for social workers.

The National Care Standards Commission

This is an independent public body that was set up under the Care Standards Act 2000 to regulate social care and private and voluntary health care services throughout England. It is responsible for registering and inspecting services. Various services are required to register with the NCSC:

- care homes
- domiciliary care agencies
- voluntary adoption agencies
- private and voluntary hospitals and clinics
- nursing agencies.

- children's homes
- residential family centres
- independent fostering agencies
- exclusively private doctors

The aim of this Commission is to ensure that all service providers meet the national minimum standards that will improve the level of protection for vulnerable people and provide a high-quality service.

The Social Care Institute for Excellence

This was established on 1 October 2001 in response to the government drive to improve the quality of social care services in England and Wales. It provides independent advice to service users and their carers, practitioners and service managers about what works in social care. This knowledge is gathered nationally and is used to produce guides on best practice for people who work in and use social care services.

The Social Services Inspectorate

This is part of the Department of Health and its work is to inspect and evaluate the quality of services. It gives advice to ministers, and monitors how the government puts policies into place for social services. It works closely with the Audit Commission and the Commission for Health Improvement.

ASSESSMENT ACTIVITY

What provision is available to different service users in your local authority area?

Find out what provision is available to different service users in your local authority area. Is the provision public, private, voluntary or a mixture of all three? You can carry out research on the Internet, or visit your local GP surgery or Social Services Department. Remember also that some information should be available at your work placement. You could do this in a small group, with each member choosing a different service user group to research. You will also need to find out how the services are structured and funded. Design a wall poster or booklet that shows the information that you have gathered. An example could be as follows:

Service provision	Where is it?	Service user group	Who provides it?	Structure of the provision	How is the provision funded?

To achieve a **pass grade** you must identify the types of provision available for different service user groups in your local authority area. You must also describe how the service provision that you have identified is structured and funded.

To achieve a **merit grade** you must explain the effects of different funding methods and structures on provision. You must explain how funding and structure affects how services are provided to the service users who require them. Think about how the types of service provision that you have researched may be affected by the way that they are structured and funded.

To achieve a **distinction grade** you must discuss the ways in which service users' health and well-being can be affected by the level and type of service provision available. Your work must focus on how service provision can affect the health and well-being of the clients who use it. What would be the effect on service users of little or no provision and of well-funded good-quality provision? How well would PIES needs be met in each case? What would be the advantages and disadvantages?

UNIT FOUR

Values and Communications in Care Settings

This unit provides an in-depth study of diversity and rights. Care values associated with confidentiality, the prevention of discrimination and rights and responsibilities are explored in detail. Relevant legislation and current policies for standards in care provide an important focus of study.

Communication skills are explored in detail and care worker skills of formal communication are explained. The protection of individuals from abuse provides another key focus of study.

This unit is internally assessed and ideas for evidencing the grading criteria are presented.

In this unit you will learn about:

- the way diversity and rights promote equality

- the way to promote effective communication

- the way to demonstrate communication skills

- the protection of individuals from abuse.

Diversity and rights

We live in a world full of new ways of communicating. Using the Internet, you can easily communicate with individuals all over the world, and you can have conversations with people hundreds of miles away using a mobile phone. Communications technology means that businesses and trade are connected across the world.

A hundred years ago the world was not like this. In 1900, you might meet only people you grew up with. But to be successful in the new world of communication, you will need to value the diversity of people all over the world. Valuing diversity is not just a central principle of care work. You have to be willing and able to understand differences in other people in order to fit in with the new interconnected world of communications. Not valuing diversity may exclude you from the future!

Diversity in individuals

You are special and no one is exactly the same as you. But you will be more like some people and less like others. Many of the differences between people are created by **cultural influences**. Culture means the values and beliefs that different social groups have. We try to make ourselves individual, but we are also influenced by the groups we belong to. Some ways in which people are different from each other (or diverse) are listed below.

Age	People may think of others as being children, teenagers, young adults, middle-aged or old. Discrimination can creep into our thinking if we see some age groups as being 'the best' or if we make assumptions about the abilities of different age groups.
Gender	People are classified as male or female. In the past, men often had more rights and were seen as more important than women. Assumptions about gender can still create discrimination.
Race	People may understand themselves as being black or white, as European, African or Asian. Many people have specific national identities such as Polish, Nigerian, English or Welsh. Assumptions about racial characteristics lead to discrimination.
Class	People differ in their upbringing, the kind of work they do and the money they earn. People also differ in the lifestyles they follow and the views and values that go with levels of income and spending habits. Discrimination against others can be based on their class or lifestyle.
Caste	The word 'caste' is used where there are rigid social divisions between groups. Caste is like social class, but much more fixed. In some cultures people are born into a caste that they cannot change,

whereas you can change social class if you change your type of work. It is important not to see some people as worth more than others in a care setting.

Religion	People grow up in different traditions of religion. For some people, spiritual beliefs are at the centre of their understanding of life. For others, religion influences the cultural traditions that they celebrate; for example, many Europeans celebrate Christmas even though they might not see themselves as practising Christians. Discrimination can take place when people assume that their customs or beliefs should apply to everyone else.
Sexuality	Many people see their sexual orientation as very important to understanding who they are. Gay and lesbian relationships are often discriminated against. Heterosexual people sometimes judge other relationships as 'wrong' or abnormal.
Ability	People may make assumptions about what is 'normal'. People with physical disabilities or learning disabilities may be labelled or stereotyped.
Health	People who develop illnesses or mental health problems may feel that they are valued less by other people and discriminated against.
Relationships	People choose many different lifestyles and emotional commitments, such as: marriage, having children, living in a large family, living alone but having sexual partners, being single and not being sexually active. People live within different family and friendship groups. Discrimination can happen if people think that one lifestyle is 'right' or best.
Politics	People can develop different views as to how a government should act, how welfare provision should be organised, and so on. Disagreement and debate are necessary; but it is important not to discriminate against people because of their views.
Presentation and dress	People express their individuality, lifestyle and social role through the clothes, hairstyle, make-up and jewellery they wear. Whilst it may be important to conform to social expectations at work, it is also important not to stereotype individuals.

Understanding diversity

Familiarity

Our own socialisation, culture and life experience may lead us to make assumptions as to what is right or normal. When we meet people who are different, it can be easy to see them as 'not right' or 'not normal'. Different people see the world in different ways. Our way of thinking may seem unusual

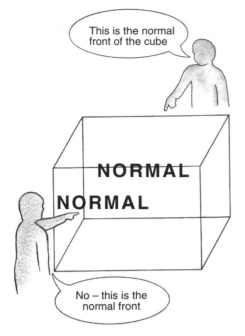

Figure 4.1 *Which is the 'normal' front of the cube?*

to others. Look at the illustration below. Which is the 'normal' front of the cube?

If a person was used to seeing the cube from only one direction, he or she might be sure that view was right. Our culture may lead us to think that some habits are better than others, but often there are many ways of looking at things. For instance, different cultures and different individuals have varying views about what is right to eat or drink.

Diversity in food

Food is quite a personal area of our lives. What we eat or drink is also strongly influenced by our culture and learning. Below is a range of views on different foods.

For	Against
Snake A good source of protein enjoyed in many countries.	Not considered acceptable to some Europeans.
Frog Eaten by some Europeans.	Once considered offensive by some English people.
Cat, dog or horse Regarded as no different from lamb or beef in many cultures.	Seen as pets and 'honorary family members' in some sections of British society.
Insects A useful source of protein and a delicacy in some cultures.	May be seen as 'inedible' or disgusting by some people in Britain.
Animals' brains and eyes A delicacy in many cultures.	Usually thrown away in Britain.
Alcohol Widely consumed in Europe.	Forbidden to many Muslims and forbidden by some Christian and other religious groups.
High-fat or sugar products Widely consumed in Europe.	Avoided by health-conscious people.

For	Against
Pork Seen as similar to lamb or beef by many Europeans.	Regarded as unacceptable by many Jewish and Muslim people.
Meat Seen as good food by many people.	Regarded as unacceptable by vegetarians and many Hindu and Buddhist people.
Genetically modified food Argued to be an effective way to produce cheap, high-quality food.	Some people think this food is dangerous or wrong because the natural environment may be damaged by genetically altered crops.
Fish Widely accepted.	Not acceptable to vegetarians, vegans and to some religions.
Milk, eggs, cheese Widely accepted.	Not acceptable to vegans.

Each person will have a similar range of views on the subjects of clothing, relationships, and social behaviour. The views we are familiar with may not necessarily be held by others. We have a right to our culture and lifestyle, but others have a right to be different from us.

Observing diversity

In order to learn about other people's culture and beliefs, it is necessary to listen and watch what other people say and do. Learning about diversity can be interesting and exciting, but some people feel that finding out about different lifestyles can be stressful. We may feel that our own culture and beliefs are being challenged when we realise the different possibilities that exist. Our emotions may block our abilities to learn.

Skilled carers have to get to know the people they work with in order to avoid making false assumptions. In getting to know an individual, carers will also need to understand the ways that class, race, age, gender and other social categories influence the person. A person's culture may include all the social groups they belong to.

Knowledge of diverse characteristics

There are many different ethnic groups in the world, many different religions, many different cultural values, variations in gender role, and so on. Individuals may belong to the same ethnic group yet belong to different

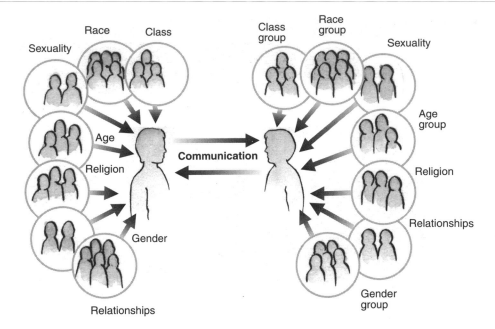

Figure 4.2 *The groups a person belongs to will influence his or her beliefs and behaviour*

religions or class groups. Knowing someone's religion will not necessarily tell you all of that person's beliefs, or general culture.

You can pick up background knowledge on different ethnic and religious customs, but it is impossible to study all the differences that might exist for individual service users. The best way to learn about diversity is to listen and communicate with people who lead different lives from ourselves.

Valuing diversity

Equality between different groups in society cannot happen if some groups are seen as being superior to others. Differences between people such as race, gcndcr, class, scxuality and age must be valued. Learning about differences and trying to understand individual beliefs and needs is an essential skill for promoting equality. Valuing diversity will help to create a fairer and more just society. The social benefits of valuing diversity are not the only reason for learning about others. Valuing diversity will enrich your own life. If you are open to understanding other people's life experience and differences you may be able to achieve the following benefits for yourself:

■ you may learn to be flexible and creative because you can imagine how other people see things

■ you may develop a wider range of social skills because you have met different people

■ learning about other cultures may provide you with new experiences, such as new foods to try and new places to visit

■ understanding other people's lives may help you to adapt your own lifestyle when you have to cope with change. For instance, if you talk to people who get married or who have children, you may be more prepared if you choose these roles

■ you may enjoy life more if you feel confident in mixing with different people

■ the more you know and have experienced diversity, the more interesting you may seem to other people. People who value diversity are unlikely to be boring!

Employers are likely to want to employ people who value diversity because:

■ effective non-discriminatory care depends on staff valuing diversity

■ GSCC codes of practice require workers to respect diversity and employers to provide training to assist workers to develop the skills

■ people who value diversity are likely to be flexible and creative

■ people who value diversity may make good relationships with one another and with service users

■ diverse teams often work very effectively. If everyone has the same skills and interests then team members may compete. If people have different interests there is more chance that the team will cover all the work and enjoy working together.

ASSESSMENT ACTIVITY

Describe cultural diversity.

Get together with some other students and make a list of ways in which people are similar or different. You could consider all the areas of diversity mentioned in this section of the book as well as other lifestyle differences. When you have made your list, design a poster that summarises 'cultural diversity'. Your list and the poster will help to provide evidence for your description of cultural diversity.

Forms of discrimination

In care work, discrimination means treating some groups of people less well than others. People are often discriminated against because of their class, race, gender, religion, sexuality or age.

Discrimination may take the following forms.

■ **Physical abuse** means hitting, pushing, kicking or otherwise assaulting a person. People may commit assault because they hate certain groups, or simply because they feel frustrated or annoyed by those who are different.

■ **Verbal abuse** means insults, 'put downs' or damaging language. Like physical abuse, it may happen because individuals feel they are more

Figure 4.3 *Discrimination through neglect can easily happen*

powerful if they can hurt other people.

■ **Neglect** occurs when people are discriminated against by being ignored or not offered the help that others might receive.

■ **Exclusion** is a more subtle form of discrimination, and may be hard to prove. Exclusion means stopping people from getting services or jobs because they belong to a certain class, race or other group. Disabled people may still be excluded from certain services because access is difficult – some buildings still do not have full disabled access. Some jobs may not be advertised in all local areas, therefore excluding certain communities.

■ **Avoidance** is where people try to avoid sitting next to people or working with people who are different from them. Those who decide to discriminate against others may try to avoid contact – perhaps so that they don't need to learn or re-think any of their prejudices.

■ **Devaluing** involves seeing some types of people as less valuable than others. Some people are helped to build self-esteem because they receive praise and their ideas are valued, but people who are 'different' may be criticised and find their ideas ignored. People who are subjected to constant discrimination and prejudice may develop a low sense of self-esteem.

Direct and indirect discrimination

Direct discrimination is open and obvious. In the 1950s and 1960s, properties for rent in London would sometimes have signs reading 'no blacks, no dogs, no Irish'. Such offensive and obvious discrimination is 'direct' – the advertisements were openly proclaiming racial discrimination.

Indirect discrimination may do equal harm, but it is less clear. An employer once produced an advert stating that applicants for a job must live in certain local areas. At first this sounded all right, but it became obvious that the areas had been carefully chosen to avoid the black and Asian communities. The advert was indirectly discriminating by identifying areas where only white people lived. Indirect discrimination involves unequal treatment which is not obvious at first.

Fifty years ago, you had to be tall to join the police. If the police still had this requirement today, it would indirectly discriminate against women, because on average, men are taller than women.

The effects of discrimination

Discrimination that results in abuse can have permanent and extremely damaging effects on people. All forms of discrimination will cause harm. Some of the possible effects of discrimination and abuse are:

- injury and death
- living in fear of others
- withdrawal from social activities
- loss of confidence
- feeling stressed or unable to cope with work.
- mental illness triggered by stress
- losing a sense of who you are
- a low sense of self-worth
- depression and anxiety

Legislation, policies and procedures

The main Acts of Parliament that deal with rights and discrimination are:

- the Equal Pay Act 1970
- the Race Relations Act 1976 (amended 2000)
- the Disability Rights Commission Act 1999.
- the Sex Discrimination Act 1975 (amended 1986)
- the Disability Discrimination Act 1995

The Equal Pay Act 1970

This Act made it unlawful for employers to discriminate between men and women in terms of their pay and conditions of work. Before this law was passed, it was possible for an employer to pay men more than women – even though the women were doing the same job!

Equal pay legislation was updated in 1975 and 1983 to make it possible to claim equal pay for work that was considered to be of equal value.

The Sex Discrimination Act 1975

This Act made it unlawful to discriminate between men and women in respect of employment, goods and facilities. The Act also made it illegal to discriminate on the grounds of marital status. It identified two forms of discrimination: direct and indirect discrimination.

The Act tries to ensure equal opportunities for both men and women to get jobs and promotion. In order to make sure that people's rights are protected, the government set up the **Equal Opportunities Commission** to monitor, advise and provide information on men and women's rights under the law. People can ask the Equal Opportunities Commission for help and advice if they believe they have been discriminated against because of their gender. This law was updated in 1986 so that it also applied to small businesses.

The Race Relations Act 1976

This Act makes it unlawful to discriminate on racial grounds in employment, housing or services. Racial grounds include colour, race, nationality, and ethnic or national origins. The Act makes it an offence to incite or encourage racial hatred. As with the law against sex discrimination, both direct and indirect discrimination are made unlawful.

The **Commission for Racial Equality** was set up in 1976 to make sure that the law against racial discrimination works. The Commission can investigate cases of discrimination and give advice to people who wish to take legal action because of discrimination. The Race Relations law was strengthened and widened by an amendment in 2000 in order to prevent discrimination in any public situation.

The Disability Discrimination Act 1995

This Act is designed to prevent discrimination against people with disabilities, in matters of employment, access to education and transport, housing and obtaining goods and services. Employers and landlords must not treat a disabled person less favourably than a non-disabled person. New transport facilities must meet the needs of disabled people and institutions such as colleges, shops and other services must ensure that disabled people can use their services.

The Disability Rights Commission was set up by the **Disability Rights Commission Act 1999.** This commission has the power to conduct formal investigations and to serve non-discrimination notices, make agreements, and take other actions to prevent discrimination against people with a disability. The commission can give advice to people who believe they have experienced discrimination.

Other important laws relevant to care

The Children Act 1989 outlined 'parental responsibility' and established children's right to be protected from 'significant harm'. **The NHS and Community Care Act 1990** established that all people who are in need of community care have the right to have their needs assessed and to have services if their needs meet certain criteria. **The Care Standards Act 2000** created a new framework for defining and controlling quality within care work.

Policies

The Care Standards Act 2000 established the National Care Standards Commission (NCSC) and the General Social Care Council (GSCC). Both of these organisations are part of the National Institutional Framework for Quality in Social Care. Further details of the National Institutional Framework can be found on pages 23–25. Both the NCSC and the GSCC specify standards and principles of good practice in social care work.

Principles of good practice

The National Care Standards Commission or NCSC started work in 2002. This organisation aims to make sure that care services, including private and voluntary hospitals and nurses' agencies, provide good-quality care. The NCSC produces a set of regulations and National Minimum Standards which care services must achieve. There are different sets of standards for different care services. The standards provide detailed guidance on how services must be delivered. Care services have to be registered with the NCSC, and the NCSC inspects services to make sure that they are providing high-quality care. The NCSC will also investigate complaints about care services. A new inspectorate called the Commission for Social Care Inspection (CSCI) is planned to take over the inspection role of the NCSC.

An example of the principles set out in National Minimum Standards for Care Homes for Younger Adults (adults between 18 and 65 years of age) is set out below:

Choice of home: Standards 1–5	
1	The registered person produces an up-to-date statement setting out the aims, objectives and philosophy of the home and its services and facilities and terms and conditions, and provides each prospective service user with a **service user's guide** to the home.
2	New service users are admitted only on the basis of a full assessment undertaken by people competent to do so, using an **appropriate communication** method and with an independent advocate as appropriate.
3	The registered person can demonstrate their home's capacity to meet the **assessed needs** (including specialist needs) of individuals admitted to the home.
4	The registered manager invites prospective service users to visit the home on an introductory basis before making a decision to move there, and unplanned admissions are avoided where possible.
5	The registered manager develops and agrees with each prospective service user a written and costed contract/statement of terms and conditions between the home and the service user.
Traditional needs and choices: Standards 6–10	
6	The registered manager develops and agrees with each service user an **individual plan**, which may include treatment and rehabilitation, describing the services and facilities to be provided by the home.

7	Staff respect service users' right to make decisions, and that right is limited only through the assessment process, and as recorded in the **individual service user plan**.
8	The registered manager ensures that service users are offered opportunities to participate in the day-to-day running of the home and to contribute to the development and review of policies, procedures and services.
9	Staff enable service users to take responsible **risks**, ensuring they have good information on which to base decisions within the context of the service users' individual plans and the home's risk assessment and risk management strategies.
10	Staff respect information given by service users in **confidence**, and handle information about service users in accordance with written policies and procedures and the **Data Protection Act 1998**, and in the best interests of the service user.

Life style: Standards 11–17

11	Staff enable service users to have opportunities to maintain and develop **social, emotional, communication and independent living skills**.
12	Staff help service users to find and keep appropriate jobs, continue their education or training, and take part in valued and fulfilling activities.
13	Staff support service users to become part of, and participate in, the local community in accordance with assessed needs and the individual plans.
14	Staff ensure that service users have access to, and choose from a range of, appropriate **leisure** activities.
15	Staff support service users to maintain **family links and friendships** inside and outside the home, subject to restrictions agreed in the individual plan and contract.
16	The daily routines and house rules promote independence, **individual choice** and freedom of movement, subject to restrictions agreed in the individual plan and contract.
17	The registered person promotes service users' health and well-being by ensuring the supply of nutritious, varied, balanced and attractively presented meals in a congenial setting and at flexible times.

Personal and health care support: Standards 18–21

18	Staff provide sensitive and flexible personal support and nursing care to maximise service users' **privacy, dignity, independence and control over their lives**.
19	The registered person ensures that the health care needs of service users are assessed and recognised, and that procedures are in place to address them.
20	The registered manager and staff encourage and support service users to retain, administer and control their own medication, within a risk management framework, and complying with their home's policy and procedures for use of medicines.
21	The registered manager and staff deal with the ageing, illness and death of a service user with sensitivity and **respect**.

Concerns, complaints and protection: Standards 22–23

22	The registered person ensures that there is a clear and effective complaints procedure, and that service users know how, and to whom, to complain.
23	The registered person ensures that service users are safeguarded from physical, financial, material, psychological or sexual abuse, neglect, discriminatory **abuse**, self-harm or degrading treatment in accordance with policy.

Environment: Standards 24–30

24	The home's premises are suitable for its stated purpose; accessible, safe and well maintained; meet service users' individual and collective needs in a comfortable and homely way; and have been designed with reference to relevant guidance.
25	The registered person provides each service user with a bedroom which has usable floor space sufficient to meet individual needs and lifestyles.
26	The registered person provides each service user with a bedroom that has furniture and fittings sufficient and suitable to meet individual needs and lifestyles.
27	The registered person provides service users with toilet and bathroom facilities which meet assessed needs and offer sufficient personal **privacy**.
28	A range of comfortable, safe and fully accessible shared spaces is provided both for shared activities and for private use.
29	The registered person ensures the provision of the environmental adaptations and disability equipment necessary to meet the home's stated purpose and the individually assessed needs of all service users.
30	The premises are kept hygienic and free from offensive odours throughout, and systems are in place to control the spread of infection, in accordance with relevant legislation, published professional guidance and the purpose of the home.

Staffing: Standards 31–36

31	The registered manager ensures that staff have clearly defined job descriptions and understand their own and others' **roles and responsibilities**.
32	Staff have the competences and **qualities** required to meet service users' needs and achieve strategy targets within the required timescales.
33	The home has an effective **staff team**, with sufficient numbers and complementary skills to support service users' assessed needs at all times.
34	The registered person operates a thorough recruitment procedure based on **equal opportunities** and ensuring the protection of service users.
35	The registered person ensures that there is a **staff training** and development programme which meets training targets and ensures that staff fulfil the aims of the home and meet the changing needs of service users.
36	Staff receive the **support and supervision** they need to carry out their jobs.

Conduct and management of the home: Standards 37–43

37	The registered manager is qualified, competent and experienced in running a home and meets its stated purpose, aims and objectives.
38	The management approach of the home creates an open, positive and inclusive atmosphere.

39	Effective quality assurance and quality monitoring systems, based on seeking the views of service users, are in place to measure success in achieving the aims, objectives and statement of purpose of the home.
40	The home's written policies and procedures comply with current legislation and recognised professional standards, covering topics set out in Appendix 3. (Appendix 3 lists 33 areas that must be covered in a home's policies and procedures.)
41	Records required by regulation for the protection of service users and for the effective and efficient running of the business are maintained, up to date and accurate.
42	The registered manager ensures so far as is reasonably practicable the **health, safety and welfare** of service users and staff.
43	The overall management of the service (within or external to the home) ensures the effectiveness, financial viability and accountability of the home.

The GSCC has designed a code of practice for both social care workers and employers of social care workers. A summary of the code of practice for social care workers can be found in Unit 1, page 36. A summary of the code of practice for employers of social care workers is set out below:

The Code of Practice for Employers of Social Care Workers

1   Employers must make sure people are suitable to enter the social care workforce and understand their roles and responsibilities.

2   Employers must have written policies and procedures in place to enable social care workers to meet the GSCC's Code of Practice for social care workers.

3   This includes written policies on:

- confidentiality
- equal opportunities
- risk assessment
- record-keeping
- acceptance of gifts
- substance abuse
- effective systems of management and supervision
- systems to report inadequate resources
- support for workers to meet the GSCC Code of Practice.

4   Employers must provide training and development opportunities to enable social care workers to strengthen and develop their skills and knowledge. This should include the following:

- induction
- workplace assessment and practice learning
- supporting staff to meet eligibility criteria
- responding to workers who seek assistance.

---

5   Employers must put into place and implement written policies and procedures to deal with dangerous, discriminatory or exploitative behaviour and practice. This should include the following:

■ bullying, harassment, discrimination
■ procedures to report dangerous, discriminatory, abusive, or exploitative behaviour
■ policies to minimise the risk of violence and to manage violent incidents
■ support for workers who experience trauma or violence
■ equal opportunities
■ assistance to care workers in relation to health needs.

6   Employers must promote the GSCC's Code of Practice to social care workers, service users and carers and co-operate with the GSCC's proceedings. This should include the following:

■ informing workers of the Code of Practice
■ informing social care users and using the code of practice to assist decision-making
■ informing the GSCC of any misconduct and co-operating with the GSCC in investigations.

Policies, procedures and the role of the care worker

By itself, the law cannot make sure that discrimination does not happen, or that people's rights are always respected. It can be difficult to prove that discrimination has happened and it can be costly in time, energy and money to fight legal battles. Policies and standards of good practice can provide an effective way of making sure that rights are taken seriously. Care services are inspected to make sure that the quality of the service they offer is acceptable. Each service will have policies on equal opportunities and confidentiality to guide staff

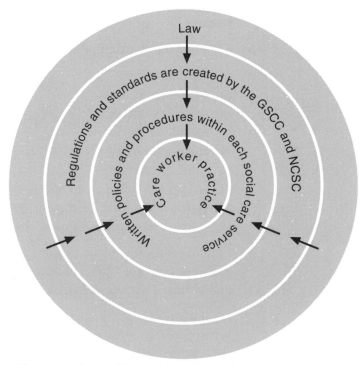

Figure 4.4 *Law, policies and procedures influence practice*

behaviour. These policies will be designed to meet legal requirements as well as NCSC standards. Together with policies, each care organisation will have procedures that staff have to follow to ensure that service users' rights are respected.

Laws provide the background to policy-making, and policies and standards guide managers when they design procedures. Just because policy and procedure documents say that care workers must meet certain standards, this does not mean that they will! The NCSC, SSI and, in the future, CSCI will undertake inspections of care services and can respond to complaints; but even inspection and complaints procedures cannot guarantee that every service user's rights will be respected. The factors listed below will influence the quality of service that an individual receives:

- the level of physical and staff resources (including the number of staff available to work)
- the amount and quality of staff training
- the amount and quality of staff supervision and support
- the values that staff believe in
- staff morale, including how tired or stressed staff feel
- the quality of team work within a care service
- the level of co-operation between different services.

Over time, standards and inspections should mean that the quality of care generally improves, but a lack of resources or the inability to change inappropriate values could still result in a poor quality of service to an individual, despite the existence of Minimum National Standards and inspection procedures.

ASSESSMENT ACTIVITY

Identify current laws, policies and procedures that affect care settings with respect to an individual's rights, responsibilities and personal beliefs.

1   Think of an individual service user whom you have met while you were on placement. Without identifying this person, draw up a list of the laws, codes of practice, and National Minimum Standards that create rights and responsibilities and protect the personal beliefs of this person. While you are on placement, make a list of the policies and procedures available in your organisation that protect the rights, beliefs and cultural diversity of service users. Use

these two lists to create a poster-size diagram which shows the influence of laws, policies and organisations' procedures on individual rights, responsibilities and personal beliefs.

2   Use your diagram as the basis for a written report that explains how legislation, standards and other guidelines can help to create respect and value for different belief systems and cultural diversity.

To achieve a **merit grade** you will need to explain how legislation and guidelines can promote cultural diversity

To achieve a **distinction grade** you will need to evaluate the effectiveness of current legislation and guidelines for promoting diversity. Your report will need to focus on the quality of service that the individual service user receives.

How far was cultural diversity understood, respected and valued during your placement? How far do you believe current legislation and guidelines are effective in creating understanding, respect and value for cultural diversity? How far do issues like staff shortages or low staff morale cause problems for care services in meeting quality standards and legal requirements?

Sources of information on rights and responsibilities

One way in which care workers can help people is by providing information. Services, rights and benefits change from time to time and from one location to another. People usually need help to find out which services they may be entitled to or can pay for. The sources of information shown in Figure 4.5 may help carers with detailed information on current support services, rights and benefits.

Figure 4.5 *Sources of information that may help carers*

The balance of rights and responsibilities

Service users have a right to choose a lifestyle and beliefs, but a person's lifestyle and beliefs must not reduce the quality of other people's lives. Rights are balanced with responsibilities – people have a right to act as they wish, but not a right to cause problems for others. For example, people have a right to smoke, even though smoking causes serious illnesses, including heart disease and cancer. But they don't have a right to make others breathe their smoke and risk their own health.

People in care have a right to:	People in care have a responsibility to:
have control and independence in their own lives	help others to be independent and not try to control other people
be valued and respected	value and respect others
maintain their own beliefs and lifestyle	respect the different beliefs and lifestyles of others
make choices and take risks	not interfere with others, or put others or themselves at risk
not be discriminated against	not discriminate against others
confidentiality in personal matters.	respect confidentiality for others.

Situations involving rights and responsibility

Graham is a 38-year-old man with learning disabilities. He gets great pleasure from eating, and particularly enjoys sweet things such as honey and jam. Graham is overweight and the staff think that he should go on a diet for health reasons. Graham cannot understand their ideas and becomes angry if he can't follow his usual eating pattern.

What are Graham's rights and responsibilities? In general, Graham has the right to choose to eat a lot of sweet things. He also has a right to be overweight! People may choose their own diet and lifestyle. But Graham has a responsibility not to behave in a way that might injure himself or shorten his life. Graham doesn't understand the issues of diet and health, so it is difficult for the staff or for Graham to decide what should be done.

In situations like this, an **advocate** should be appointed to help decide on the balance of rights and responsibilities. An advocate is someone who tries to understand the needs and wishes of a service user, and then argues for them. In Graham's situation the advocate might argue that Graham should continue to enjoy his favourite food, but that the care staff should keep an eye on his weight in case this becomes more of a risk to him later.

The balance between rights and responsibility is often hard to decide. Sometimes it is important to involve an advocate for the service user, and there is often a need for negotiation and problem-solving work. Care workers should not have to make decisions on their own – they should at least be able to get advice from managers before having to negotiate about rights and responsibilities.

Confidentiality

Confidentiality is an important right for all service users. It is important because:

■ service users may not trust a carer if the carer does not keep information confidential

■ service users may not feel valued or able to keep their self-esteem if their private details are shared with others

■ service users' safety may be put at risk if details of their property or their habits are widely known

■ a professional service that maintains respect for individuals must keep private information confidential

■ there are legal requirements to keep personal records confidential.

Trust
If you know that your carer won't pass things on, you may feel able to tell him or her what you really think and feel.

Self-esteem
If your carer promises to keep things confidential, it shows that he or she respects and values you; it shows that you matter.

Safety
You may have to leave your home empty at times. If other people know where you keep your money and when you are out, someone may be tempted to break in. Carers need to keep personal details confidential to protect service users' property and personal safety.

Staying professional
Medical practitioners and lawyers have always strictly observed confidentiality as part of their professional role. If service users are to receive a professional service, care workers must copy this example.

Legal requirements

The Data Protection Acts of 1984 and 1998, the Access to Personal Files Act 1987 and the Access to Health Records Act 1990 made it a legal requirement to keep recorded information confidential.

The 1998 Data Protection Act establishes rights to confidentiality covering both paper and electronic records. This Act provides people with a range of rights including:

- the right to know what information is held on you and to see and correct this information
- a right for you to refuse to provide information
- a right that data held on you should be accurate and up to date
- a right that data held on you should not be kept for longer than necessary
- a right to confidentiality; information about you should not be accessible to unauthorised people.

The law set out in the Data Protection Act 1998 has been incorporated into the regulations set out by the NCSC and the GSCC. For example, Standard 10 of the NCSC's National Minimum Standards for Care Homes for Younger Adults is set out in full below:

	Standard 10
10.1	Staff respect information given by service users in confidence, and handle information about service users in accordance with their home's written policies and procedures and the Data Protection Act 1998, and in the best interests of the service user.
10.2	Service users and their families have access to their home's policy and procedures on confidentiality and on dealing with breaches of confidentiality, and staff ensure service users understand the policy.
10.3	Service users' individual records are accurate, secure and confidential.
10.4	Staff know when information given to them in confidence must be shared with their manager or others.
10.5	Information given in confidence is not shared with families/friends against the service users' wishes.
10.6	The home gives a statement on confidentiality to partner agencies, setting out the principles governing the sharing of information.

All services now have to have policies and procedures on the confidentiality of recorded information.

Boundaries to confidentiality

Service users have a right to confidentiality, but also a responsibility in relation to the rights of others. Confidentiality often has to be kept within boundaries, or even broken when the rights of others must be balanced with the service user's rights. Keeping confidentiality within boundaries means that a carer may tell his or her manager something learned in confidence. The information is not made public, so it is still partly confidential. Information may need to be passed to managers when:

- there is a significant risk of harm to a service user

- a service user might be abused

- there is a significant risk of harm to others

- there is a risk to the carer's health or well-being.

Some examples of these situations are given below.

- An old person in the community refuses to put her heating on in winter; she may be at risk of harm from the cold.

- A person explains that his son takes his money – he might be suffering financial abuse.

- A person lives in a very dirty house infested with mice and rats. This may be creating a public health risk.

- A person is very aggressive, placing the carer at risk.

Case Study – Ethel

Ethel is 88 years old and receives home care. One day she says to you: 'Keep this confidential, but I don't take my tablets – I'm saving them so that I can take them all at once and finish my life if my pain gets worse.' Ethel manages to say this before you can tell her that some things can't be kept confidential.

Do you have to keep this information confidential? Ethel has a right to confidentiality, but she has a responsibility not to involve other people in any harm she may do to herself – she doesn't have a right to involve you. The information about the tablets should be shared with managers and her GP, who can discuss the matter with Ethel.

Ethel's neighbour stops you as you are leaving one day. The neighbour asks: 'How is Ethel, is she taking her tablets?'

Can you tell the neighbour of your worries? Before giving any information to anyone, carers have to ask the question: 'Does this person have a need to know?' A need to know is different from wanting to know. Ethel's neighbour might just be nosy, and it would be wrong to break confidentiality without an important reason. If the GP knows Ethel doesn't take her tablets, this information may save her life. But the neighbour does not need to be told.

Effective communication

Forms of communication

Working effectively as a carer involves learning about the individual people you work with. Learning about other people includes listening to what they say and watching the messages that people send with their body language. The skills of listening, taking part in conversation and understanding other people's body language help us to understand each other and to build relationships. It is not always easy to get to know people.

Body language

Within a few seconds of meeting your service users you will usually be able to tell what they are feeling. You will know whether they are tired, happy, angry, sad or frightened – even before they say anything. We can usually guess how people feel by looking at their body language.

Another term for body language is **non-verbal communication**. 'Non-verbal' means without words, so this refers to the messages we send without putting them into words. We send messages using our eyes, the tone of our voice, our facial expression, gestures with our hands and arms, the angle of our head, the way we sit or stand – known as body posture – and the tension in our muscles.

When a person is sad, he or she may signal this emotion with eyes that look down – there may be tension in the face, and the mouth will be closed. The muscles in the person's shoulders are likely to be relaxed, but the face and neck may show muscle tension. A happy person will have wide-open eyes that make contact with you – he or she will smile. When people are excited they move their arms and hands to signal their excitement.

Most people can recognise such emotions in the non-verbal behaviour of others. The skill that care workers need is to go one stage further, and understand the messages that they send with their own bodies when working with other people.

Non-verbal messages

Our body sends messages to other people, often without us deliberately meaning to send these messages. Some of the most important body areas that send messages are shown in the diagram opposite.

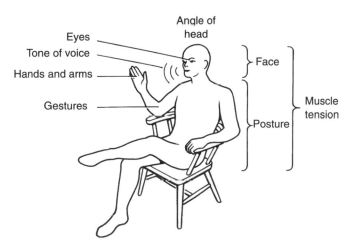

Figure 4.6 *Areas of the body that send out non-verbal messages*

The eyes
We can guess the feelings and thoughts that another person has by looking at his or her eyes. Our eyes get wider when we are excited, attracted to, or interested in someone else. A fixed stare may send the message that someone is angry. Looking away is often interpreted as being bored or not interested.

The face

Our face can send very complex messages and we can read them easily, even in diagram form.

Voice tone

It is not just what we say, but the way that we say it. If we talk quickly in a loud voice with a fixed voice tone, people may see us as angry. A calm, slow voice with varying tone may send a message of being friendly.

Body movement

The way we walk, move our head, sit, cross our legs and so on, send messages about whether we are tired, happy, sad or bored.

Posture

The way we sit or stand can send messages. Sitting with crossed arms can mean 'I'm not taking any notice'. Leaning can send the message that you are relaxed or bored. Leaning forward can show interest.

Muscle tension

The tension in our feet, hands and fingers can tell others how relaxed or how tense we are. If someone is very tense her shoulders might stiffen, her muscles might tighten and she might sit or stand rigidly. A tense face might have a firmly closed mouth with lips and jaws clenched tight. A tense person might breathe quickly and become hot.

Figure 4.7 *Our faces send messages to other people*

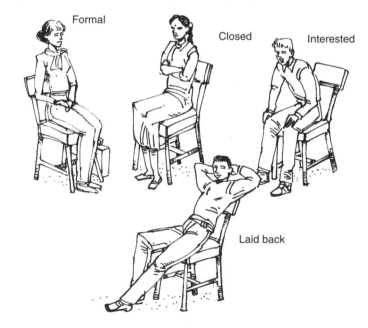

Figure 4.8 *Our body posture can send messages about the way we feel*

'I don't know'

'stop, don't do that'

'success – everything's going well'

'perfection' or 'perfect'

Figure 4.9 *Some gestures commonly used in the UK*

Gestures

Gestures are hand and arm movements that can help us to understand what a person is saying. Some gestures carry a meaning of their own. Some common gestures are shown in Figure 4.9.

Touch

Touching another person can send messages of care, affection, power over them, or sexual interest. The social setting and other body language usually help people to understand what touch might mean. Carers should not make assumptions about touch. Even holding someone's hand might be seen as trying to dominate them!

How close people are

The space between people can sometimes show how friendly or 'intimate' the conversation is. Different cultures have different behaviours with respect to space between people who are talking.

Face-to-face positions

Standing or sitting eye to eye can send a message of formality or hostility. A slight angle can create a more relaxed and friendly feeling.

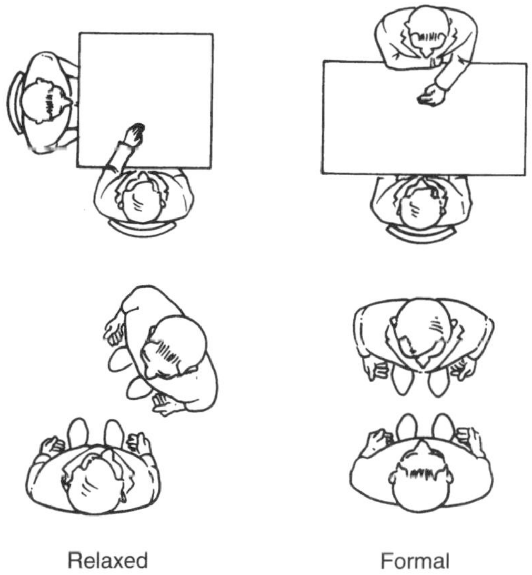

Relaxed

Formal

Figure 4.10 *Face-to-face encounters*

Verbal communication

When we talk to people we have to start the conversation off. Usually we start with a greeting or asking how someone is. Conversations have a beginning, a middle and an end, and this means that we have to create the right kind of atmosphere for a conversation at the beginning. We might need to help someone relax, so we might need to show that we are friendly and relaxed. When we end a conversation we usually say something like 'See you soon'. Ending a conversation has to involve the right emotional feelings.

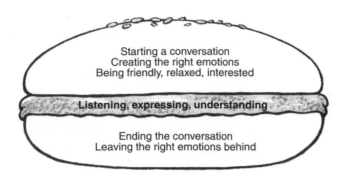

Starting a conversation
Creating the right emotions
Being friendly, relaxed, interested

Listening, expressing, understanding

Ending the conversation
Leaving the right emotions behind

Figure 4.11 *The conversation sandwich*

The communication cycle

Communication is not just about giving information to people. While we are having a conversation we go through a process or 'cycle' of:

- hearing what another person says

- watching the other person's non-verbal messages

- having feelings

- beginning to understand the other person

- sending a message back to the other person.

The communication process might look something like the diagram in Figure 4.12.

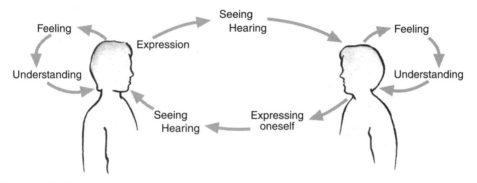

Feeling

Seeing
Hearing

Expression

Feeling

Understanding

Understanding

Seeing
Hearing

Expressing
oneself

Figure 4.12 *The communication cycle*

Listening skills

We can understand other people's emotions by watching their non-verbal communication; but we can't usually understand what is on someone's mind without being good at listening.

Listening is not just hearing the sounds that people make when they talk. Listening skills involve hearing another person's words, thinking about what they mean, then deciding what to reply to the other person. Some people call this process **active listening**. As well as thinking carefully and remembering what a service user says, good listeners will make sure that their non-verbal behaviour shows interest.

Skilled listening involves:

- looking interested and ready to listen
- hearing what is said
- remembering what is said
- checking understanding with the other person.

THINK IT THROUGH

Take a piece of paper, divide it into four areas and write out four headings: 'Where I live', 'An important thing that happened in the past', 'Something I am looking forward to', and 'Where I work or study'. Any other titles will do, as long as you can talk in detail about the areas. Think through what you can tell another person about yourself under each heading, then get together with a colleague who has also planned what to say.

Explain your thoughts on the four areas to each other. This should take at least ten minutes. Then see what you can remember about the other person, and how detailed and accurate your memory is! How good are you at understanding and remembering?

Confirming information and reflection

It is usually easier to understand people who are similar to ourselves. We can learn about different people by checking our understanding of what we have heard.

Checking understanding involves hearing what the other person says and asking questions. Another way is to put what a person has just said into your own words and say it to them to check that you did understand. When we listen to complicated details of other people's lives, we often begin to form mental pictures based on what they tell us. Listening involves checking these mental pictures to make sure that we are understanding correctly. Good listening involves thinking about what we hear while we are listening and checking our understanding as the conversation goes along. Sometimes this idea of checking our understanding is called 'reflection', because we reflect the other person's ideas.

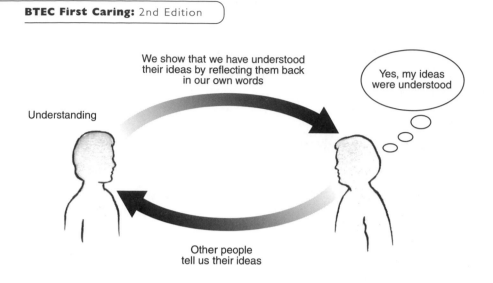

Figure 4.13 *Reflecting back to the other person proves you have listened*

Cultural differences

Skilled carers use a range of conversational techniques when working with others. These include being sensitive to cultural differences and social contexts.

Culture means the history, customs and ways that people learn as they grow up. The expressions that people use and the meanings of non-verbal signs can vary from one culture to another. People from different regions of Britain use different expressions. Non-verbal signs vary from culture to culture. White middle-class people often expect others to 'look them in the eye' while talking. If a person looks down or away, it is a sign that he or she may be dishonest, or perhaps sad. In other cultures, for example among some black communities, looking down or away when talking is a sign of respect – a way to show you are using your listening skills!

Care workers have to be careful not to assume that statements and signs always have the same meaning. Culture, race, class and geographical location can alter what things mean. There are a vast range of meanings that can be given to any type of eye contact, facial expressions, posture or gesture. Every culture develops its own special system of meanings. Carers have to respect differences, but it is impossible to learn all the possible meanings which phrases, words and signs may have.

Getting a conversation going and keeping it going (interaction)

It can be hard to get to know people unless you keep a conversation going. Starting a conversation is often easy – we ask someone how he or she is today, we introduce ourselves or we ask a question. If we remember the service user, we can mention things that have been talked about before, such as 'How did you get on at the dentist yesterday?'

Once a conversation has started, the trick is to keep it going long enough. Skills that help with this are turn-taking, using non-verbal communication to show interest, being good at asking questions and using silence at the right times.

Turn-taking in conversations means taking turns to listen and talk. If you are trying to get to know a service user you will probably do less talking and more listening. People normally show when they want you to talk by slowing down the rate at which they speak their last few words, changing the tone of the voice slightly and looking away from you. The person will then stop speaking and look directly at you. If you are sensitive to these messages you will be ready to ask a question or say something that keeps the conversation going.

Showing interest involves giving the other person your full attention. Appropriate body language includes:

- eye contact – looking at the other person's eyes

- smiling – looking friendly rather than 'cold' in expression

- hand movements and gestures that show interest

- slight nods of the head to mean 'I see', or 'I understand', or 'I agree'.

Showing interest can be a good way of keeping another person talking.

Asking questions

It is important to ask the kind of questions that encourage people to talk. Questions that don't do so are called closed questions, and are not very useful when trying to get to know people. Questions like 'How old are you?' are closed, because there is only one simple answer the person can give: 'I'm eight', 'I'm 84', and so on. Closed questions don't lead on to discussion. 'Do you like butter?' is a closed question – the person can only say yes or no.

Open questions encourage people to think and discuss their thoughts. A question like 'How do you feel about the food here?' asks the other person to think about the food and then discuss it. Open questions keep the conversation going. Sometimes closed questions can block a conversation and cause it to stop.

Silence

Sometimes a pause in conversation can make people feel embarrassed, but silence can mean 'let's think' or 'I need time to think'. Silent pauses can show respect and interest, and don't always stop the conversation. Some carers use pauses in a conversation to show that they are listening and thinking about what the service user has said.

The skills used in individual communication are also needed for communication in formal and informal group situations. (See Unit 6, pages 228–231, for more information on formal and informal situations.)

Constraints on effective communication

There are three main ways that communication becomes blocked:

1 A person can't see, hear or receive the message.

2 A person can't make sense of the message.

3 A person misunderstands the message.

Examples of the first kind of block, where people don't receive the communication, include visual disabilities, hearing disabilities, and environmental problems such as poor lighting, noisy environments, and speaking from too far away.

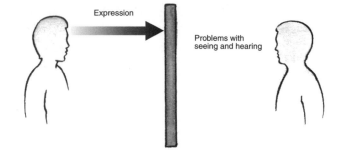

Examples of not being able to make sense of the message include:

Figure 4.14 *Environmental problems like noise and poor light can create communication barriers*

- the use of different languages, including signed languages

- the use of different terms in language, such as **jargon** (technical language), **slang** (different people using different terms), or **dialect** (different people making different sounds)

- physical and intellectual disabilities, such as being ill, or suffering memory loss, or learning disability.

Reasons for misunderstanding a message include:

- cultural influences – different cultures interpret non-verbal and verbal messages, and humour, in different ways

- assumptions about people – about race, gender, disability and other groupings

- emotional differences – very angry or very happy people may misinterpret communication from others

- social context – statements and behaviour that are understood by friends and family may not be understood by strangers.

Because people are so different from one another, the communication cycle can easily be blocked if professional listening skills are not used.

The effects of communication difficulties

Constantly being unable to communicate with others can make it very difficult to meet any of your personal needs.

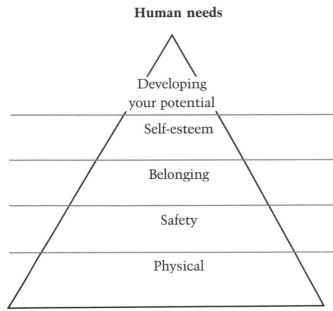

Human needs	Communication difficulties
Developing your potential	It is difficult to develop well without communication with others.
Self-esteem	It is difficult to value your life if people don't communicate with you.
Belonging	It is difficult to feel that you belong if you can't communicate with others.
Safety	You may feel threatened if people do not understand you.
Physical	If you do not communicate hunger, thirst or pain – people may not respond even to your physical needs.

Labelling and stereotyping

People who have difficulty hearing or seeing are sometimes assumed to be awkward or mentally limited. Older people are sometimes seen as demented or confused if they do not answer questions appropriately.

People can also be labelled or stereotyped when they use different language systems. Some people will shout at those who don't speak the same language, as if increasing the volume would help. People who sign to communicate are sometimes thought to be odd or to have learning difficulties, because they don't respond to written or spoken English.

Ways of overcoming difficulties

Visual disability

- Use language to describe things.

- Assist people to touch things (e.g. touch your face to recognise you).

- Explain details that sighted people might take for granted.

- Check what people can see (many registered blind people can see shapes, or tell light from dark).

- Check glasses, other aids and equipment.

Hearing disability

- Don't shout, keep to normal clear speech and make sure your face is visible for people who can lip-read.

- Show pictures, or write messages.

- Learn to sign (for people who use signed languages).
- Ask for help from or employ a communicator or interpreter for signed languages.
- Check hearing aids and equipment.

Environmental constraints

- Check and improve lighting.
- Reduce noise.
- Move to a quieter or better-lit room.
- Move to smaller groups to see and hear more easily.

Language differences

- Communicate using pictures, diagrams and non-verbal signs
- Use translators or interpreters.
- Be careful not to make assumptions or stereotype.

Jargon, slang and dialects

- Re-word your messages – find different ways of saying things.
- Speak in short, clear sentences.

Physical and intellectual disabilities

- Use pictures and signs as well as clear, simple speech.
- Be calm and patient.
- Set up group meetings where people can share interests, experiences or reminiscences.
- Check that people do not become isolated.

Misunderstandings

- Watch out for different cultural interpretations.
- Avoid making assumptions about or discriminating against people who are different.
- Use reflective listening techniques to check that your understanding is correct.
- Stay calm and try to calm people who are angry or excited.
- Be sensitive to different social settings and the form of communication that would be most appropriate.

ASSESSMENT ACTIVITY

Use different forms of communication, and describe the stages required in order to communicate clearly and effectively.

I   While you are on placement, make some notes on conversations that you have experienced or taken part in. These conversations could be between staff or between staff and service users. Try to identify examples of the 'conversation sandwich' and the 'communication cycle'. Think about communication difficulties and how you can reduce barriers to communication.

2   Think about your own communication skills with service users. How good are you at using the range of verbal and non-verbal skills set out in the grid below? Give yourself a mark out of five for how well you use each skill. Next, try to remember a conversation you have had in a care setting and write a short report that explains how you used the 'conversation sandwich' and the 'communication cycle' during this conversation. Your report should also describe different verbal and non-verbal skills that you have used. Your report might also explain how you have reduced constraints on effective communication.

To achieve a **distinction grade** you must prepare an action plan for developing and improving your communication skills. You might like to refer back to the section in Unit 1 on developing your own skills (pages 51–53). You could also use the grid set out below to help you identify your current level of communication skills, and develop a plan for improving your skills. You will need to practise communication skills and achieve feedback from tutors or placement supervisors to help you develop. Outline areas for development could be chosen using the grid below. Target dates to discuss these skills could be negotiated with tutors or supervisors. You might like to adapt the grid below to suit your own needs.

Skill	Mark out of 5	Develop this skill further yes/no?	Date for review	Name of person who can give feedback
Using eye contact effectively				
Using facial expression effectively				
Using an appropriate tone of voice				
Using other aspects of body language				
Using the conversation sandwich				
Using the communicaton cycle and active listening				
Using questioning skills effectively				
Recognising cultural differences				
Overcoming difficulties and barriers to communication				

Communicating formally in care settings

Working as a carer involves being part of a large network of people. Each person you work with will have a network of friends, relatives and other professional people who communicate with him or her. You will be working with other people, including professionals and managers, who also work with your service users.

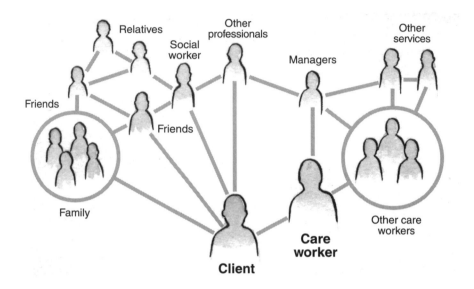

Figure 4.15 *Care workers and service users are part of a network of communication*

It is an important task to make sure that information gets to the people who need it, and that personal information does not go to those who have no right to know it. Carers may also need to establish how important information is, in order to prioritise passing it on.

The law on information: the Data Protection Act 1998

The **Data Protection Act** was passed by Parliament to protect people's rights in relation to the way information about them can be stored. The Data Protection Act 1998 replaced an earlier law from 1984. All information about people now has to be kept in accordance with the following principles:

- Information or data must be **fairly and legally** obtained. People must not be misled about the purposes for which information is gathered.

- Data must be gathered with the **permission** of the people involved and processed for limited purposes.

- Data gathered has to be **adequate, relevant** and not **excessive.**

- Data must be accurate and kept up to date.

- Data must **not be kept for longer than is necessary** for the purpose it was originally gathered for.

- People have the right to find out or **access personal data** being kept about them and certain other **rights** about the way in which data can be used.

- Data must be kept **secure.** Organisations must make sure that data are not lost or made available to unauthorised persons. The security principle means that data must be kept confidential.

- Data **must not be transferred** to any country outside of the European Union unless there are guarantees of data protection.

Good practice: *information*

- Keep information confidential, and pass information only to people who have a right and a need to know it.

- Record information accurately.

- Keep records safely so that they can't be altered or lost, or seen by people who do not have a need to use them.

Access to records

Not all care staff may have access to all the information about service users. Some homes maintain personal files on residents to which all permanent staff have access, although some sections may be restricted to senior staff.

The information available to all permanent staff may include personal details such as the person's doctor, next of kin, age and religion. Details about personal finance, action to be taken after a resident's death, and legal arrangements, may be restricted to managers because other staff don't need this information in order to care for residents.

Personal files should be kept for at least three years after a service user leaves care. Each home or service will have its own policies on recording information and on who has a need to know it.

Confidentiality and the need to know

Good care practice involves asking service users if we can let other people know things they tell us. It would be wrong to pass on even the date of a service user's birthday without asking him or her first. Some service users might not want others to know about a birthday – Jehovah's Witnesses believe that it is wrong to celebrate birthdays! Whatever we know about a service user should be kept private unless the service user allows us to share the information.

The exception to this rule is that information can be passed on when others have a right and a need to know it. Some examples of people who have a need to know about your work with service users are:

- your manager – he or she may need to help you make decisions that affect the service user

- your colleagues – these people may be working with the same service user

- other professionals – they may also be working with your service user and need to be kept up to date.

Giving information

When information is passed to other professionals it should be passed on with the understanding that they keep it confidential. It is important to check that other people are who they say they are. If you answer the telephone and someone says he is a social worker or other professional you should explain that you must phone him back before giving any information. Phoning back enables you to be sure that you are talking to someone at a particular number, or within a particular organisation. If you meet a person you don't know, you should ask for proof of identity before passing on any information.

Relatives will often say that they have a right to know about service users. Sometimes it is possible to ask relatives to discuss issues directly with the service user rather than giving information yourself, for example:

Relative: Has the doctor said anything more about my mother's illness?

Care worker: I expect your mother would like to talk to you directly – shall I show you to her room?

It is important to explain that you cannot share confidential information without the service user's consent. It will be important to discuss procedures for handling requests for information with your supervisor or manager at work or on placement.

The accuracy of information

Because social care work involves communicating with complex networks of people, it is vital that information is carefully checked and recorded.

When you take phone calls or other messages it is vital that key details are written down, because your memory for what was said will soon disappear. Compare the following two notes in Figure 4.16.

The Ba phoned for you said it was important.

Date:	Mon 20th Aug
Time:	9.55am
Message for:	'You'
Person calling:	Theba Timms
From:	S E Area Social Work team
Tel no:	01291 532107
Message:	Please call back between 11am–12 noon about visit tomorrow
Message taken by:	Sarosh

Figure 4.16 *Two telephone messages*

The first note is inaccurate and contains little information. The second note follows a set of headings which helps the worker to take accurate information.

The dangers of inaccurate information include:

- delays in meeting people's needs
- not being able to follow up enquiries
- making mistakes with arrangements for people's care
- missing meetings or important arrangements
- not being able to organise services for service users properly
- other professional workers not having the right information.

Many organisations use printed forms to help staff to ask important questions and check that they have taken accurate information. Service users' personal records arc likely to be written on forms which use headings. When writing information down, it is a good idea to:

- check that the other person agrees with what you are writing
- check the spelling of names and repeat phone numbers back to the person in order to check that they are correct.
- use a form or a prepared set of headings to help you check that you are collecting the right information.

Information can be gained by:

- watching what service users do
- listcning to what they say
- asking service users questions
- asking relatives or friends for information
- asking other professional workers for information.

Recording information

When recording personal information it is important to be as factual and accurate as possible. Say just what you see and what you hear.

It is important to describe only the facts or the events that happened, without giving your own interpretation or saying how you feel about the person.

Storing and retrieving records

Personal records and information may be kept electronically on a computer disk, or manually in handwritten or printed files. Whichever way records are kept, there should be a range of security measures to make sure the information stays confidential and is not lost or inappropriately altered.

Manual records

■ Keep records in a locked room or a locked cupboard to which only authorised staff have access.

■ Do not take records out of a particular room or area, to avoid the risk of their being lost or left where others might see them.

■ File records using a system such as an alphabetical one so that they can be found easily.

■ Find out about the policy as to who should update or change details.

■ It may be good practice to record the initials of the person who made the records and the date of any changes.

Electronic records

■ Keep a back-up copy in case the original is lost or damaged.

■ Use a password security check to ensure that only appropriate staff have access.

■ Find out about the policy on the printing of details so that hard copies don't get lost, or seen by others.

■ Find out about the policy on who is authorised to update or change records. The recording system must prevent information being altered or lost by accident.

■ Print out faxed documents in an appropriate confidential area and keep them in a manual system to prevent inappropriate people having access to confidential material.

If service user records are not managed in accordance with the Data Protection Act and NCSC regulations service users might suffer a range of damaging consequences. These consequences might include:

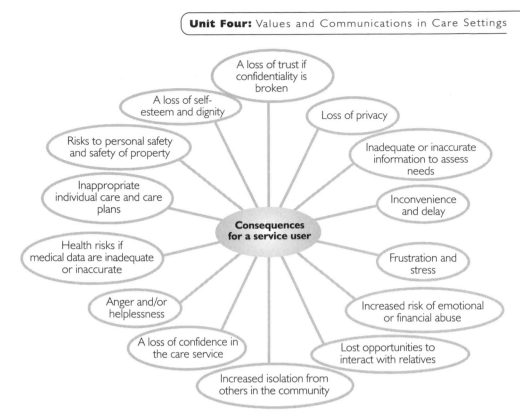

Figure 4.17 *Consequences for a service user if records are not managed correctly*

If care workers fail to follow appropriate policies and procedures for handling service user's information, they may experience a range of negative consequences. These consequences may include:

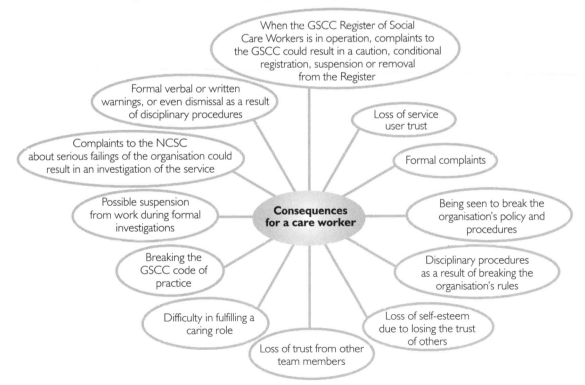

Figure 4.18 *Consequences for a care worker if records are not managed correctly*

ASSESSMENT ACTIVITY

Describe the responsibilities of a care worker in respect of service user information.

1 While you are on placement, ask your supervisor if you can have a copy of the organisation's policies and procedures that are relevant to the handling of service user information. Talk to a senior member of staff and ask them to explain the responsibilities of care workers in relation to recording and using personal information about service users. Ask if you can take some notes during this conversation. Use your notes to make a list of the responsibilities of a care worker within a specific organisation.

2 Ask the senior member of staff what the consequences might be for service users if policies and procedures were not followed. Ask the senior member of staff what the consequences for care workers might be if they failed to follow procedures. Use the information you gather from your conversation, together with the ideas in the section above, to help you write a report that explains the possible effects and consequences of failing to follow procedures for handling service user information.

To achieve a **merit grade** you must explain the possible effects and consequences for both service user and care worker of failing to follow procedures for handling service user information.

To achieve a **distinction grade** you must evaluate the effectiveness of current legislation and guidelines for handling service user information. At this level your report should explore the quality of service that people in your placement organisation receive. How far do issues such as staff shortages or low staff morale influence the handling of service user information? How far does legislation, standards, other policies and procedures result in a high quality of service?

Protecting individuals from abuse

The word 'abuse' covers a wide range of behaviour. Abuse can include criminal acts of violence, or acts of neglect. Abuse can be caused by the way organisations work, as well as by individuals. Carers need to understand their own and others' behaviour in order to minimise abuse in care settings and care relationships.

Forms of abuse

- **Physical abuse** includes hitting, pushing, pulling, restraining or causing pain or distress by physical actions.

- **Sexual abuse** means sexually exploiting or humiliating others.

- **Emotional abuse** includes bullying, blaming, threatening and damaging others' feelings of self-esteem (this is sometimes called psychological abuse).

- **Financial abuse** involves taking others' property or money, theft and the exploitation of other people's resources.

- **Neglect** means not giving food or physical care, or not giving attention.

Causes of abuse

People abuse children, adults, older people or relatives for complicated reasons. Some different causes of abusive behaviour are listed below.

- **Stress:** When people become tired or exhausted they are more likely to lose their temper – perhaps resulting in emotional abuse, physical abuse or neglect.

- **Past learning:** Some people have experienced abuse in their past and have come to regard physical or emotional abuse as a way of relating to others.

- **Power:** Some people desire to, or believe they have a right to, control and exploit others. A desire for power may motivate sexual abuse as well as bullying and financial abuse. Some people believe that their needs and wishes should come before the rights of others.

- **Social and organisational systems:** service users who are young, or otherwise unable to protect themselves, are vulnerable. Where staff think they ought to control these vulnerable people, there is a risk of abuse. If staff also become stressed because of lack of time or too much work, they may start to abuse their service users.

Abuse in care settings is often due to stress and a lack of supervision or other systems to prevent abuse. It would be wrong to think that all abuse is caused by individuals who intend to harm other people – when people are under pressure it is easy to neglect the needs of others.

Signs of abuse

It is important not to jump to conclusions, but the following list of possible signs of abuse might alert you to the risk that someone had been physically or emotionally abused. You should always discuss issues with a supervisor or manager before concluding that a person has been abused.

Physical signs

- Bruising or other injuries that are not explained.

- Bruises that look as if they have been caused by objects, such as belts, buckles, shoes or hands.

- Multiple small bruises – which may have been caused by poking.

- Black eyes.

- Bruising to the ears.

- Burns that could have come from a cigarette.

- Burns or scalds in unusual areas of the body.

- Marks to wrists, arms or legs, which could mean the person has been restrained.

- Ulcers or bed sores in older people.

- Unusual sexual behaviour.

Emotional signs

- A service user becoming quiet and withdrawn.

- A service user having problems with sleeping.

- Children with a sudden change in sexual behaviour or obsession with sexual language.

- Children who are unwilling to change their clothes or participate in sports.

- A child appearing tense or frightened with a particular adult.

- A child finding excuses not to go home.

- Depression or fear of making decisions or choices.

- Disappearance of benefit, pension or bank account books.

- Difficulty getting to see the service user (relatives always find a reason why he or she is not available).

- New financial agreements, or arrangements that the service user doesn't understand.

- Relatives speaking in a negative way about the service user.

Figure 4.19 *How would it feel to be in her shoes?*

The effects of abuse

Abuse can cause long-term damage to a person, and can limit a person's ability to develop his or her potential. The effects of abuse can vary from person to person, but some likely effects are listed below:

- fear and anger
- loss of self-confidence
- self-destructiveness
- copying the abusive behaviour
- mental illness.

- withdrawal and depression
- loss of self-esteem
- attention seeking
- increased dependency

The law and abuse

Criminal law covers many serious offences such as assault, sexual offences, theft and crimes against property. The police have powers to investigate and take action where many forms of abuse are suspected.

The Children Act 1989 requires that local authority Social Service departments provide protection from abuse for children in their area. In an emergency, a social worker can apply to a magistrate for an Emergency Protection Order to care for a child. The police can also take action to protect a child. Protection Orders are granted if there is reasonable evidence to show that a child may suffer 'significant harm'. Later, court hearings decide what should happen in the longer term. Very often, social workers work with families to prevent abuse and to protect children.

The Mental Health Act 1983 enables Social Service departments to assume responsibility for people who are not able to be responsible for their own affairs. This is called guardianship. However, for adults there is no specific legal duty to protect people from abuse.

Most Social Service departments will have procedures and guidelines to enable them to investigate suspected abuse of vulnerable adults. Where an adult may be at risk, a case conference may be called so that a plan of action can be worked out.

The National Care Standards Commission established by the Care Standards Act 2000 The NCSC has establish National Minimum Standards for various care services. These standards provide detailed regulations for protecting vulnerable service users from abuse. For example, Standard 23 of the Standards for Care Homes for Younger Adults states:

23.1	The registered person ensures that service users are safeguarded from physical, financial, material, psychological or sexual abuse, neglect, discriminatory abuse, self-harm or degrading treatment in accordance with policy.
23.2	Robust procedures for responding to suspicion or evidence of abuse or neglect ensure the safety and protection of service users.
23.3	All allegations and incidence of abuse, and action taken, are recorded.
23.4	Staff who may be unsuitable to work with vulnerable adults are referred in accordance with the Care Standards Act for consideration for inclusion on the Protection of Children and Vulnerable Adults registers.
23.5	Physical and verbal aggression by a service user is dealt with appropriately, and physical intervention is used only as a last resort by trained staff in accordance with the Department of Health guidance.

23.6	The home's policies regarding service users' financial affairs ensure service users access to their financial records, safe storage of money and valuables, consultation on finance in private, and preclude staff benefiting from wills.

Residential homes and nursing homes have to be registered with the NCSC. All homes are subject to inspection and the NCSC can investigate allegations of abuse. Inspectors have the power to take action against unsatisfactory homes. Homes will have detailed complaints procedures which may be used to challenge incidents of abuse.

What to do if you see or hear abuse happening

If you witness abuse you must report what you have seen or heard to your supervisor or manager, who will help you follow the correct procedures. Your manager will make a decision about how to follow up your information. If you think your manager is involved in the abuse, you should report the information to someone more senior.

Sometimes a range of professionals may need to be involved. If there are injuries, a medical examination may be necessary. Decisions about investigating abuse should be taken by senior staff. They will decide what risks can be taken, what should be kept confidential and whether legal action is appropriate.

Very often your information and observations about possible abuse will be shared within the team of people who work with a service user. A case conference may be necessary to decide on the best course of action. You must record exactly what happened. Your memory for details will change with time, so it is important that you make a record soon after the event. Your work setting may have a form or a series of headings to help you. Your reports should state just what you saw or heard and any actions you took, not give opinions or try to judge who was right or wrong.

If you find it difficult to write a report, you could describe what happened to another person who might write the report and ask you to check it and sign it. If no report is made, it can be difficult for managers or social workers to take further action.

Methods of preventing and dealing with abuse

Abuse can happen in any setting or situation, but some common situations where abuse can occur are listed below.

Abuse of children may happen where:
- parents put their own needs first – before the needs of their children
- parents or carers want to dominate others

■ parents have had difficult childhoods or been abused themselves

■ families are living in stressful circumstances

■ families have a history of violence.

Abuse of adults may happen where:
■ carers feel stressed because they have had to change their lifestyle

■ the service user shows difficult or challenging behaviour such as aggression, or has serious communication problems

■ carers have no support

■ carers are dependent on drugs or alcohol

■ carers have no privacy.

Abuse in care settings may happen where:
■ staff are poorly trained or untrained

■ there is little supervision or management support

■ staff feel isolated

■ staff are stressed – perhaps by their workload

■ staff feel that service users should be controlled

■ relationship and communication skills are poor.

To prevent abuse, it is important that carers receive support and guidance for working with difficult or stressful situations. Some abuse in the community happens because parents or carers do not have enough support or help. One way of preventing abuse to adults is to provide respite care. This is short-term care for a service user, to enable his or her carers to have a break.

Staff working in care can take steps to prevent abuse by:
■ attending regular supervision and team discussions

■ understanding service users' needs and care plans

■ learning how to cope with stressful situations, including challenging behaviour

■ understanding the risks that can lead to abuse

■ believing others when abuse is reported

■ challenging bad practice and reporting abuse.

It is important to work as a team member in order to understand service user needs, and to cope with the stress that challenging behaviour can cause. Both younger and adult service users can make offensive remarks or physically attack care staff. It is critically important that care staff never decide to 'get their own back' – users of care services are vulnerable. Most have low or insecure levels of self-esteem. If carers return physical or verbal abuse, they are committing an act of abuse themselves. If you work in a care role you have a responsibility never to lose your temper or return abuse when you are with service users.

To avoid reacting to stress and abusing service users, it is important to learn to:

- prevent others from becoming stressed and aggressive
- stay calm in tense situations
- help others to be calm
- use assertiveness skills, rather than becoming aggressive
- know when you should seek assistance.

Staff training and supervision may help with the development of these skills.

If service users tell you about abuse that has happened to them, it is very important to take what they say seriously and to believe them. It may often be unpleasant to listen to stories of abuse, but it is important not to give in to these feelings and damage the person further by not taking him or her seriously.

If you see or hear other staff failing to respect the rights of service users, it is important to challenge and, if appropriate, report what you have seen. It is vital that you know the procedures you should follow in your work setting.

Referral to professionals

Case Study – Mrs McKendrick and Jamie

Mrs McKendrick lives alone but has regular home care. One day she says, 'Don't tell anyone, but it makes me so upset – my son is always helping himself to my pension money. But I don't want anything to happen to him – he's my son.'

Jamie is nine years old. He often has bruising to his face, and recently you have noticed bruising on the back of his legs. Jamie has become quiet lately and when asked about his marks he will only say that he has been in a fight.

In both these situations there is a serious possibility that the service users are being abused. In both situations it would be vital to report what you had seen or heard. Both situations may be complex; but both Mrs McKendrick and Jamie need any abuse to stop. If you report what you know, it is likely that Social Services will become further involved.

Professional assessment of the situation may result in new services being made available to both service users' carers. Perhaps Mrs McKendrick's pension can be managed differently. Jamie's family may need a range of support services, together with careful monitoring of his situation. Your own role is to report and seek help – you should not try to sort out these types of situations by yourself.

Preventing and dealing with abuse can often require professional skills, knowledge and experience. Always refer situations to your manager or other senior staff as soon as possible.

May contribute to preventing abuse

Youth worker · Teacher · School staff · Care staff · Carer · Health visitor · Probation officer · Nurse · Social worker · Service manager · Advocate · Police · GP

Figure 4.20 *People who may be involved in working with abuse*

A wide range of services may become involved in preventing and dealing with abuse. Social Services can provide social worker support to assess, advise and plan appropriate care packages. Some services may be provided by the voluntary or private sectors. The NSPCC (National Society for the Prevention of Cruelty to Children) may enquire into potential abuse of children. Clients are sometimes unable to explain what is happening to them because of disability or dementia. In this situation, an advocate may be appointed to argue for the rights of the person.

ASSESSMENT ACTIVITY

Outline the ways in which service users can be protected from different forms of abuse, and the action that has to be taken when abuse is suspected.

1   On your placement, ask your placement supervisor if you can have a copy of the organisation's policies and procedures for protecting vulnerable people from abuse. Ask your supervisor to explain the policies and procedures to you. Use this information to help you write a brief report of how service users can be protected and what to do if abuse is suspected.

2   Discuss your report with a senior member of staff at your placement. Discuss the risks of abuse that service users may face and the ways in which service users may be harmed by abuse. With a senior member of staff, work out the reasons why the organisation's procedures are designed in the way they are. Use this discussion to develop your report so that it explains the reasons for the steps taken to protect service users from the different forms of abuse.

3   Again with a senior member of staff, discuss the positive role that care workers can play in protecting vulnerable people from neglect, physical, sexual, emotional and financial abuse. Discuss how care workers may work with more senior staff and the actions that senior staff might take in order to protect service users. Use this discussion to develop your report so that it includes an analysis of the significance of the care worker role.

To achieve a **merit grade** you need to discuss the reasons for the steps taken to protect service users from the different forms of abuse and the actions taken when abuse is suspected.

To achieve a **distinction grade** you need to analyse the significance of the role of the care worker in protecting, identifying and reporting abuse.

PHYSICAL CARE

This unit looks at the way in which carers can ensure that they provide good-quality physical care for their clients. Meeting a client's basic needs by helping them to be clean, well fed, warm and comfortable will have a positive effect on their sense of well-being and self-esteem. This includes encouraging them to be as independent and self-managing as possible.

In this unit you will learn about:

- the hygiene requirements of service users
- preparing food and drink

- the factors involved in moving and handling service users safely
- enabling service users to achieve physical comfort.

Hygiene requirements

The skin

The skin is the largest organ of the body. It provides a complete covering and protection for the body, and needs to be kept clean. The skin consists essentially of two layers, the outer layer called the epidermis and the inner layer, the dermis.

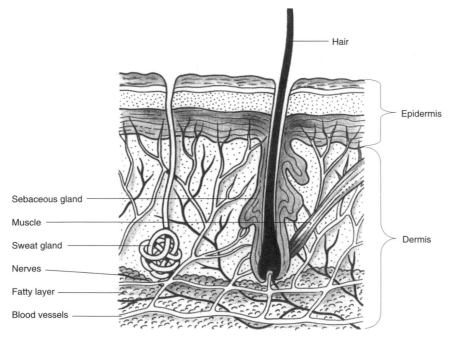

Figure 5.1 *A cross-section through the skin*

The epidermis is constantly being renewed – it sheds cells, and new cells are grown to replace them. You will have noticed how skin cells are shed when you undress or change bed sheets. The skin also contains glands that produce sweat and others (the sebaceous glands) that produce sebum, which is an oily substance that maintains waterproofing of the skin.

Skin becomes dirty because of exposure to the environment, but it also collects dried sweat, dead skin cells and oily sebum. All of these factors combine to provide a breeding ground for an assortment of bacteria. These bacteria can cause offensive odours and lead to infections, so skin needs to be regularly washed so that the bacteria are removed from the skin.

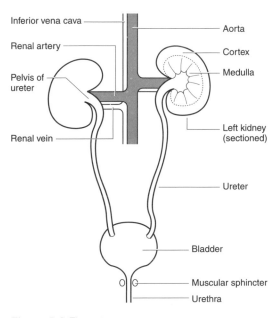

Inferior vena cava

Renal artery

Pelvis of ureter

Renal vein

Aorta

Cortex

Medulla

Left kidney (sectioned)

Ureter

Bladder

Muscular sphincter

Urethra

Figure 5.2 *The urinary system*

Personal cleanliness is also important because it improves the way people feel about themselves – they tend to feel better after having a bath or shower, so it is good for morale.

The urinary system

The urinary system is made up of two kidneys, two ureters, the urinary bladder and the urethra. Its function is to filter the blood to remove waste products such as urea formed from the breakdown of protein. This waste is known as urine and is collected in the bladder until it is excreted via the urethra.

The oral cavity

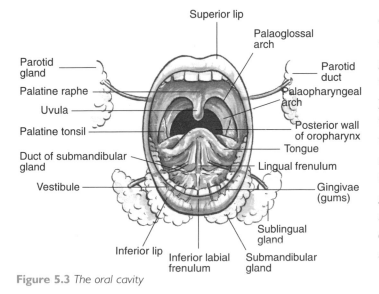

Superior lip

Palaoglossal arch

Parotid gland

Palatine raphe

Uvula

Palatine tonsil

Duct of submandibular gland

Vestibule

Parotid duct

Palaopharyngeal arch

Posterior wall of oropharynx

Tongue

Lingual frenulum

Gingivae (gums)

Sublingual gland

Inferior lip

Inferior labial frenulum

Submandibular gland

Figure 5.3 *The oral cavity*

The mouth contains the teeth, the tongue and the salivary glands. Children have 20 milk teeth and adults have 32 permanent teeth. Teeth are used to cut, grind and chew food. The tongue is a muscle and is used to aid swallowing and for speech. Saliva is produced by the salivary glands to help lubricate the food and to start the digestion of carbohydrates. Saliva also acts as an antiseptic.

The hair

Hair is found on all parts of the body except the palms of the hands and soles of the feet. Most hair on the body is soft and short. Hair grows much more thickly on the head, under the arms and in the pubic region. Hair growth continues throughout life, but hair may become thin due to damage to the follicles or hormonal changes, especially in old age. The scalp contains sebaceous glands that produce an oily substance onto the skin's surface. Sebum and dead skin cells can make the hair greasy and dirty.

Personal hygiene care

Service user	Considerations
Older, not disorientated, quite active	Little support needed, may need a check from time to time. Discuss with service user the level of assistance required.
Older, disorientated	Needs assistance, extra time necessary to carry out processes, needs supervision.
Service user with a physical disability	Unless recently disabled, is likely to have own system of personal hygiene. Discuss the help required, and be guided by the service user.
Service user with learning disability	May need assistance with particular tasks, depending on level of difficulty. Discuss with service user, if possible, the level of help required.

If you are providing care for service users in their own homes, you will need to check:

■ that they are able to reach their own bathing facilities – if the bathroom is upstairs it may be necessary to refer your service user for special access arrangements such as a stair lift, or a downstairs shower room

■ that you have found out about all the equipment that is available to assist service users, and discussed it with them.

Where you are dealing with a service user in a residential or supported living setting, it is likely that bathrooms and bathing facilities will have been built to ensure the necessary ease of access.

Bathing and showering

Don't forget that sometimes a bathing or showering aid can provide the same sort of help that a care worker could provide, but will enable the service user to maintain his or her privacy and dignity. This may be considered preferable to having a carer present. Always make sure that you offer a bath aid as an alternative, if it is available. Some of the aids used are shown in Figure 5.4.

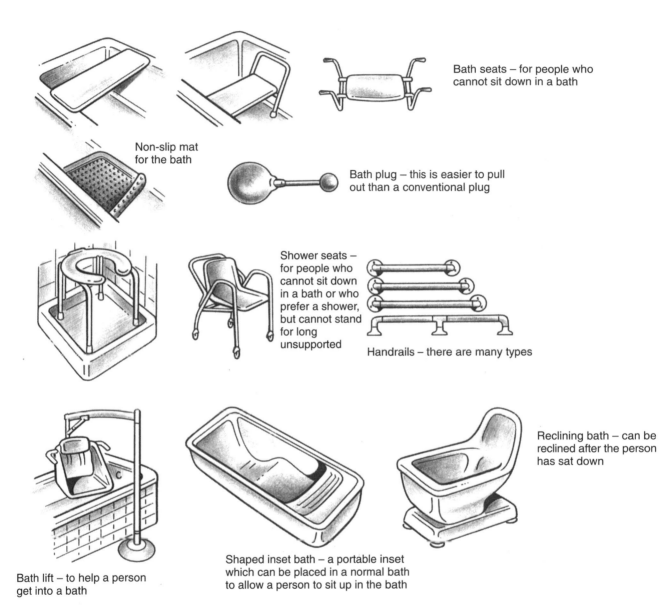

Bath seats – for people who cannot sit down in a bath

Non-slip mat for the bath

Bath plug – this is easier to pull out than a conventional plug

Shower seats – for people who cannot sit down in a bath or who prefer a shower, but cannot stand for long unsupported

Handrails – there are many types

Reclining bath – can be reclined after the person has sat down

Bath lift – to help a person get into a bath

Shaped inset bath – a portable inset which can be placed in a normal bath to allow a person to sit up in the bath

Figure 5.4 *A selection of bathing and showering aids*

DID YOU KNOW?

It is the responsibility of your employer to carry out risk assessments for all service users who require assistance with personal hygiene. Your employer must ensure that the necessary equipment is available to enable you to assist the service user safely. However, it is your responsibility to use it.

Showering can be a valuable way of keeping clean. It allows people to stand or sit, unlike bathing, which can avoid the problems some people have climbing in and out of a bath. It is also compatible with the religious views of some people, and the personal preferences of others who like to clean themselves in running water rather than static water. Some service users are able to shower with the assistance of a shower seat or a plastic chair placed in the shower. Others are happy to shower provided that there are grab handles and a non-slip surface.

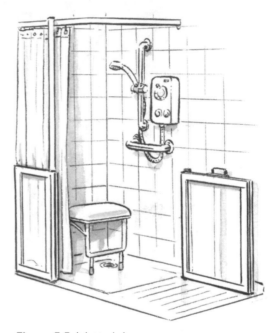

Figure 5.5 *Adapted shower*

Don't forget that sometimes a bathing or showering aid can provide the same sort of help that a care worker could provide, but will enable the individual to maintain his or her own privacy and dignity. This may be considered preferable to having a carer present. Always make sure that you offer a mechanical aid as an alternative, if it is available.

There is a wide range of aids to help people with bathing. They range from devices to help with removing the bath plug to mechanical hoists and baths which recline. Most care settings are likely to have a selection of these aids, although items like reclining baths are very expensive and are not necessarily available in all care settings.

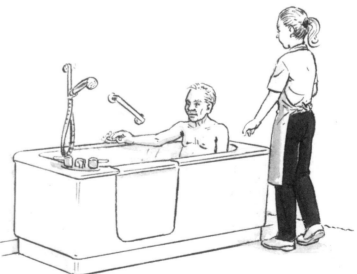

Figure 5.6 *Adapted bath*

There will be situations in which it would not be safe to allow someone to bathe alone, or where a person does not feel confident and prefers to have assistance from a care worker. As in all caring situations, manual lifting and assistance should be avoided if at all possible – mechanical aids, like bath chairs and slings, should be used. They should be available in your workplace and should have been assessed as being appropriate for the person you are helping.

Washing

If you work with service users who are bedridden, either temporarily because of an illness or permanently, then there may be occasions when bathing or showering is not needed or wanted but a wash would be welcome, and would help to make someone feel a little better.

In all situations, you will need to assess what level of help a service user is likely to need, and this should be discussed with the care team and detailed in the service user's care plan. The most important views to take into account are those of the service user.

Shaving

Shaving is important for most men, because they find it uncomfortable and irritating to have stubble on their faces. If a service user is not able to shave himself, you will have to arrange to carry this out. Ask him what kind of help he needs – it may be that he can carry out the shaving himself if you are able to put the soap on his face. Where you need to carry out the whole procedure of shaving, you should remember that it is not a straightforward procedure and is not the same for every individual. You will need to establish whether the service user shaves with a safety razor or an electric razor.

A safety razor

An electric razor

Figure 5.7 *Find out whether the person shaves with a safety razor or an electric razor*

Mouth care

Mouth care, or oral hygiene, is extremely important for all service users because bacteria will multiply in a mouth that is not kept clean and this will lead to infections.

As long as people maintain a sufficient intake of fluids, the saliva in the mouth normally carries out a great deal of cleaning. However, various illnesses and conditions, as well as the natural ageing process, can change the way the mouth works. Saliva production can be reduced and people may suffer from dry and crusted mouths, and infections such as thrush (a fungal infection), a sore tongue or ulcerated gums or cheeks can develop. A reduction of saliva production will also increase the incidence of bad breath (halitosis).

Oral hygiene involves:

- cleaning teeth or dentures
- cleaning between teeth to ensure the removal of all food particles
- cleaning of gums and soft parts of the mouth
- checking for problems
- moisturising the lips if they are cracked and sore.

Eye care

When people are fit and well their eyes are kept moist and clean naturally by the fluid that fills the eyes and drains into the nose. However, when people are ill their eyes can often become dry, irritated and sore, and you may need to bathe the eyes to soothe them and treat any infection.

Hair washing

Washing the hair of someone who is confined to bed can be extremely difficult. If a service user is able to have a bath or a shower, washing the hair is not a problem, but for those who are restricted to bed you need to be able to wash hair.

The most effective way is with an inflatable hair wash tray, which allows you to wash the hair and drain the water away without the service user having to move from the bed. This is very important for people who are suffering from back injuries or paralysis.

Figure 5.8 *Inflatable hair wash tray*

Service user requirements and preferences

Cultural beliefs and preferences

You may find that people have religious beliefs related to maintaining cleanliness, and you must find out about these and make sure that people have the opportunity to carry out cleaning rituals and bathing in whatever way they wish.

- Muslims and Hindus will need to be provided with running water in which to wash, if at all possible. Muslims need to be able to wash their hands, face and feet in running water.

- Hindus will prefer a shower to a bath, and will use a bidet rather than paper to clean themselves after using the toilet.

- Sikhs and Rastafarians believe that hair should not be cut.

- Both Hindus and Muslims will accept treatment or assistance only from a carer of the same gender.

Make sure that you always take into account people's personal beliefs and preferences in the question of clothing, hairdressing and personal grooming. They are just as important as in the area of personal cleanliness. For example, many Orthodox Jewish women wear wigs. Always ensure that you ask the service user or seek advice from members of the family or others if it is not possible to ask the service user directly.

Consequences of poor personal hygiene

The problem you are most likely to come across in the area of personal cleanliness is the service user who refuses to wash and bathe, or to be bathed or washed, as often as is necessary in order to maintain hygiene. This situation can often cause problems when service users are living in a residential or hospital setting and there are other people who object to the odour that can come from someone who fails to wash regularly. This is a situation where tact and gentle persuasion are likely to be most effective. An explanation of the reasons for keeping clean should be given, followed by some fairly firm but friendly advice. It may be better to suggest that the service user begins slowly – rather than a full bath, he or she should be offered the option of a wash and gradually encouraged over time to accept a bath or shower.

Case Study – Phil

Phil is 25 years old and has spina bifida. He is a wheelchair user, but has achieved a high degree of independence and is as mobile as it is possible to be – he plays sports and has a full-time job. Phil lives in a small group of supported flats. However, his standard of personal hygiene leaves something to be desired. Even after playing basketball or five-a-side football, he does not see the need to bathe or shower. The care staff have begun to get complaints from Phil's workplace and from his team mates. Other tenants in the flats have also demanded that something be done.

1   How do you think this should be handled?

2   Does Phil have the right to decide his own level of hygiene?

3   Is it a different situation if he shares living space with others?

4   Is this the responsibility of the staff?

Equipment required for personal hygiene and grooming purposes

Bath and shower aids

Some clients will be self-caring and able to bath or shower themselves. Sometimes you may have to provide support and this will depend on the client's level of ability and independence. Remember that sometimes the need for help can be caused by a client lacking confidence, perhaps due to fear of falling. There is a good selection of bath and shower aids available, some of which are shown in Figure 5.4.

Helping people get dressed

There are many aids that can assist people in dressing themselves. Several of them are shown in Figure 5.9. They can make the difference between a service user having to ask for help and being totally independent. Managing zips and pulling on shoes, stockings and tights can be difficult with limited movement or weak hands. A well-designed dressing aid can make it perfectly possible for a person to dress himself or herself without relying on help from a carer.

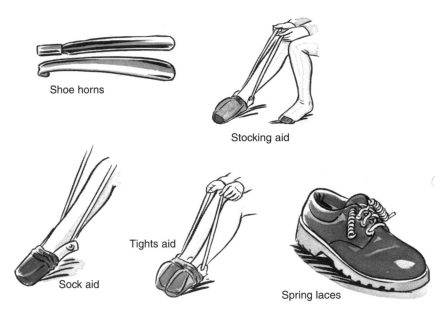

Shoe horns

Stocking aid

Sock aid

Tights aid

Spring laces

Figure 5.9 *Dressing aids*

Grooming

Grooming is important – if service users are not able to carry out grooming for themselves you need to offer help. The main areas of grooming where you may need to assist are likely to be:

■ hair care   ■ make-up   ■ manicure.

Hair care

The way that hair is styled and groomed is a matter of individual choice and most people have strong feelings about how they like their hair to be done. If

you work in a residential, day-care or hospital setting, hairdressers may be available to service users on a regular basis. If you are visiting and supporting service users in their own homes, you may be able to arrange for a hairdresser to visit periodically in order to cut and perm or colour hair.

Specially designed combs and brushes can allow service users to continue grooming their own hair – many will prefer this to having to ask for help.

Figure 5.10 *Aids for hair grooming*

Make-up

You will need to discuss the type of make-up a service user uses and establish what sort of help is needed to apply it. Always check with a service user if they wish to use perfume or cologne.

If you have to apply make-up you should ensure that each service user has her own make-up and that it is not shared – this reduces the risk of cross-infection.

Manicure

The day-to-day care of the nails will be partly undertaken during bathing, when you should use a nail brush to keep the nails clean. You will need to ensure that fingernails are regularly cut or filed to a rounder shape, following the shape of the finger.

Toenails can be difficult to cut, particularly in older people where they can become very hard and almost impossible to cut with normal nail clippers. Where it is possible to cut toenails they should be cut in a straight line and never rounded, because this can encourage in-growing toenails.

If there are difficulties in cutting nails, a visit from a chiropodist should be arranged as these professionals have the proper equipment to deal with the needs of service users.

Personal clothing

It is no good paying attention to washing and grooming if a clean body is then going to be dressed in soiled clothing. However, some elderly people may be reluctant to wear clean clothes every day as they may have been brought up in an age where washing machines were not widely available and all washing would have been done by hand.

Most residential and nursing care homes today have access to their own laundry facilities and so a supply of clean clothing should be readily available. Underwear should be changed daily and outer clothing should be changed on a regular basis and always if a service user has spilt something down themselves or had an accident. It is never pleasant to sit in dirty clothes. Always remember to protect a service user's clothing when they are eating by using a napkin, or a bib for babies and small children.

In a residential setting, clothes are named so that they do not get lost or given to another client by mistake.

Personal laundry that is soiled with urine and faeces can be placed in red bags that are put directly into the washing machine. These dissolve during the washing cycle. This helps to prevent cross-infection and protects carers from having to handle heavily soiled clothing.

Clothing should always be folded neatly or put on coat hangers and then put away in drawers or wardrobes. This helps to prevent creasing. Clothing that is laundered regularly and stored properly will look better and may last longer.

Access to and use of toilet facilities

One of the key areas in maintaining independence is to give service users choice, and this applies no less to toilet facilities than to other matters. It is of course a difficult area to discuss, and you may find it far from easy to talk to service users about their use of toilet facilities and about their body waste. They may be embarrassed by the discussion, but it will be made worse if you show that you are also embarrassed. Try to think about toileting and body waste as a necessary physical process to be undergone in the same way as any other aspect of care. If it is possible for a worker of the same gender to talk with a specific service user at his or her request, then that should be offered.

Getting to the toilet

The question of accessing the toilet facilities will need to be looked at in terms of:

- a service user's mobility
- the frequency with which the service user usually needs to use the toilet
- the urgency with which the service user usually needs to use the toilet.

For example, somebody who has poor mobility may still be able to reach the toilet independently. But a service user who suffers with urgency (a feeling of urgent need to empty the bladder) may become incontinent as a result of poor mobility simply because he or she is not able to reach toilet facilities in time. Similarly, frequency (a condition where someone needs to empty the bladder often) can also present problems for a person with mobility problems – it is one thing to undertake a painful, slow walk to the toilet every two to three hours, but it is quite another to do it every half-hour.

Adjusting clothing

The other area that can present difficulties for people with limited mobility is adjusting their clothing once they reach a toilet facility. To undo trouser flies, or adjust buttons, or reach to remove underclothes, may be extremely difficult for people who have limited use of their arms or who are unsteady and need to support themselves with both hands.

Accessing the toilet

You may find that you need to offer assistance to a service user who needs help to get on and off the toilet. Service users may have difficulty in sitting down or in rising from a seat without help. If a person needs help to get in and out of a chair, it is possible he or she will need similar help with a toilet – but may find it much more difficult to ask, or to accept help.

How to provide help

It is important to bear the following points in mind when arranging help for service users to use toilet facilities.

- have discussions in private
- agree the level of help needed
- agree how the service user will indicate when he or she needs help
- ensure privacy for a service user using the toilet – do not interrupt, or allow anyone else to do so
- offer help quietly and unobtrusively.

Helping service users to clean themselves is another area of assistance that requires discussion with the service user. If you are providing assistance in terms of accessing the toilet, you may be able to observe what a service user is able to achieve in terms of cleaning himself or herself appropriately. You will need to:

- establish the level and type of help a service user needs
- wear an apron and gloves
- wash or wipe the genital and anal areas gently
- if washing, use clear water, and not use soap
- if using wipes or paper, make sure the area is clean and free from faeces
- wipe from front to back – never from back to front
- after cleaning, dispose of the cleaning materials in a sluice or toilet
- wash your hands.

Make sure that you always assist service users to wash their hands after using the toilet, regardless of the facility they have used.

Checking for abnormal body waste

The waste expelled from a person's body is a good indicator of any problems that may be developing within the functioning or health of the body. It can often be an early indicator of illnesses or potentially serious conditions, so it is vitally important that you establish a service user's normal body waste so that you can identify any changes occurring that would give rise to concerns.

Abnormalities can indicate many potential illnesses or changes, and they can range from the common and easily treatable to serious. It is important that you always report any changes in a service user's normal pattern of waste. For example, a change from large, soft stools to small and hard stools indicates that a service user is constipated. This may be dealt with by a simple change in diet, or it could be an early indicator of a more serious condition. Stools changing in colour from brown to pale and yellowish may indicate problems with the liver or pancreas. This should be reported immediately as it requires urgent medical attention.

Changes in urine must also be reported – for example, a dark colour may indicate that there is inadequate fluid intake. Cloudy urine or an offensive odour could be indicators of infection. Blood in the urine is always a cause for concern, as is pain on opening the bowels or passing urine. All of these conditions should be recorded in the service user's notes.

Collection and disposal of body waste

You may be required to care for service users who are not able to use the lavatory. You may have to change nappies or pads, empty catheters or change soiled clothing or bed linen. In all cases it is vital to prevent cross-infection so you should always wash your hands before and after undertaking any tasks where body waste needs to be disposed of. You should also always wear disposable gloves and an apron, which must be changed between clients.

Nappies and pads should be disposed of directly into a waste bag, which should be tied up and disposed of promptly. When emptying a catheter bag, a clean jug should always be used. The contents should be flushed away in a lavatory or sluice and the jug should be disinfected after use. Urine bottles should also be emptied and disinfected or placed in the sluice for cleaning. Faeces should also be disposed of in this way and a bedpan should be cleaned in the sluice or disinfected. Always remember if a client has used a commode to clean it thoroughly after use.

Soiled clothing and bed linen should always be placed directly into linen bags and should never be put on the floor. Very soiled linen should be placed in a red bag before sending to the laundry.

ASSESSMENT ACTIVITY

Describe how service users' hygiene needs are met.

1   Describe how you would meet the hygiene needs of service users. Produce an information sheet (no more than two sides of A4) for new care workers stating what parts of the body you must pay close attention to. You must include other aspects of hygiene that you would need to consider when caring for clients.

2   If a service user was reluctant to maintain basic levels of personal hygiene, what would be the consequences to the service user, and to the care setting and other service users?

To achieve a **merit grade** you must explain the consequences for both the service user and the care setting of poor personal hygiene.

Prepare and provide food and drink

Safe food handling and preparation

If you are preparing areas or equipment for people to eat or drink, it is important that you follow basic hygiene procedures. It is also vital that you know how to store and prepare food safely so that people's health is not endangered.

Personal hygiene

If you have long hair, it must be tied back or covered. You should ensure that your nails are short and clean, and that you are not wearing any jewellery in which food could become trapped, such as rings with stones. Wash your hands thoroughly at each stage of food preparation and between handling raw food and cooked food, or raw meat and any food which will not be cooked. You must of course wash your hands after going to the toilet, and avoid touching your nose, face or hair with your hands during food handling or preparation.

If you have a cut or sore on your hands, you must wear a special blue adhesive plaster dressing. This is because no food is blue, so if the plaster should come off during food preparation it will be easy to locate. The plaster should also be waterproof to protect the food from being contaminated.

Hygienic food preparation

Food is contaminated by bacteria, which can be spread by infecting food directly if it is not heated or chilled properly, or by cross-contamination, which is caused by bacteria spreading from one item of food to another.

The main bacteria that cause contamination of food are *Salmonella*, *Campylobacter* and *E. coli*. Any of these bacteria can cause food poisoning, which can be very serious in people who are elderly or ill, or in young children.

Raw meat is a source of bacteria, and you should be sure to use separate utensils and chopping boards or surfaces for raw and cooked food. For example, do not chop the raw chicken breasts and then chop the lettuce for the accompanying salad on the same chopping board or with the same knife. This is a recipe for giving everybody who eats your salad a nasty dose of salmonella poisoning. You should keep separate chopping boards for meat and vegetables, and ensure that you use different knives. Remember to change knives and wash your hands in between preparing different types of food. Colour-coded chopping boards are available. For example, red boards and knives should only be used for raw meat.

It is possible to kill most bacteria by cooking food, but be very careful with foods that are not cooked, such as salads or mayonnaise, that you use clean utensils to prepare them.

A core temperature of 75°C will kill most bacteria, so hot food should be heated or reheated to at least this temperature.

Food storage

By law, food should be stored in a refrigerator at 8°C or lower. However, good practice dictates that food should be stored between 5°C and 8°C, and food deteriorates quite quickly at higher temperatures. Food that has been left in a fridge with the door open or where the power has been switched off should be discarded.

ASSESSMENT ACTIVITY

Describe how to handle and prepare food in a safe manner.

1   Prepare a booklet that could be given to students undertaking work experience that describes safe ways of handling and preparing food. You must include personal hygiene and hygiene in the kitchen, including keeping surfaces and equipment clean and how to store food correctly.

2   Add a separate section at the back of your booklet that explains the consequences of failing to maintain the correct hygiene standards when handling and preparing food. Which groups of people are most vulnerable, and what diseases could they contract by eating contaminated food?

To achieve a **merit grade** you must explain the consequences of poor hygiene in food handling.

Healthy diet

All human beings require certain essential nutrients in order to survive. They are classified into five major groups: proteins, carbohydrates, fats, vitamins and minerals. Humans also need to drink about two litres of liquid each day. The liquid can be water, fruit juice, tea, coffee or any kind of non-alcoholic drink. A good intake of fibre is also recommended to prevent constipation and to help to keep the gut healthy.

Nutrient	Where found	Purpose
Proteins	Meat, fish, eggs, milk, cheese, nuts, cereals, tofu and beans.	Proteins promote growth and they are also essential for the replacement and renewal of body cells. They are essential for everyone and must be eaten each day.
Carbohydrates	Sugar, potatoes and some root vegetables such as yams, sweet potato, bread, flour, rice, cereals, and pasta.	Carbohydrates, also known as starches, are used by the body to provide energy and heat. They are essential to provide an energy source, but if they are eaten to excess they will be stored as fat.
Fats	Butter, margarine, cooking oil, dripping, meat fat, cream, soured cream, milk, cheese, egg yolks.	Fats are a very concentrated source of heat and energy, but if they are eaten to excess they will be stored by the body in the adipose layer just beneath the skin. Fish and seed oils, such as linseed or olive oil, can help to protect against heart disease.

Vitamins and minerals

Vitamins are essential to maintaining good health and keeping the body in good condition. Some vitamins are in certain foods in very small quantities, but they are nonetheless essential. Minerals similarly may be found only in quite small quantities, but like vitamins they are essential and have very specific purposes in the body.

It is important that a healthy diet balances the amounts of different nutrients taken each day. Clearly, the necessary amounts will vary depending on the individual. Some elderly people will require less food, for example, than an active teenager. Lifestyle and the amount of exercise taken must be considered when deciding on the overall amounts of food that people will consume. It is important to get the balance right, however, regardless of quantity.

Nutrient	Where found	Purpose
Vitamin A	Liver and fish oils, milk, butter, eggs and cheese, and can be made by the body from carotene which is found in carrots, tomatoes and green vegetables.	Protects from infection and contributes to growth. Lack of vitamin A can cause eye problems.
Vitamin B (there are several)	Cereals, liver, yeast and nuts.	This is a large group of complex vitamins, all of which are essential for maintaining good skin. Lack of vitamin B may be responsible for some diseases of the nervous system.

Nutrient	Where found	Purpose
Vitamin C	Citrus fruits, strawberries, potatoes and some green vegetables.	Vitamin C cannot be stored so it must be taken each day. Lack of vitamin C can cause scurvy, a disease that causes bleeding in the gums and is extremely serious. People who have a lack of vitamin C are also more likely to be affected by viral infections and coughs and colds.
Vitamin D	Eggs and fish oils, and made by the body when the skin is exposed to sunlight.	Vitamin D enables calcium to be absorbed to strengthen and develop bones and teeth. A severe shortage of vitamin D will lead to rickets, a deforming disease seen in children whose bones do not develop adequately.
Vitamin E	Wheatgerm, cereals, egg yolk, liver and milk.	This helps to prevent cell damage and degeneration.
Minerals	A wide range of minerals are essential for health and are found in eggs, cocoa, liver, baked beans, cheese and milk.	Iron is important for the formation of red blood cells, and a lack of iron can lead to anaemia. Calcium is used for developing firm bones. Sodium is important for maintaining the fluid balance of the body, but an excess of sodium can be a contributory cause of oedema (fluid retention).

Energy requirements

The amount of energy provided by different types of food is measured in calories, which are 'burned' by the body to provide the energy for carrying out activities. The amount of energy needed depends on a person's level of activity; for example, watching television or sitting at a computer does not require much energy, so not many calories are used. Doing housework or running up flights of stairs takes much more energy.

Salads, fruit and vegetables provide fewer calories than fatty foods like chocolate or cream cakes. For people to remain healthy, not only must they eat a diet that is balanced in terms of nutrients (carbohydrates, proteins, fats, etc.) but they must also consume the right amount of calories. If they have too many calories people will gain weight, with too few they may become seriously underweight.

The average adult woman needs 1,940 calories a day to remain healthy and to provide the necessary energy for normal activities. An adult man requires 2,550 calories on average – this is because men generally have a greater weight and body size. Even though children have a smaller body size than adults, they still need approximately the same calories as an adult because they are growing rapidly, which takes a great deal of energy, and they are usually very active. It is especially important that the correct balance of nutrients is maintained for children as this will ensure proper growth and development.

Pregnant women require additional calories in the last three months of pregnancy – but only about 200 extra per day. There is no truth in the old saying about 'eating for two' – in fact, it is not good for women to gain too much weight during pregnancy. However, if a woman is breast-feeding a baby, then she really is 'eating for two' and will need quite a significant number of extra calories, because milk production uses up a great deal of energy. She should increase her calorie intake by approximately 500–600 calories per day.

People who are disabled and not mobile, and older people who are unable to get about as much as they used to, may need to reduce their calorie intake to avoid gaining weight. Calorie intake should not be drastically reduced, however, and even for a very inactive person should not drop below 1400 calories for women and 1700 for men daily.

A balanced diet

Carbohydrates should make up more than 50 per cent of the calories consumed each day – that is, fruits, vegetables, cereals, bread and pasta. The remaining 50 per cent should include about 20 per cent from protein, which comes from lean meat, poultry, fish, nuts and beans.

Special dietary needs or preferences

People who have a dietary problem	Special dietary needs
Diabetes	Regular meals/snacks, controlled amounts of sugar.
Allergies; commonly nuts, dairy products, or food additives	Strict avoidance of problem foods, ensuring that information is recorded and people are aware of the allergy.
Coeliac disease	Gluten free diet, i.e. no flour or cereals. Rice can be given as an alternative.

People who choose a particular diet	Special dietary needs
Vegetarians	No meat, poultry, game or possibly fish.
Vegans	No meat, poultry, game, fish, eggs or dairy products.
Cultural preferences	For religious or other reasons, need to eat or not eat certain foods (e.g. pork) or to observe rules at certain times.

Total fat intake should be no higher than 30 per cent of daily calories. Eating a variety of foods is the most likely way to ensure a balanced diet and a good intake of vitamins and minerals.

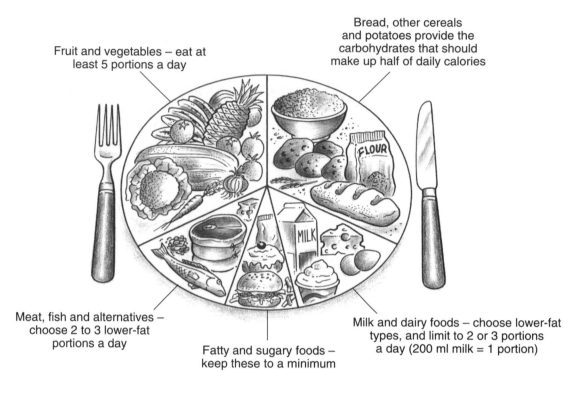

Fruit and vegetables – eat at least 5 portions a day

Bread, other cereals and potatoes provide the carbohydrates that should make up half of daily calories

Meat, fish and alternatives – choose 2 to 3 lower-fat portions a day

Fatty and sugary foods – keep these to a minimum

Milk and dairy foods – choose lower-fat types, and limit to 2 or 3 portions a day (200 ml milk = 1 portion)

Figure 5.11 *A balanced diet*

Cultural and religious preferences

People from different religions may follow certain rules regarding food and drink. For example, Jews and Muslims do not eat pork and Hindus do not eat beef. It is very important to be aware of particular rules about food for different religions, as service users may be offended if they are offered food or drink that they cannot consume.

How food is served

The way in which food is served can often reflect the quality of the care setting and can show a great deal about the way in which the service users who use the facility are considered. The significant factors are:

- presentation of food
- the variety of food offered
- choice of seating plan – whether at large tables, in small groups or individually

- whether service users can have a tray on their knees in front of the television

- whether times of the serving of meals are flexible.

All these factors are indications of how much choice and individuality is available for service users in a particular setting. Obviously, for service users who are in their own homes these issues are not so relevant, although those who are dependent on others to prepare and serve their meals may still have some of the same concerns.

Mealtime support

The most important thing to establish first is whether the service user requires your assistance. You should never impose help on a service user – it is far better to encourage independence, if necessary through the use of specially adapted utensils rather than to offer to feed the service user yourself. Some service users would be perfectly capable of feeding themselves if they were given a minimal amount of assistance, perhaps in the form of specially designed eating and drinking aids such as the ones shown in Figure 5.12.

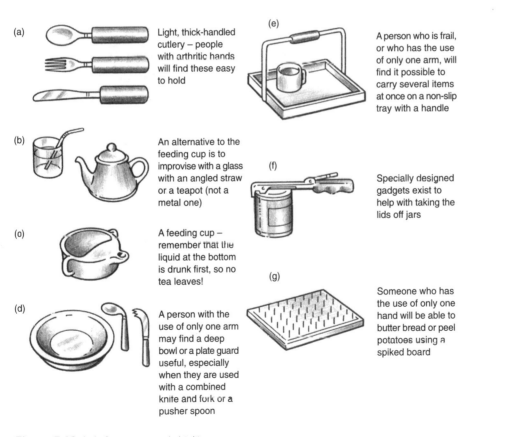

(a) Light, thick-handled cutlery – people with arthritic hands will find these easy to hold

(e) A person who is frail, or who has the use of only one arm, will find it possible to carry several items at once on a non-slip tray with a handle

(b) An alternative to the feeding cup is to improvise with a glass with an angled straw or a teapot (not a metal one)

(f) Specially designed gadgets exist to help with taking the lids off jars

(o) A feeding cup – remember that the liquid at the bottom is drunk first, so no tea leaves!

(d) A person with the use of only one arm may find a deep bowl or a plate guard useful, especially when they are used with a combined knife and fork or a pusher spoon

(g) Someone who has the use of only one hand will be able to butter bread or peel potatoes using a spiked board

Figure 5.12 *Aids for eating and drinking*

There are special ways of helping service users who have particular needs. For example, visually impaired service users are often able to feed themselves if you can help to prepare the plate of food in advance. If you arrange the food in separate portions around the plate and then say, using a clock as a comparison, that potatoes are at 2 o'clock, meat at 6 o'clock, sprouts at 8 o'clock and so on, this is often enough to allow the person to enjoy the meal independently (see Figure 5.13).

Figure 5.13 *Compare the meal to a clock face – potatoes are at 2 o'clock*

When feeding people who cannot feed themselves, remember to go through the following steps:

■ Help the service user to use the toilet or commode if necessary and to wash his or her hands.

■ Wash your hands.

■ Check that you have everything you will need: the meal, salt and pepper, feeding utensils, etc.

■ If the service user is completely unable to feed himself or herself because of lack of use of the arms, you should position the service user comfortably either propped up in bed or sitting in a chair. The upright position is necessary to assist digestion.

■ Ensure that the service user is comfortable before you begin the meal.

■ Establish whether the service user likes to eat food piping hot or to give it the opportunity to cool down.

■ Offer the chance to see the meal before you begin to feed, and ask which food the service user would like to start with – for example, the potatoes first or meat first.

■ Sit down beside the service user, slightly to one side and in front.

■ Regardless of whether you feed with a fork or spoon, make sure that you leave enough time for each mouthful to be properly chewed and swallowed and that not too much food is put on the spoon or fork.

■ Bear in mind that if a service user is ill it may take a considerable amount of time to finish the meal. Do not rush the service user and hover with the next spoonful before the last one is finished.

■ Keep up an interesting conversation throughout the meal, even if your service user is unable to respond to you – but beware of the dentist's trick of asking a question that requires an answer just after you have put a spoonful of food into the service user's mouth!

■ Help the service user to wash if he or she wishes at the end of the meal, or wipe the mouth and rinse the hands. Remember that some service users may have religious requirements for particular types of washing and cleaning after food.

- Make sure that the service user takes regular drinks before and/or after the meal.

People who have been ill, or who have specific disabilities, can experience problems in eating and drinking. This is not restricted to those who have physical difficulty in using eating utensils or sitting at a table – other problems may arise. For example:

- people may find difficulty in swallowing and chewing following a stroke

- some disabilities can cause swallowing problems or digestive difficulties

- people who are ill may lose their appetite and find it difficult to eat

- people who have an illness that affects their sense of smell or taste will find eating difficult or even unpleasant.

Always ensure that you check for these problems with the service user and by consulting the care plan. It may be necessary to record and monitor food and drink intake for some service users who are experiencing difficulties.

ASSESSMENT ACTIVITY

Describe the components of a healthy diet and identify common special dietary needs and preferences (both religious and personal).

1 What are the main components of a healthy diet? Describe how each component helps to maintain health, and give at least two examples for each component. Produce a table of the common food rules for religions such as Judaism, Hinduism, Sikhism and Buddhism. You may also include others. What personal or health factors other than religion may need to be taken into consideration when offering food to service users?

2 Why is it important to provide service users with a healthy diet? Refer back to the work you have done on the components of a healthy diet. Why is it important to meet the dietary needs of service users? Consider religious requirements, personal preference and special dietary needs.

3 Consider all the work that you have completed in the assessment activities in this unit so far. How effective would the care provided be in providing the appropriate level of care to meet physical needs? Remember that you need to address all aspects of care that have an impact on physical well-being.

To achieve a **merit grade** you must explain the importance of providing service users with a healthy diet and meeting special dietary needs.

To achieve a **distinction grade** you must analyse the effectiveness of the steps that care workers can take to meet the physical needs of service users.

Moving and handling service users safely

Physical and psychological factors affecting mobility

Some service users have problems that affect their mobility. These may be physical or psychological.

Physical factors

- **Broken bones or damaged ligaments.** Such damage will generally cause pain and discomfort, and strapping or plastering will protect the affected part of the body by keeping it immobile until it has healed. Some fractures such as a broken hip may require surgery and may be painful for some time after the operation. Gentle physiotherapy and pain relief can assist with movement.

- **Stroke.** A clot in a blood vessel in the brain can cause brain cells to die. If the area of the brain affected controls movement, there can be a degree of paralysis. Some people can recover well with the support of a physiotherapist, but others will never regain full use of the affected part of the body.

- **Neurological diseases.** Diseases such as multiple sclerosis or motor neurone disease affect the nerves and result in mobility problems. These diseases can be progressive and a person's ability to move about may become reduced over time. People will need to be assessed on a regular basis to allow carers to provide the right level of support.

Psychological factors

- **Fear of painful movement**. People may become afraid to move if they experience pain. If you are caring for such a person, you might want to make sure that pain relief is given before attempting to provide personal care that will necessitate movement.

- **Loss of confidence and fear of falling.** There may be many reasons why people lose confidence and be afraid that they might fall, for example suffering from an illness that has resulted in a long period of bed rest. A person may feel very wobbly and be worried about standing and walking. In such cases encouragement and support is very important. Initially it may be necessary for two or even three carers to assist the person until he or she becomes more confident.

- **Loss of interest and motivation.** People can become withdrawn or depressed for many reasons, and as a result do not wish to undertake activities that require movement. As a carer you can listen and provide support and encouragement, but the services of a specialist worker such as a counsellor or psychologist may be required.

Mobility appliances

Mobility appliances assist a service user to become or continue to be mobile, either by providing support or, like a wheelchair, by providing the means to mobility.

Mobility appliances such as walking sticks, crutches, quadrupeds, and walking frames provide support where people have become unsteady or where joints or muscles are weak or painful. They also provide additional security where someone has had a fall or is recovering from illness – often the loss of confidence after an incident such as a fall is as damaging to mobility as any injury sustained.

Mobility aids can make a significant difference to a service user's quality of life. Rather than be dependent upon assistance for everything, the service user with a mobility aid can often maintain his or her independence and freedom to choose.

Walking sticks, quadrupeds and tripods

The amount of support a service user needs will determine whether a walking stick, a tripod or a quadruped is appropriate. A walking stick would be used for someone who is generally unsteady, needs to regain confidence, or who is recovering from an injury.

A quadruped would only be used for a service user who has considerable difficulty in walking on one particular leg, either because of hip or knee degeneration or a stroke. It is not an appropriate aid for somebody who is generally unsteady.

Walking frames

The decision to provide a service user with a walking frame would be taken when the service user had reached the stage of needing considerable support from one or two care workers, and when he or she is no longer steady on a walking stick or quadruped.

Frames on wheels

The frame on wheels is similar to a walking frame, except that it has wheels on the front legs. This is very useful for service users who are too disabled to be able to cope with learning the walking pattern necessary for an ordinary walking frame, and is also useful for people with particular arm or shoulder problems who would be unable to lift the frame.

Wheelchairs

Where an assessment has concluded that a service user requires a wheelchair, the service user is entitled to be correctly measured and assessed by a physiotherapist. Wheelchairs come in a range of sizes and styles, ranging from chairs that have to be pushed, to chairs that allow service users to propel them, and electric wheelchairs. Many younger people with disabilities have decided views about the types of wheelchairs they will use, the amount of equipment and features they should have, the colours they are and the speed at which they travel around in them.

Figure 5.14 *Different types of wheelchair*

Movement

As you may remember from Unit 3, employers have a responsibility under health and safety legislation to examine and assess all risks in your working environment. All risks must be noted and assessed, and steps must be taken to minimise them as far as possible. This is known as risk assessment. Employers are required to provide adequate equipment for such tasks as moving and handling individuals who require assistance.

Each time you move or lift any individual, you are responsible for making an assessment of the risks involved in carrying out that particular manoeuvre. You also need to consider the environment. You should take into account all of the following factors:

- Is the floor surface safe, or are there wet slippery patches?

- Are you wearing appropriate clothing – low-heeled shoes, tunic or dress with enough room to stretch and reach?

- Is the immediate area clear of items that may cause a trip or fall, or items that could cause injury following a fall?

- Is all the equipment to carry out the lift available, and is the place to which the individual is to be moved ready?

- Does the individual have privacy and can dignity be maintained during the move?

Many people who have a long-standing disability will be experienced and skilled in dealing with it. They are the best people to ask for advice as they know the most effective ways to lift in a way that will avoid pain and discomfort as far as possible.

Once you have carried out all of the necessary assessments, you should explain carefully to the service user what you intend to do and what the service user's own role is in contributing to the effectiveness and safety of the move.

> ### *Good practice: moving and handling service users*
>
> ▪ Assess risks to the service user and to yourself before starting any lift or move.
>
> ▪ Ask service users about the best way of moving or assisting them.
>
> ▪ Explain the procedure to service users at each stage, even where it may not be obvious that you are understood.
>
> ▪ Explain how the equipment operates.
>
> ▪ Check that you have the agreement of the person you are moving.
>
> ▪ Stop immediately if the service user does not wish you to continue – you may not move anyone without consent.

A wide range of equipment is available and technological advances are being made continuously in the field of medical equipment. Regardless of the individual products and improvements that may be made to them, lifting and handling equipment broadly falls into the following categories:

▪ hoists, slings and other equipment to move the full weight of an individual

▪ equipment designed to assist in a move and to take some of the weight of the individual, such as transfer boards

▪ equipment designed to assist individuals to help themselves, such as to pull themselves up. This category includes grab handles, raised toilet seats, and lifting chairs.

There are very few situations in which manual lifting should be carried out. Unless it is an emergency, or a life-threatening situation, there should be no need to move anyone without the correct equipment. Manual handling should be carried out only in situations that do not involve lifting all or most of a service user's weight.

Shoulder lifts (like the Australian lift) are no longer considered safe, and there is no safe weight limit for lifting. The only workplaces where lifting should now take place is in units caring for babies and small children. Even there it is important to ensure that risk assessments are carried out to avoid the likelihood of injury.

If you need to move someone manually in order to change a service user's position or provide assistance, you should follow the principles of effective manual moving and handling which are:

▪ it should be well planned and assessed in advance, and technique rather than strength is important

■ it should be comfortable and safe for the service user, thus creating confidence that being moved is not something to be anxious about and the service user can co-operate with the procedure

■ it should be safe for the worker carrying out the procedure – a worker injured during a badly planned or executed transfer is likely in turn to injure the service user, and similarly a service user injured during a move is likely to cause injury to those assisting the move.

Reasons for moving service users

One of the main reasons for moving service users is to prevent the development of pressure sores. Pressure sores are the result of an interruption to the blood supply, which can cause the tissue in that particular area to break down. The interruption to the blood supply is caused by various types of pressure, exerted in different ways, but the effect is the same – the tissue in the affected area begins to degenerate into a sore. Every one of us would get pressure sores if we were not able to move regularly each night while we were asleep. For individuals who are unable to change their own position regularly, whether that is lying down or sitting in a wheelchair, the pressure can result in a sore. Some areas of the body are particularly vulnerable:

■ the back of the head
■ the shoulders
■ the sacrum (the bottom of the back)
■ the buttocks
■ the backs of the legs and the calves
■ the heels.

Figure 5.15 shows the most common sites for pressure sores.

Preventing pressure sores

It is always better to work on preventing pressure sores than to have to treat them once they have developed. The best way to ensure that pressure sores do not develop is to keep people as active as possible, so that they are less likely to remain in one position. It is also important for individuals who are confined to bed or a chair that they have a special mattress or cushion (such as a Roho cushion), designed to distribute weight more evenly so that the downward pressure is evenly spread.

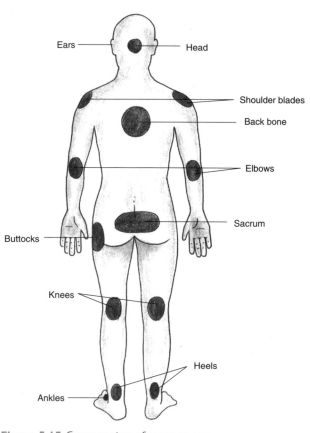

Figure 5.15 *Common sites of pressure sores*

It is important to ensure, also, that individuals eat a good balanced diet with a significant protein content, as protein is required for cell renewal and can help reduce the risk of tissue breakdown and development of pressure sores.

It is vital to ensure that service users who are incontinent are never left sitting in wet clothes or incontinence pads – the effect of wet, urine-soaked clothing on skin is to make it vulnerable to sores in the pressure areas.

Sheepskin, or artificial sheepskin, is a useful tool in preventing the development of pressure sores, and tends to be used particularly for heels in the form of sheepskin booties. It has the effect of relieving pressure and spreading weight more evenly.

To help prevent pressure sores, remember to:

- move people regularly

- turn an unconscious or paralysed person every two hours

- use aids such as a Roho cushion, special mattress, or fleece pads

- check that the service user's diet contains adequate protein.

See the next section of this unit for information on the signs and indications that a service user is in pain, and the ways to meet service users' need for rest.

Rest

Rest, not necessarily sleep, is important for individuals who are in a care setting. The rest can be relaxation, a period of quiet, the opportunity to read or meditate, or simply a quiet time alone.

Barriers to sleep

A range of factors can make it difficult for people to sleep. These broadly fall into the following categories: psychological and emotional, physical and social.

Psychological and emotional factors include:
- anxiety
- fear of incontinence
- fear of a strange place.
- distress
- fear of disturbing dreams

Physical factors include:
- pain or discomfort
- disturbed body clock
- illness
- too many stimulants, e.g. caffeine or alcohol.
- lack of exercise
- feeling hot or cold
- overeating

Social factors include:
- noise
- uncomfortable bed or bedding
- temperature
- light.

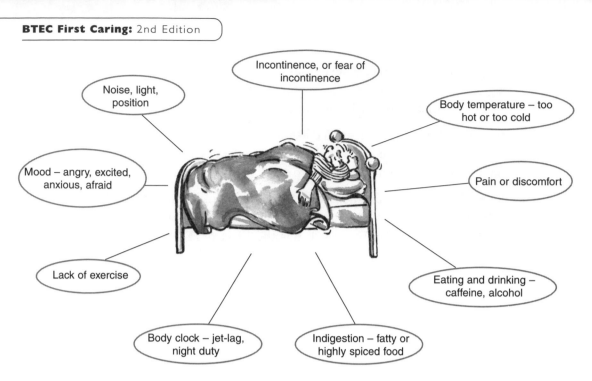

Figure 5.16 *Barriers to rest and sleep*

How to assist rest and sleep

You have an important role in helping people to sleep and to rest. You will need to know how best to support people to sleep well at night and to rest at times during the day.

You can help people to sleep at night:

- by reassuring them and making sure there is nothing they are anxious about

- by encouraging them to carry out some relaxation exercises, which will help both mentally and physically to prepare for sleep

- by offering a warm drink, preferably a milky drink without any caffeine or stimulants

- by offering a hot water bottle

- by ensuring that the individual is comfortable

- by checking whether service users need their position adjusting or their pillows or bed to be made more comfortable

- by offering to take them to the toilet or to provide them with a bed pan – often a full bladder or bowel will prevent people from going to sleep.

The environment in which the individual is sleeping is just as important as the care of the individuals themselves.

■ Ensure that noise is kept to a minimum and that squeaking trolleys, noisy shoes, loud laughter or talking amongst the staff are avoided.

■ The lights should be dimmed and rooms should be warm but ventilated.

There is much that can be done during the day to help ensure sleep at night. If an individual has physical exercise coupled with mental stimulation, he or she is far more likely to achieve satisfactory rest than somebody who has been left with nothing to do either physically or mentally, and has had little activity of body or brain during the day.

Rest at other times of the day is also important. When planning care, thought should be given to times in the day when individuals are able to rest.

Rest periods should preferably be uninterrupted by treatments, procedures, observations or activities. They may be fitted in best immediately after lunch – an early afternoon nap is welcome for many. Rest may not involve sleeping – reading, relaxing or just being quiet and undisturbed may be equally useful.

Everyone who is receiving care should have a plan of that care drawn up by the care team. It is important that plans for rest and sleep are included in the care plan. Establish each individual's normal pattern of sleep and rest by talking to the service user and by observation. Any indications of change in an individual's normal sleeping or resting pattern should be recorded and concerns must be passed on immediately to your supervisor or manager.

ASSESSMENT ACTIVITY

Identify the factors that may affect service user mobility and describe how the care worker can promote mobility. Describe ways in which care workers can assist service users to be comfortable.

1 Observe three service users in your work placement to identify the factors that affect mobility. Address such factors as level of mobility and the use of particular aids that can help clients to remain as mobile as possible. What can a care worker do to ensure that his or her clients are as comfortable as possible?

2 The three examples that you choose could be presented in the form of case studies of three clients who have different levels of mobility. The use of different aids should be considered as well as other factors. If you are using real clients from a work setting,

you must ensure that you maintain confidentiality of the client.

To achieve a **merit grade** you must use at least three examples to explain the ways in which improved mobility and physical comfort can affect the health and well-being of a service user.

To achieve a **distinction grade** you must evaluate the ways in which care workers can contribute to service user mobility and comfort. You must evaluate these carefully. How useful or beneficial are they to the service users? Are there any ways in which a care worker could improve what is already offered to the service users?

Enable service users to achieve physical comfort

Care planning

For every service user who is being cared for, there will be a written plan called a 'care plan' or 'individual service user plan'. The care plan outlines the service user's present and future needs and describes how these needs will be met. The following is an example of a care plan for Mrs J, who is 85 years old and mentally alert. Following a fall in which she broke her pelvis, she is confined to bed.

	Care plan for Mrs J
Mobility	Mrs J needs to be moved every four hours to prevent her developing pressure sores.
	She has a one-hour physiotherapy session every day to improve circulation and muscle strength.
	She is confined to bed, so needs assistance with toileting.
Food and drink	Normal diet, but small portions as she is overweight.
	Frequent drinks.
Pain control	Pain relief morning and evening as prescribed by Dr N.
	Extra pain relief can be given if requested by Mrs J. Refer to main carer, Mr F.

The care plan is very important as it shows exactly how a service user is being cared for and what can be done if he or she is in pain or discomfort. In the case of Mrs J, the care plan says that she can be given extra pain relief if she needs it, so you can reassure her that she does not have to suffer.

Observation of services users' condition and reporting

Emotions play a considerable part in the experience of pain. If someone is afraid or tense or has no knowledge of what is happening, he or she is likely to experience more pain than someone who is relaxed, and knows exactly what the cause of pain is. Sometimes the fear of pain can not only make pain worse but can cause additional pain by anticipation. This is commonly seen in a person who has an illness or injury in which movement is extremely painful, and he or she reacts in anticipation of being moved.

There is also compelling evidence that people who have had limbs removed can continue to feel pain in the limb. The evidence shows that pain is more common in a limb that had been painful prior to removal, and would suggest that pain pathways can continue to function after the cause has been removed.

How to help people to express their pain

Because of people's beliefs, values and culture they may not find it easy to say that they are in pain. This can result from a feeling that they do not want to make a fuss, be a nuisance or bother anyone.

It is important that you create as many opportunities as possible for people to express their pain and that you contribute towards creating an atmosphere where people know it is acceptable to say that they are in pain and they want something done about it. You can help by:

- noticing when somebody seems tense or drawn
- noticing facial expressions, if someone is wincing or looking distressed
- observing if somebody is fidgeting or trying to move around to get more comfortable
- noticing when somebody seems quiet or distracted
- checking if someone is flushed or sweating or seems to be breathing rapidly.

All of these are signals which should prompt you to ask a person if he or she is in pain and if any help or relief is needed. Even in the absence of any obvious signals, it is important to check regularly and ask if any of the people that you care for are in pain or discomfort or need any assistance.

You will need to be particularly aware of possible pain when you are providing care for people who are not able to communicate directly with you, including:

- people who do not use English as a first language
- people with speech or hearing difficulties
- people with severe learning difficulties or multiple disabilities
- people who have an illness such as dementia.

You will need to be especially vigilant if you provide care for anyone who comes into these categories.

Allowing service users to express feelings of pain and minimising pain and discomfort

Consulting service users

It is important that you talk to your service users about the best way to make them comfortable. After all, they probably have more experience with their illness or disability than you have. Make sure that you ask the service user first before carrying out any procedure or activity. Consider the following conversation.

Carer: Oh dear, Edith, is your arthritis bad today? You look a bit uncomfortable. Would it help to put your leg on this stool, or are you more comfortable in the upright chair?

Edith: My foot on the stool is usually best – the upright chair always gives me a sore neck after a while.

Carer: OK then, here's the stool. Is that better? Can I get you a cushion, or is there anything else that usually helps?

Edith: No thanks, cushions make me uncomfortable. They always seem to end up in a hard lump. A hot water bottle is usually good, and if you could bring me one of my tablets, that would help.

Carer: No problem. Would you like a cup of tea to take the tablet?

Edith: That would be lovely.

Bodily position

Service users who have difficulty in moving, such as after suffering a stroke, may find it difficult to get themselves into a position where they are comfortable. It is always important to ask them if they are comfortable when you have helped them into a chair or into bed. You may need to help them to reposition by moving their head or limbs or by using pillows or other aids to provide support. Some service users may have difficulty in communication so it may take several attempts to discover the problem. It is important to persevere or ask for help if you have difficulty understanding.

Self-help

The service user can be encouraged to try various self-help methods for the relief of pain, or may have preferred methods of his or her own, including:

- moving or walking about if possible
- imagining himself or herself in a pleasant and comfortable location
- taking a warm bath
- taking recommended exercise
- finding a task to distract from the pain
- having a conversation.

Alternative therapies

The so-called 'alternative therapies' are increasingly accepted into mainstream western medicine, and have an invaluable role to play in the reduction of pain and the improvement of general well-being. These can include the practices shown in the following table.

Aromatherapy	Natural oils are used for massage. Their aroma has a beneficial effect.
Homeopathic medicine	The illness or disease is treated with minute quantities of naturally occurring substances, which would cause similar illness if taken in larger amounts.
Reflexology	Specialised foot massage stimulates particular areas of the feet, which are said to be linked to parts of the body.
Acupuncture	This must be administered by an expert, and uses ancient Chinese medical knowledge about specific points in the body which respond to being stimulated by very fine needles. Acupuncture is now increasingly recognised by western medical practitioners and is available from the National Health Service in many places.
Yoga and meditation	Yoga and meditation work essentially on the emotional component of pain. Meditation works by dealing with the mental response to pain, whereas yoga combines mind and body in an exercise and relaxation programme.

Drugs

Drugs that are effective in the relief of pain are:

- analgesics (aspirin, paracetamol, etc.)
- anti-inflammatory (ibuprofen)
- opiates (morphine, heroin)
- anaesthetic spinal block (epidural).

Drugs supplied on medical prescription for the relief of pain are likely to be analgesics, but in cases of severe or prolonged pain they may be opiates.

The effects of culture, background and personal belief

People from different cultures have different attitudes to pain. Some may express pain by wailing or moaning while others will suffer in silence. People will often not complain about the amount of pain that they are in because they do not want to be a nuisance. As a carer your observation skills are very important. It is not acceptable for people to be in pain if some effective form of relief is available. If you think that someone is suffering, you must always report it, and you must always ensure that their personal beliefs and preferences are respected.

Organisational policy on pain relief

Organisations will generally have their own policy on the administration of all drugs and normally only senior care workers or qualified nurses will be able to administer drugs. Any drugs administered must be recorded, stating the time and dose given.

Service User Support

This unit explores the impact of change on service users and the support that service users may need. The importance of relationships, activities and interests, confidentiality and privacy are emphasised. The fourth section of this unit explores the support a service user might need in a home care setting.

This unit is internally assessed and ideas for evidencing the grading criteria are presented.

In this unit you will learn about:

- the effects of change on service users and ways of providing support to service users

- the importance of relationships and how they can contribute to health and well-being

- the importance of activities and interests in maintaining service users' health and well-being

- ways of supporting service users in a home setting.

Effects of change and ways of providing support

Unit 2 explored life stages and some of the changes that are likely to happen to people as they grow and develop. Life involves constant change, and change can create stress. A list based on research in 1997 by some American psychiatrists shows the 15 most stressful life events as in the following table.

1997	
1. Death of partner	9. Pregnancy
2. Divorce	10. Major business readjustment
3. Death of close family member	11. Loan repayment demand
4. Marital separation	12. Gain new family member
5. Fired from work	13. Marital reconciliation
6. Major illness or injury	14. Change in health of family
7. Jail term	15. Change in financial state
8. Death of close friend	

Researchers claim that life stress appears to have increased in recent times and that, in general, unmarried people experience higher life stress than people who have a partner to support them.

The table above shows how stressful general life events can be. Most people do not go into residential care, but if they did, this change would probably come high up on the list of stressful life events.

Why does change cause stress?

Change can cause:

- uncertainty
- a sense of loss
- a need to learn new things
- pressure on time, money and emotional energy
- a need to change our view of ourselves, or our self-concept.

Uncertainty

When you start at a new school or job, you don't know how the other students or staff will behave; whether they will like you, and whether you will get on all right. Moving house or moving to live with someone can create a lot of worry – all sorts of things could go wrong. Not knowing how things will work out can cause a feeling of stress for many people.

A sense of loss

Serious changes such as redundancy, sudden disability or bereavement can involve multiple losses. Bereaved people may have lost:

- the person they talked to most and who gave them advice
- their sexual partner
- the person who made social life fun
- the person who shared life's tasks with them
- the focus of life at home
- the person who provided most emotional support
- the person who protected them
- a person who helped bring in money.

A person who loses both legs in a road accident may feel that he or she has lost the ability to get out easily, and may fear being labelled and stereotyped as a wheelchair user, or feel like a burden and unattractive. A person may believe that he or she is of no use and that his or her partner might leave. If such a person ends up alone, he or she might also have all the problems listed above for the bereaved person!

A need to learn new things

Moving house, starting a new job, becoming disabled or moving into a care home all involve a great deal of new learning. Moving home may involve organising the move, getting to know new neighbours and learning how to use new household equipment. A new job involves learning new routines, learning about new roles, new tasks and new people. Disability involves learning new ways to be independent and learning to cope with other people's assumptions about you. Going into care might involve learning a whole new lifestyle.

Learning a lot of new things can be tiring and even stressful if you have to learn in a hurry.

Pressure on time, money and emotional energy

It takes time to learn a new job or to make new relationships. Time is often limited. Moving home or getting married may cost a lot of money, and these events may also be emotionally draining.

Changes such as redundancy, serious illness, and bereavement may also involve extra expenditure, additional work and more emotional involvement in order to sort everything out. In these situations you are spending your time and money to sort out things that you never wanted to happen.

A need to change self-concept

The way we see ourselves is partly a result of the way our friends, relatives and other important people see us. When we change friends, relationships, jobs or school, the people we mix with will change. New people might see us differently. Our ideas of our skills and our importance might have to change.

You may have been very good at a previous job, and seen yourself as efficient. When you change jobs, your new colleagues might work in different ways, and they might not see you as efficient. Your concept of yourself might drop in value.

Redundancy, serious illness and bereavement may also damage your self-concept. You may have seen yourself as efficient, physically fit, a partner in a loving relationship, only to find it has all been taken away. You can no longer be the person you used to be. You have to change your whole way of understanding yourself. Having to rebuild your idea of yourself can be a painful process.

What is stress?

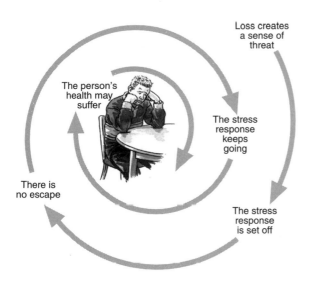

Loss creates a sense of threat

The person's health may suffer

The stress response keeps going

There is no escape

The stress response is set off

Figure 6.1 *The stress response can continue until health begins to suffer*

Physical and mental pressure can damage health. When a person feels under pressure, he or she often becomes tired. This exhaustion can cause people to worry about aches and pains, and to have migraines, headaches, back pains, sleep disturbances and emotional tension. When stress continues for a long time, it can affect a person's health. Heart disease and strokes have been associated with stress in older adults. Other physical illnesses associated with stress include diabetes, stomach problems and skin problems including eczema and rashes. People who are stressed may be more likely to catch colds, flu, or other infections.

People suffer all these physical reactions because of the way our **stress-response** mechanism works. We have all experienced a biological reaction called the stress response, which helps us to jump, run or fight if we feel threatened. If you were crossing the road and suddenly realised there was a speeding car coming towards you, you would feel scared. Because you were in danger your stress response would help you to escape – your senses (eyesight, hearing, etc.) would become clearer, your muscles would become efficient to enable you to jump or run. If you feel threatened, you can run or jump more quickly than normal.

After escaping from the speeding car, you will feel 'wobbly' for a few minutes. You might breathe quickly and feel your heart pounding, but soon you will feel safe and your stress response will switch off.

Major changes in life can cause a feeling of being threatened, and because we feel threatened our stress response is switched on. We want to escape, fight or run away, but there is nowhere to run and no way to escape. The threat is not physical, so we cannot escape it in this way. Our stress response might keep going until we feel exhausted and ill.

Change can make people feel as if they are being attacked. People who feel attacked and threatened are at risk of developing physical and mental illnesses. We might describe such people as being vulnerable.

THINK IT THROUGH

Imagine how you would feel if the following happened to you. You can either read this story and think about it, or listen carefully while someone reads it to you.

Imagine that you have lived to reach old age. Perhaps you have lived to the age of 85. Imagine that you are living alone in the same house or flat that you have lived in for over 30 years.

It is a damp, cold morning and you are sitting in your normal chair in the living room of your own home. You can see a large window – try to imagine it. What colour are the curtains? Are there any blinds at the window? Can you hear bird song, or traffic noise? What sound would come into the room?

Look around, look at your furniture, and notice the colour of the carpet. Perhaps you have a pet dog or cat – imagine whether you would have a pet.

Now imagine your own hands. As you look at your hands you think these do not look right, the skin is wrinkled and hangs too loosely, the veins stand out. These hands don't look the way that you remembered them. Your knees, legs and arms look too thin – not the way you remember them. You think about how painful it can be to move, and how difficult it can be to make meals and drinks. No one has visited you for over a week, you are lonely.

Imagine it is now the afternoon, and you have had a visit from a relative and a government official you have never met before. They both explained that you owe a lot of money for your health care! You do not understand this. They said that you will have to move – because of your debts. Tomorrow at 10 o'clock an ambulance will come to collect you and take you to a little room in a hostel. You have seen this little room with its thin, narrow bed. The room has one locker and a small wash basin.

This is the last day you can be with your pet dog or cat. Tomorrow someone will take him to an animal refuge, as pets are not allowed in the hostel. This is the last day you can look at old photos, books or videos – tomorrow they will be thrown away. You can take only two suitcases with you to the hostel.

How do you feel? How will you act when they come for you? What are you living for at this time?

Imagining yourself in this story may help you to understand the idea of vulnerability and a threat to self-concept. Just imagining this situation might make you feel sad or angry – you might have wanted to withdraw, or to fight the authorities who say you are in debt.

The person in this story was going to a hostel and would be warm, well fed and have a place to sleep there. But meeting a person's physical needs is not enough. The person in this story has lost control – others have all the power. Some people would want to give up on life as a result of this situation.

Ways of supporting service users

Caring means working with people, not working 'on' them. Carers need to be able to understand service users and imagine what they might be feeling. service users should be able to make choices and feel in control of their lives. Supporting service users may involve the following skills:

- listening and talking with a service user in order to understand his or her needs

- listening and talking with other staff, and friends and relatives of a service user, in order to understand his or her needs

- helping friends and relatives to keep in touch with a service user

- using a service user plan to help understand individual needs

- good communication skills that show respect for the service user and his or her rights, and help to meet the service user's emotional needs

- helping a service user to make choices and to be as independent as he or she wants to be

- helping a service user to relax using activities and interests (see below).

Ways of helping a service user cope with change

1 Give useful information and advice if asked. Information and advice can help reduce feelings of uncertainty. Advice on welfare benefits might help with money worries.

2 Be available to listen. When people are feeling a sense of loss it can help to be able to talk. Advice cannot help people to cope with loss, but talking seems to help many people. Carers can help others just by listening.

3 Provide help with learning new routines or using new equipment. Coping with new learning is easier if you have a friendly guide to help you.

4 Provide physical and practical care. When people are tired and stressed it can be comforting if someone else does housework or cooking, or gives other kinds of help.

5 Show respect and value for the service user. People going through change may experience a loss of self-esteem, a carer can show that the service user matters. Listening carefully to a service user can demonstrate a feeling of concern and respect for a person.

Further information on listening and communication skills can be found in Unit 4. Further detail on service users' rights can be found in Unit 1.

ASSESSMENT ACTIVITY

Describe the effects of change on the physical and emotional needs of service users and identify ways of supporting them and their carers through the process.

While you are on placement, talk to senior staff about the experiences of change that service users face. If possible read service user plans that aim to meet individual needs. Use your discussions and observations, together with the diagram below, to help you write a report that describes the effects of change on the physical and emotional needs of service users. Use the list above to help identify some ways of supporting service users through change.

Physical needs
• anxiety
• tiredness
• needs associated with disability such as mobility, or hearing needs
• can the person manage his or her daily living activities?
• does the person need help with cleaning, shopping, or food preparation?

Emotional needs
• self-esteem needs, including respect and value
• does the person have support from friends and relatives?
• how do care staff provide emotional support?

Figure 6.2 *A service user's needs*

To achieve a **merit grade** you must explain how life changes can affect the health and well-being of service users in a care setting. Your report must explain why people will have individual physical and emotional needs. You will need to explain why self-esteem could be threatened and why some people may experience stress.

To achieve a **distinction grade** you must use a case study to analyse the effects of change on the physical and emotional needs of service users and prepare a plan to support them and their carers through the process. Your report must include a case study. Coping with change can be a threatening experience; and you may find it difficult to get permission to work with a service user to explore their experience. You may however, be able to gather some general ideas about the physical and emotional needs of service users while on placement. You may also be able to find out about service user plans. You could use your knowledge to invent a character and invent a plan to meet the needs of this character.

Losses

Illnesses, disabilities and moving into care can mean that a person might experience loss in relation to any of the following factors:

- Body image – a person may feel he or she looks 'different'.

- Mobility – a person may not be able to walk or get up from a chair.

- Vision or hearing – sensory loss may isolate a person.

- Health – illness may restrict what a person can do.

- Friends – it is easy to lose contact with friends if you can't get out and about.

- Status – a loss of self-esteem may result from the way a person is treated by others.

- Income – illness, disability or moving into care may reduce the amount of money a person has to spend on other things.

- Self-worth – the above problems may cause a person to feel that he or she is not worth so much.

Feeling unsafe

Some people feel that illness, disability or moving into care involves an attack on their self-esteem. Other people might attack you by:

- stereotyping or labelling you, perhaps with labels like 'senile', 'wheelchair', or 'daft'

- discriminating against you – you may have needs that can't be met if everyone is treated the same.

People may also feel attacked by their own body if they suffer pain or impairment. They may live in fear of further losses, including losing independence and control over their lives.

Roles and responsibilities of carers

The National Vocational Qualifications (NVQ) in Care defines the values that carers must have in their work with others. The NVQ defines three basic values:

■ foster the equality and diversity of people

■ foster people's rights and responsibilities

■ maintain the confidentiality of information.

From these values it follows that carers have certain responsibilities to service users and to their own organisations, as shown in the following table.

Responsibilities towards service users	Responsibilities towards the organisation
Not to stereotype, label or discriminate against people who are different.	To understand the relevant law and policies related to equal opportunities and confidentiality.
To show respect to service users.	To follow policy or guidelines on staff behaviour in order to show respect and value for service users.
To develop an understanding of service users' beliefs and preferences.	To manage time to make it possible to get to know the service users.
To offer choices to service users.	To clarify the choices available and the resources needed to offer choice.
To respect service users' rights and support service users to uphold their rights.	To discuss care needs with other team members and managers in order to support service users.
To develop a caring relationship.	To undertake self-development and training to improve communication and supportive skills.
To maintain confidentiality.	To operate record-keeping systems effectively and check if people have a right to know information.
To help service users develop or keep their self-esteem.	To be responsible and reliable regarding other team members.
To contribute to the full development and independence of others.	To understand and discuss the problems that can arise when trying to respect rights and maintain confidentiality.

Sources of support for carers

Informal carers

Meeting the needs of vulnerable people cannot be achieved by one person alone. As well as a relationship with individual care workers, vulnerable people may have relationships with friends and family. Carers must work effectively within the organisation and within the service user's network of relationships. This network could include family, neighbours, friends, even pets.

Supporting vulnerable people can be tiring work. Sometimes a partner or relative will be the only carer for a vulnerable adult. People who develop mobility problems may rely on a partner to do all the housework and shopping, and people who develop dementia may rely on a partner or relative to provide round-the-clock help. People with dementia may forget where they are; they may constantly ask the same questions, or become lost if they leave their house. The stress put onto a carer can be very great.

Lone carers will often need assistance in supporting their vulnerable relatives. Organisations that may help include both statutory and voluntary services. Services such as home care can take some pressure off carers by working directly with a service user or by doing household tasks that the carer has been unable to do because of spending time with a service user.

Respite care involves caring for a service user for a limited period of time. This allows relatives to take a holiday or other break from caring work. Some residential homes for older people offer this 'respite' or 'short-stay' service.

When people care for their own relatives, they run the risk of becoming not only stressed, but isolated. Lone carers may lack advice or help with problems that they face. **Self-help groups** can provide a source of advice and support. Voluntary groups like the Alzheimer's Society may provide advice and guidance to carers in the community.

Professional carers

Professional care workers also need a source of advice and support to guide their work. Professions such as nursing require that their staff undertake professional training to update their skills at regular intervals. Professional counsellors receive regular supervision to ensure that their counselling practice is satisfactory and ethical. Care workers need supervision sessions on a regular basis to check that their practice respects service users' rights. This is vital, because people who feel cared for and supported themselves may tend to treat others in a caring and supportive way, whereas those who feel devalued or stressed may tend to devalue and stress others.

Care workers may also provide more effective care if they can take part in regular training and discussion groups (see Unit 1).

Relationships

Relationships are very important to the health and well-being of most people. Studies show that people who have good relationships with others are usually happier and are often healthier than people who do not enjoy good social relationships. Why are relationships important to people? One answer is that we have an inbuilt need to be with others and that doing so can meet many of our physical, intellectual, social and emotional needs.

THINK IT THROUGH

If you had to draw a simple sketch of yourself in 20 years' time, or write a description of your life, would you include in the picture friends, partners or family? It is likely that you would because many people find it hard to imagine a happy and full life without friends and family around them.

How relationships help

Relationships with other people can help us in many ways, including offering us practical help, enabling us to feel safe, and maintaining our self-esteem.

Practical help that relationships can bring include the following:
- Friends and relatives might help us with shopping, with maintaining a home or car, and other practical activities.

- Close friends or relatives might support us by lending money, sharing or lending things we need.

- People we know may give us useful advice.

Feeling safe is easier if we have supportive relationships.
- Friends and family create groups to which we belong. Many people feel relaxed and safe when they are with their friends or 'at home'.

- Relationships can protect us from feeling stressed about money or other problems in our lives.

Happiness and self-esteem often come from relationships.
- If we get on well with friends and relatives, we may feel that we are valued – relationships can give us a feeling of self-worth.

- Friends and family can provide us with a 'social life'. Without relationships, people often feel lonely and bored.

- Talking and listening to people and planning things with others can create a sense of purpose in life.

- Relationships can meet people's social, love and sexual needs.

- People can be interesting – relationships may help to keep us mentally active.

Different types of relationships

We make relationships with individual people, but we may also feel that we belong with groups, such as groups of friends, groups of colleagues at work and

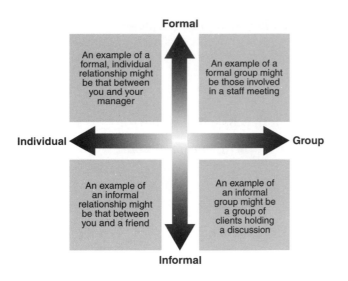

Formal

An example of a formal, individual relationship might be that between you and your manager

An example of a formal group might be those involved in a staff meeting

Individual ← → Group

An example of an informal relationship might be that between you and a friend

An example of an informal group might be a group of clients holding a discussion

Informal

Figure 6.3 *Types of relationships*

family groups. Sometimes our relationships might be part of a formal role that we play – we may get on well with our supervisor or manager at work, but the relationship might be quite formal. Relationships can be very informal, or formal, or somewhere in between. Relationships can be with individuals, with small groups or with large groups.

Types of relationships could be described in a chart like the one in Figure 6.3.

Social and family relationships

Social and family relationships normally involve people who:

■ are well known to us and whom we meet regularly

■ will be with us throughout life

■ we feel are trustworthy and feel tied to emotionally

■ support each other, and may share similar views

■ help us develop and keep a sense of who we are.

Because we are involved with family and friends, we share their happiness and celebrate things with them. We also share their pain and grief, and we may become upset if things go wrong for them.

Being closely involved with people causes a great deal of happiness; but it can also create stress and tension. Arguments and anger can easily break out between people who are emotionally involved with each other. When relationships break down, this can cause a great deal of unhappiness and stress.

Professional relationships

When we work with people in social care, we take on a professional role. We have to use personal skills in order to understand and try to meet individual needs. Workers have to make skilled decisions minute by minute in order to help people. Further discussion of professional roles can be found in Unit 1.

Professional relationships mean that we have to:
■ work with people we don't know at first

■ provide an equal quality of service for everyone

- provide an equal quality of service regardless of whether we like people or think they are attractive

- work with people whether or not we feel like it

- be prepared to learn about new people

- understand the idea of 'boundaries' in working with people (see Unit 1)

- become involved with people sufficiently to care for them, but not become so involved that we worry

- behave responsibly as a member of a team (see Unit 1).

Helping service users to maintain or develop relationships

When people are being cared for by others, their needs for relationships are still strong, but it may be difficult to develop or maintain them. For example, a young person may have lost touch with his or her parents; an elderly person may be in care away from his or her old home and friends.

Care workers can help people to develop or maintain relationships in the following ways.

1   Get to know the individuals you work with and build a sense of trust with them. This will involve good listening and conversation skills. Sometimes the care relationship becomes an important part of a service user's support network – older people in the community may sometimes rely on their care worker for company and social support.

2   Organise activities and social events so that people have a chance to meet and develop new relationships. Planning and leading groups are important skills that care workers may need in order to organise activities.

3   Show respect and value for a service user's family and friends. Many older people get a sense of purpose in life from contact with children and grandchildren, and parents are key people in the lives of many younger service users.

4   Create a setting where friends and relatives can visit or support the person you work with. It is important to do everything you can to keep people in touch with their support network. This might include

Your daughter is here to see you, Mr Rajiah

Figure 6.4 *It is important to create a setting where friends and relatives feel welcome to visit*

providing a private setting where people can meet and talk confidentially. Relatives and friends need to be able to trust you and to feel welcome.

Loss or breakdown of relationship

When people lose relationships they may experience strong emotions such as grief, depression, anger and guilt. The loss of a partner or the loss of contact with friends or family can greatly reduce a person's self-confidence and self-esteem. Grief can sometimes make people feel that there is no purpose to their life – they can lose their sense of who they are through the shock of losing a close friend or partner.

If people lose touch with their entire network of friends and family, perhaps because of illness or disability, they can become socially isolated. Some older people can lose touch with relatives because their relatives live so far away, and a partner may die. Such an isolated person may feel vulnerable and threatened, and may experience anxiety or depression.

ASSESSMENT ACTIVITY

Describe the main different types of relationship and the role of care workers in helping to develop and maintain these relationships.

1   Think of a person that you have worked with in care. Draw a diagram of this person's network of family and friends, being careful not to use any real names in your diagram. Use your diagram to help you write a report that explains the main different types of relationships service users may have. In theory, what help can you provide in order to help the service user to stay in contact with his or her network of family and friends? Discuss your ideas with others and then write them in your report.

2   To help you to prepare your report, work with others to design a poster that shows the importance of social relationships for service users. After the posters have been designed it will be important to discuss the various benefits which they have identified. This discussion might help to identify benefits and ideas for encouraging social support.

Figure 6.5 *Some posters on the theme of social relationships*

To achieve a **merit grade** you must explain how individuals benefit from relationships and suggest ways in which the care setting can encourage them. Your report must explain the importance of relationships and set out some ideas for ways in which a care service can encourage supportive relationships.

Activities and interests

Young children might learn a range of practical and social skills from joining in activities like singing, playing musical instruments, drawing, painting and making things. Young children learn to develop their imagination with play activities like using a sandpit or using shapes to build structures.

Adults with learning disabilities may need the opportunity offered by activities and interests to mix with people and develop their relationships. As well as social activities, adults with learning disabilities might enjoy relaxation activities, and activities that develop independent living skills such as cookery.

Older people may be mainly interested in social activities, but these may include games and pastimes they have enjoyed in the past (for example, card games like bridge). Some older people may wish to take part in activities such as music and movement, which exercise muscles as well as providing social contact. Other older people may be interested in thinking and talking about their past. This activity is called 'reminiscence', and it may help some older people keep a strong sense of self-esteem.

Many types of activity can be relevant to social care work and different activities can meet different types of need. Some examples are set out in the table below:

Physical needs

Physical exercise can keep muscles working and joints moving. Exercise may help people to develop control of muscles and improve general fitness. Exercises might be linked with games, music or dance activities.

Intellectual needs

Some activities help people to learn new skills. Activities like shopping and cooking can help people to learn skills that will make them more independent. Sport or dance might help children to learn to co-ordinate their hands or their bodily movements. Social activities like a quiz might help some people to feel mentally fit and active.

Social needs

Activities like sport, card games, discussion groups, quizzes, gardening and cooking involve mixing with people and talking with them. Activity and interest groups can help people to meet others and perhaps make new relationships.

Emotional needs

If you can think 'I'm good at this', you may develop a feeling of self-worth. If you make good social relationships during activities it may help you to develop a higher level of self-esteem. Discussion and reminiscence activities may help some older people to keep a high level of self-esteem.

THINK IT THROUGH

Below are some sample lists of activities, of care settings and of service user groups. Looking at the activities, work out which care settings and service user groups they would be appropriate for. Work out how the activities might meet the physical, intellectual, social or emotional needs of service users.

Activites	Care setting	Client groups
Building a house using boxes	School or day nursery	Children
Sand play		Adults
Cutting out shapes	Home in the community	Adults with learning disability
Drawing or painting pictures		
Shopping for food	Day centre	Older people
Making masks	Residential home or care home	
Cooking		
Exercising to music		
Being part of a team playing a quiz game		
Using old photos to reminisce about the past		
Playing card games		
Using lighting and music to create a relaxation session		
Discussing shared interests with other people		

Who decides on service users' needs?

Activities can have many benefits, but not all activities are equally valuable to all service users. A young person might not find a reminiscence discussion very useful. An older person with poor eyesight and arthritis – who had never been interested in painting – might not find an art class very valuable.

Care workers can make some general guesses as to the value of an activity for certain groups of people, but they are unlikely always to guess people's needs accurately. The only person who really understands a service user's needs in relation to activities is the service user.

Imagine you lived in a country where you were required by law to walk or run five miles every day, to spend half an hour doing mental arithmetic, and to go to bed early. Imagine all this was checked by the secret police. The government might, quite rightly, point out that this lifestyle would be very good for you. Your mind and body would probably be much fitter than they are now. The government would be meeting your physical and intellectual needs!

But most people do not like being told how to live their lives. In a democratic society, we believe that people have a right to choose the interests and activities that make up their lifestyle. If people are pushed into doing things they have not chosen to do, they may feel that their opinions and views are of little importance.

> Remember: service users should actively choose to join in activities or interest groups – if they don't choose to join in, the activities may do more harm than good.

One elderly woman in a care home was asked why she refused to join in activities. She explained that, at 85, she felt differently to the way she had earlier in life. 'I want to sit and think and rest – I don't want to do anything else. I've worked all my life, and I want some peace now. You may feel the same if you get to my age!'

Different people see their needs differently. It is a service user's right to choose to opt in or out of activities.

Planning activities

Most activities have to be planned, although sometimes you can just get talking to people or just show someone how to do something. If you are trying to get a group together to learn about cooking or to reminisce, you will need to do some planning.

Aims

The first thing is to work out the aim or purpose of the activity. What value will a game or an activity have for a group? Will it meet social needs? Is the activity intended to help people become more independent? Is the activity intended to give people a sense of achievement? Unless the aim of an activity is clear you can't be sure that it will meet people's needs.

Appropriateness

The next issue is to be sure that the activity is culturally and individually appropriate for the people you want to work with. If you want to lead a cooking session, you will need to check service users' views on food and food handling. Different cultures and religions have strict views on what may be eaten and how food should be prepared. In some cultures and age groups, men may feel that cookery is inappropriate for them. Some people dislike certain activities and certain foods.

Figure 6.6 *Service users may have differing views about levels of activity*

Choice

Before starting any activity you need to know the background and views of the people involved. You must also check that they really would like to do the activity – it is a service user's right to choose! Pressurising adults into doing things may threaten their self-esteem.

Safety

There are two aspects to safety – physical safety and emotional safety. Physical safety involves checking that people won't injure themselves. If you were showing people how to cook, the issues to check would include sharp objects like knives, hot things like boiling water and cooker hobs, and food hygiene.

Emotional safety means that the activity won't lead to individuals feeling upset, discriminated against or threatened. If you were going to lead a reminiscence session you might want to check that the pictures or objects you would show people were appropriate. Pictures of working-class children from long ago might offend an older person who saw himself as middle class! Some memories – perhaps of the war – might be upsetting for some people.

Environment

Next, you need to check you can have an appropriate room or setting for your activity and that all the equipment and materials you need are available.

You need to have a plan for how you will work with people. For example, you should decide how you will demonstrate cooking. Will you explain things step by step? How will you get people talking? What prompts or ideas will you use?

Finally, you should check all your planning with a supervisor or tutor before trying to lead any activity. If you are not experienced it may be important that there is someone to help you. Showing people how to do things or leading a discussion can look easy; but you can easily go wrong or forget what to do next. Having an experienced member of staff to work with you can create a sense of confidence for everyone.

Feedback

When you have led an activity it will be important to find out if the activity met the needs of the service users. You will get some feedback from service users while you are doing the activity. You will be able to see if they are happy and if they are enjoying what they are doing. Many service users will tell you if they are comfortable and benefiting from the task.

As well as informal verbal and non-verbal feedback from service users, you may want to prepare some questions that you can ask in order to find out if the activity was successful. If a senior member of staff has watched you lead an activity, they may also be able to give you some feedback, which will help you to judge the benefits that service users may gain from your work.

Good practice: planning an activity

- Set out the aim of the activity.

- Check that the activity is appropriate.

- Check that people want to be involved.

- Check for any physical safety risks.

- Check for any emotional safety risks.

- Decide which rooms/equipment/materials are needed.

- Decide on the methods or steps involved in the activity.

- Decide what feedback you will get in order to help judge the success of the activity.

- Check on the support and help available.

ASSESSMENT ACTIVITY

Plan two different activities for each of two different service user groups

1 While on placement you will have watched service users taking part in activities. Choose two activities that you have watched with two different groups and work out what rooms, equipment and materials are needed in order to lead these activities. Work out what steps and methods are needed in order to get the activities to work. Use the 'planning an activity' checklist above to help you and then write a plan for the four activities.

2 Use the theory on physical, intellectual, social, and emotional needs in this unit to help you explain what needs your activities might be expected to meet. Explain why your activities will be appropriate for the service user group.

To achieve a **merit grade** you must explain the purpose of your planned activities and the results you intend to achieve.

To achieve a **distinction grade** you must explain how you will judge the benefits service users gain from your planned activities. You will need to explain what kind of feedback you plan to gather and how you might know whether your work had been successful or not.

The risk of isolation

Residential and day-care settings can help to meet people's social and emotional needs by providing a social atmosphere where care staff use conversation and activities to encourage people to get to know each other and perhaps to get on well with each other.

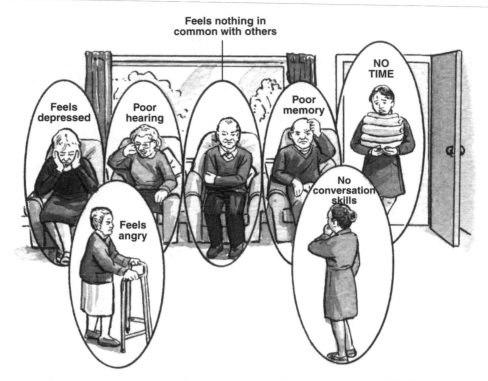

Figure 6.7 *There is a danger in care settings that people will live inside 'isolation bubbles'*

Without conversation and activities, a care setting may not be a sociable place to be. It is possible for members of a day centre or residential centre to live in their own 'bubble' of experience and not to communicate with others. If service users have lost touch with their friends and relatives, they may experience total isolation. Visits from friends and family may be very important for preventing a feeling of isolation.

THINK IT THROUGH

Imagine a day in the life of a resident who lives in a large home where there is a low staff to resident ratio. The staff have time only to get the residents up, provide meals and help them with going to the toilet and other basic care. The residents all come from different backgrounds and have different disabilities. During the day, residents sit around in the lounge or wander about the home. Think about how the residents might feel isolated in this home.

Support the service user in a home setting

The place where you live is very important. It is your home. Imagine how you might feel if for some reason a stranger had to come and live in your home – or even your room. How would this affect you?

For people who need to be cared for in their own house it is particularly important for the carer to be sensitive to possible feelings of anger or fear.

Service users are likely to feel nervous when a care worker comes into their home, so it is very important that the worker is supportive. Carers should:

- develop a good sense of trust with the service user

- build a relationship using listening and conversation skills

- show respect for service users and make them feel that their beliefs and preferences are understood and valued

- reassure service users that workers keep their information confidential

- explain their work role

- work within care plan guidelines

- respect service users' rights including the right to choose their own lifestyle, routines and standards.

When working with a new service user, a care worker has to work hard to get to know the person. As well as being friendly, the care worker has to find out exactly what kind of help is needed and how the service user would prefer things to be done. Care plan details are likely to explain only the general tasks that have been agreed. The care worker has to discover how to meet the service user's needs in detail.

Case Study – Mr Wilson

Mr Wilson's care plan simply states that he needs help with shopping and general household cleaning. When you meet Mr Wilson, you discover that his needs are not straightforward. Mr Wilson is lonely because he can't get out. He is a member of a local church; it seems a good idea for someone to contact the church to arrange visits or transport to church services.

Mr Wilson grew up in the Caribbean. He has a preference for certain fruits and vegetables, which can be bought at the local street market but not in the local supermarket.

Care workers may have to help service users with clothing, managing their own budget, making choices about food, with shopping or with cleaning. All these depend on the carer working in a supportive way.

Care of clothing and linen

Care of service users' clothing and linen involves:
- washing clothes
- ironing
- taking clothes to cleaners.
- drying and folding
- storing

Many service users will have their own routines for washing, ironing, folding and storing clothes. It is usually important not to take over and impose new ways.

Service users may need help only with particular tasks. Perhaps a service user may have difficulty with loading, setting and unloading a washing machine, but may be able to fold items of clothing. It is important to agree what work you can help with and how that work should be done.

Service users may have their own system for storing clothes in different drawers or cupboards. It may be very important to work within their system they have invented. If clothes are stored in new places, service users may become frustrated and confused.

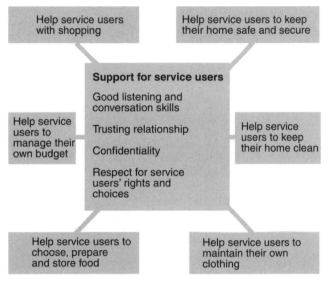

Figure 6.8 *Practical help depends on using supportive skills*

Carers should discuss all procedures for washing, ironing and storing clothes with the person they care for. It is always important to show respect for service user choice.

There may be laundry services for people who have problems with incontinence. These might be run by local or health authorities. Soiled laundry can be collected and cleaned, and then delivered back to the service user.

Choosing, preparing and storing food

Food is a very personal area of life. Many people express their individuality through their choices about food and food preparation.

Religion, culture, life experience and the amount of money available may all influence what a service user will choose to eat and drink. Service users who are depressed or withdrawn may not want to eat. Encouraging service users to make choices is one way of showing you value them and helping to increase levels of self-esteem.

Case Study – Mrs Soros

Mrs Soros is 90 years old and has been on her own for nearly a year since her husband died. Mrs Soros has difficulty in preparing and cooking food because of breathlessness and partial sight. She says 'everything tastes the same anyway!'

Mrs Soros has home care. Her carer, Jenny, encourages her to take an interest in food and cooking, but at first Mrs Soros would just ignore advice. She was happy to eat only sweets and fruit. After a few weeks Mrs Soros came to like and trust Jenny. They talked a lot and Mrs Soros started to take an interest in Jenny's life. Jenny decided to talk about the meals she liked to cook, and how they could easily be bought and prepared. Jenny suggested that Mrs Soros might like to try some of the new meals from the supermarket. Mrs Soros agreed – because she had become interested in Jenny's life, and because she trusted Jenny.

Relationships are often very important in motivating service users to make choices – especially if they have become depressed.

A home carer may often need to spend time finding out about a service user's beliefs and preferences connected with food. Many people have strong views about diet and the way food should be prepared. Carers may also need to spend time learning about different cultures' methods of food preparation so that they can understand service user need. Carers must be careful not to push their own beliefs and preferences onto service users or to criticise a service user's choices.

As with other activities, a particular service user may need help only with one particular activity. Some service users can't get to the shops, but can manage their own routines for cooking at home. Some service users may need help with lifting heavy pots or pans, and others may need help to choose appropriate food if they have developed problems with memory. Each person will be different and the care worker needs to work out how best to support each service user with his or her chosen diet and routines.

Food safety

There are some important principles care workers should follow when preparing food or assisting service users to do so, because of the need for hygiene and safety.

Good practice: food preparation

- Always wash your hands before touching food.
- Cover any cuts or sores with a waterproof dressing.
- Try not to handle food any more than is necessary.
- Keep raw and cooked food on separate work surfaces.
- Clean utensils between using them for different foods.
- Keep food covered.

■ Keep food refrigerated or very hot.

■ Get rid of waste food quickly and properly.

■ Keep all equipment and work surfaces clean.

■ Check 'use by' dates on manufactured food products.

■ Do not sneeze or cough near food.

Healthy eating

Current advice on healthy eating includes:

■ cut down on fatty foods, which include red meat, cheese and cream

Figure 6.9 *Eat plenty of fresh fruit and vegetables*

■ eat plenty of fresh fruit and vegetables, and cereals with a high fibre content

■ try to avoid eating too much and becoming overweight

■ if you drink alcohol, drink only moderate amounts.

It is important not to impose health education advice on service users, as some may feel that being given such advice is an attack on their dignity.

THINK IT THROUGH

You could try this in pairs. Wear a blindfold or use glasses that limit your vision so that you can play the role of a service user with a visual disability. Work with another student who will act as your carer and will help you choose and prepare a sandwich.

At the end of the exercise think about how it might feel to be cared for. In particular, did your carer:

■ *check your beliefs and preferences – or just tell you what to do?*

■ *talk you through things?*

■ *respect and value you?*

■ *try to find out what you could do for yourself?*

■ *give you choices?*

■ *help you to do things for yourself?*

■ *follow food safety rules in relation to the storage and preparation of food?*

Maintaining a clean, safe and secure environment

There is detailed advice on hygiene and safety, and the issues of health and safety at work, in Units 3, 5 and 7. Unit 7 also addresses the issue of security.

Care workers often work with people who have different standards, beliefs and preferences from their own. It is important not to argue with service users or to insist that your standards are the right ones. Instead, you need to estimate the risk that may be involved in a service user's behaviour. For example, does the service user let strangers in or light fires? If you feel there is a risk to safety or health, you should discuss the problem with a manager.

THINK IT THROUGH

What should a care worker do if:

- *a service user hoards newspapers? Some people have been known to fill whole rooms with newspaper – never to throw them away, but save them 'because they could be useful'.*

- *someone has a dusty and dirty home but doesn't want it cleaned?*

- *someone refuses to put the heating on because he or she wants to save money to leave it to the grandchildren?*

Hoarding

Hoarding newspaper always increases the risk of a fire starting, and of a fire spreading quickly. However, many people keep old books and papers, and people have a right to store things that they want in their own homes. If the service user is at risk of setting the paper on fire, some sort of emergency action may be needed to reduce this risk. But the action may not necessarily be to remove all the newspaper!

Dirt and dust

Dirt and dust are not good for people, but individuals have different standards. If a property is a public health risk, it may be necessary to clean the house to remove the risk. Some dust and dirt may be acceptable, however, and it is important to respect service users' wishes unless there is a risk to the care worker or the public.

Cold

Under-heated rooms can be a serious risk to old people and it may be that something needs to be done. However, carers cannot force their views onto service users. It may be possible for a care worker to keep an eye on a service user at risk and get the service user to turn the heating on when the temperature falls below a mark on a thermometer placed in the service user's living room. However, a carer can't argue that the service user must not save money on heating.

Security and access

You need to ensure that any access arrangements you have to the service user's home do not create a security risk. It is not safe to leave front door keys under mats or pots or on a string through the letterbox. Systems for securing access to a service user's property may have to be negotiated with managers. It may be that keys to service users' properties will be kept in a locked safe and that you sign them out and back in after you have visited a service user. Keys should never have names and addresses attached to them in case they become lost.

Shopping for household and personal goods

Service users may not be able to get out to the shops to buy food, clothes and household goods such as cleaning materials and washing powder. Care plans often state that service users need help with shopping.

Some people know what they want – which brand of washing powder, and so on. It is important to respect a service user's choices even though we may make different choices. Some people may have a fixed routine and want a set list of shopping every week. Other people will like change and will like to vary what they eat and drink.

It is important not to make assumptions that people will always want a fixed lists of things to buy. Part of the carer's job is to help service users to plan their shopping, and people may want to try different things from time to time.

Budgets

Many service users have to be careful with their money, and some service users may ask for your help in working out their shopping bills. Service users may also welcome any advice you can give about how much things cost. You should always keep the till receipts when you go shopping; usually you will need to check them through with the service user. Checking the receipts not only proves that you have been honest, but it may also help to give the service user up-to-date information on shopping.

THINK IT THROUGH

You return from shopping and the service user is so pleased with you that she says: 'Keep the change – it's a little present, no one will know.' It is very important that carers never accept money from service users. Care agencies will have strict rules that forbid accepting money. The reasons for these rules is to protect service users from financial abuse, and also to protect workers from complaints about money.

Financial abuse can happen when people are expected to offer gifts or extra payments for services. If you never accept money, you can make sure that you can't be accused of trying to win trust so as to get money out of people.

Storage

When you return with shopping, many service users may ask you to help with putting the shopping away. There are two important principles to think about here.

1 **The system the service user uses**. Some people have difficulty in seeing or remembering where things are kept. If they have a set place for things, it is important that the carer understands and stores things in the right place.

2 **Safety**. Heavy things should be stored where they can't fall out and hit someone. Older food purchases should be moved to the front of a cupboard with new goods stored behind them so that food is used before its 'use-by' date. Many types of food need to be refrigerated. Care workers may sometimes be able to offer useful suggestions on managing storage – but the service user has a right to manage this as he or she wants to.

The supportive role of the care worker

Professional care is not just about meeting physical and practical needs. People in the community who need care often feel threatened by having a stranger come into their home. Service users will have a need to feel 'safe'.

Some people will have lost touch with relatives and friends, and sometimes the care worker may be the main person a service user talks to. The care worker may become someone who helps to give a service user a sense of belonging or a sense of purpose in life.

Carers need to think about all the 'levels of need' that people have – not just their physical needs. Working supportively involves trying to meet social and emotional needs, as well as physical needs.

Risks to service users

Although most people want to live in a clean, safe and secure home, many people are more worried about maintaining their dignity and control over their home than they are about cleanliness. Some service users feel threatened by having a stranger in their home. If a care worker suggests changes to a service user's routines this could make the service user feel threatened. If the care worker takes over jobs like cleaning and shopping it can sometimes make the service user feel that he or she has lost control. If the care worker puts the shopping away, service users may feel that they no longer know where things are. People with visual disabilities may feel safe only if important belongings are kept where they placed them. Having to have a care service can make some older people feel that they have reached the end of their useful life. Some service users may lose self-esteem if their lack of independence is brought home to them.

Some service users may fear becoming more independent in terms of daily living activity because they are afraid that relatives, friends, or carers will spend less time with them if they are independent. Independence might increase the loneliness of some service users.

Some benefits and risks of a clean and safe and secure environment are set out below:

Benefits	Risks
Being safe from physical harm.	Loss of self-esteem because of the loss of privacy and perhaps dignity.
Lowered risk of infection and other health risks.	Being afraid of increased loneliness.
Maintaining self-esteem because the environment is socially acceptable to others.	Lowered self-esteem if you do not feel in control.
Feeling comfortable because the environment is clean, safe and secure.	Feeling threatened by new routines or difficulty in finding things.
Lowered risk of accidents.	Being afraid of a loss of independence if others take over.
Improved physical health and freedom from stress.	Increased stress if independence, privacy or dignity feel threatened.

In order to limit the social and emotional risks to service users the following can be considered:

- build a supportive relationship with individuals
- use effective communication skills including active listening
- communicate respect and value for service users
- find out about service users' beliefs and preferences
- recognise the rights of service users, including the right to take risks

- follow safety procedures and guidelines to protect yourself and service users

- offer choices about the way you work

- negotiate plans with service users and with friends and relatives if the service user wishes this.

ASSESSMENT ACTIVITY

Explain how service users may be encouraged to maintain cleanliness, safety and security in their physical environment and in food preparation.

Imagine that you have to work with an older man who has become depressed and neglects the house where he lives alone. The man has a limited ability to walk, and needs help with shopping and cleaning. He shows little interest in doing anything for himself or in preparing or eating food. Discuss the situation with another student and make a list of ideas for encouraging a service user to cope with daily living activities. Use this list in order to write a report.

To achieve a **merit grade** you must discuss the benefits and potential risks to a service user of being able to maintain a clean, safe and secure environment. You also need to identify some of the potential threats to self-esteem that the person might experience when working with care staff. You should also identify the possible risks of a loss of social support that might come with independence.

To achieve a **distinction grade** you must analyse ways to limit the potential risks to a service user of maintaining the cleanliness, safety and security of his or her environment. Your report should explain the values, communication skills and ways of working which will help to limit the social and emotional risks to a service user.

The Caring Environment

This unit explores how to maintain a clean, safe and secure living environment. In addition to the study of practical issues, this unit provides an explanation of how a clean, safe and secure living environment can meet different levels of service user need. The unit provides a study focus on skills needed to meet service users' needs. The unit also provides a very practical focus on how to deal with emergencies and the importance of health and safety.

This unit is internally assessed and ideas for evidencing the grading criteria are presented.

In this unit you will learn about:

- creating and maintaining a clean, safe and secure living environment

- working with other people in the care setting

- dealing with emergencies in a care setting.

A clean, safe and secure living environment

There are two main reasons for keeping clean the environment that we live in:

1   to meet people's social and emotional needs

2   to meet people's physical health and safety needs.

Social and emotional needs

People have different beliefs and values about how clean a home should be. Some people believe that everything should be neat and tidy, with a place for everything and everything in its place. Many people find dust or dirt offensive.

Someone used to living in tidy, spotless surroundings may become distressed if he or she can no longer keep to former standards of cleanliness. If you were forced to live in an untidy or dirty care setting you might feel that other people did not value you or think you deserve good treatment. Having to live in untidy or dirty surroundings could take away a person's self-esteem or cause depression.

Health and safety

Some people do not worry about how tidy or clean their environment is, and their self-esteem is not influenced by cleanliness. However, it is still important to clean the environment for health and safety reasons.

Controlling infection

Many illnesses and diseases are caused by micro-organisms such as viruses or bacteria. Once a person has an illness such as diarrhoea or a respiratory (throat or chest) infection it can spread to other people if they do not have sufficient resistance to infection, and there is a way in which the infection can spread.

How are infections spread?

Infection can be spread by:

- breathing in infectious viruses and bacteria

- taking in infectious organisms through the mouth

- infection through cuts, through mucous membranes, or just by skin contact.

Figure 7.1 *Infections can be spread through air*

Breathing in infections

When a person sneezes or coughs, infection can be carried through the air on tiny droplets of moisture. People may develop an illness if they breathe in these infected droplets. Droplets can settle and dry to particles that mix with dust. When the dust is disturbed it can mix into the air again – making it possible for people to breathe in the infection. Do you know the rhyme: 'Coughs and sneezes spread diseases'?

Good practice: protecting yourself and others

- Cover your nose and mouth if you cough or sneeze, to try to limit the spread of droplets.

- Ensure good ventilation. Fresh air circulation will help to remove infected particles. Closed, crowded rooms may make it easier for infection to spread.

- Do not mix with service users or colleagues if you think you have a serious illness such as flu.

- Prevent dust from building up by dusting or vacuuming domestic surfaces and floors.

Taking in infections by mouth

Putting unwashed fingers into your mouth may be enough to pass on an infection. Some infections are passed on through contaminated food, or food that has touched infected surfaces. Water and other drinks can also become contaminated.

Good practice: handling food

- Keep all food handling areas and equipment clean by regularly washing and wiping down.

- Follow food hygiene rules (see Unit 5, pages 197–198).

- Always wash your hands before touching any food or working in a kitchen. Always wash your hands after using the toilet.

- Do not prepare food for other people if you have a skin or stomach infection.

Infections through contact

Some infections can be spread by skin contact, or contact between harmful micro-organisms and an individual's mucous membranes (the thin membranes in your mouth, for example) or blood system.

Good practice: safe contact

- Take great care with knives and other sharp instruments. If you do cut yourself, encourage the wound to bleed and wash the wound as soon as possible. Report any injuries that happen, and cover all cuts.

- Wear protective gloves to provide a barrier against infection on any occasion where you have contact with body fluids including blood, vomit, urine or faeces, or with soiled linen or dressings. Take the gloves off by turning them inside out so that your skin does not come into contact with the outside surface of the gloves.

- Wash your hands before and after contact with other people's skin.

- Wear protective clothing such as a plastic apron for any procedure that involves bodily contact or deals with body fluids.

- Tie up long hair – to prevent contact with others.

- Clean all equipment and surfaces that come into contact with body fluids, using a disinfectant or antiseptic solution.

- Avoid sharing towels or other linen or clothing. Ensure that towels and other laundry are handled and washed according to appropriate procedures. Laundry should not come into contact with food preparation areas or be left on the floor.

- Clean all toilets, hand basins, showers, baths and bidets on a regular basis (usually at least once every 24 hours where different people use the same facilities).

- All waste material soiled with blood or other body fluids should be disposed of using yellow plastic bags to indicate that they contain hazardous material.

- Regularly clean play equipment or toys that are shared by children.

- Make sure you know the procedures for cleaning and for controlling infection within the care settings you work in. Make sure you have adequate protective equipment and that you know how to use the equipment provided.

Safety

It is vitally important that everyone who works in care checks for safety hazards. Safety hazards are explained in Unit 3, and also later in this section.

THINK IT THROUGH

Look at the diagram in Figure 7.2. How many safety hazards can you spot? (Answers are given at the end of the unit.)

Figure 7.2 *How many hazards can you spot?*

The National Minimum Standards for Care Homes for Younger Adults defines the following standards for cleanliness in Standard 30:

30.1	Premises are kept clean, hygienic and free from offensive odours throughout and systems are in place to control the spread of infection (in accordance with relevant legislation, published professional guidance and the purpose of the home)
30.2	Laundry facilities are sited so that soiled articles, clothing and infected linen are not carried through areas where food is stored, prepared, cooked or eaten and do not intrude on service users
30.3	Hand washing facilities are prominently sited in areas where infected material and/or clinical waste are being handled
30.4	The laundry floor finishes are impermeable and these and wall finishes are readily cleanable
30.5	Policies and procedures for control of infection include the safe handling and disposal of clinical waste; dealing with spillages; provision of protective clothing; hand washing
30.6	The home has a sluicing facility where appropriate and, in care homes providing nursing, a sluicing disinfector

30.7 Foul laundry is washed at appropriate temperatures (minimum 65 degrees centigrade for not less than 10 minutes) to thoroughly clean linen and control risk of infection

30.8 Washing machines have the specified programming ability to meet disinfection standards (where applicable)

30.9 Services and facilities comply with the water supply (water fittings) regulations 1999

Security

If people are to feel safe there must be appropriate arrangements. In a care setting security arrangements can protect people from:

- loss or theft of personal possessions
- financial abuse or fear of losing money or possessions
- physical threat or attack
- loss of confidentiality.

It is important that equipment and materials within a care setting are not damaged or stolen. Staff should also feel safe and not at risk from intruders. Some security issues which may need to be checked are described below.

Access to care settings

Care settings should not be 'public places' where anyone can come or go. It is important to be able to check who people are and why they are in a setting.

Ideally, care settings should be organised so that visitors enter through a main entrance where they can be greeted and their identity checked. Many centres have a reception area where staff can record people entering and leaving a building. Doors and windows should have a locking system to prevent people entering without being noticed.

Knowing who people are is important in order to prevent theft and worse crimes such as assault. Service users have a right to choose who they see and who they do not see. If visitors are always met by staff, it will help to protect residents' rights.

Security of residents' property

Personal possessions can be very important to people. A wedding or engagement ring might have tremendous emotional importance. Losing a personal possession like a ring could create a deep sense of loss or pain; the ring might have much more value than just its monetary value.

There should be systems for recording witnessed accounts of the money and valuables that residents possess.

Personal security

Service users may sometimes be at risk of verbal or physical attack by other service users. It is important that staff can identify potential risks with respect to other residents' behaviour. Records of incidents and past behaviour can be important to help staff identify risks.

Where service users have poor memory or limited ability to understand where they are, it is important that they cannot simply wander out of the building to become lost or perhaps walk into dangerous traffic.

Security of records

Details of written or electronic records on service users must be kept confidential (see Unit 4). Files and other records should be kept in locked rooms or cupboards, and computer records should be protected by password security. It is important that staff follow appropriate procedures and do not leave files or records where they can be seen by people who do not have a right to read them. It is also vitally important that personal details, records of medication and so on do not become lost.

Supplies and equipment

Running a home or a care setting efficiently depends on keeping an adequate stock of food, cleaning materials, clean towels, clothes and linen.

Storage

It is important to store food separately from cleaning materials to help to prevent the spread of micro-organisms or the contamination of food. Certain foods such as cooked and raw meat should also be stored separately (see food hygiene points on pages 197–98).

Monitoring stores

If you work with an individual in the community you may be able to monitor the person's needs by getting to know him or her and checking supplies in the fridge or cupboard. Even in this situation, however, it is important to organise fridge and cupboard space so that food is eaten in the order of its 'use-by' date and the stock of materials can be seen clearly.

In larger care settings, just leaving stock in cupboards would usually cause problems. Care homes have to **monitor** what is being used and how long different supplies last in order to:

- know how often to re-order supplies, so that they do not run out
- check best value for money (some cleaning liquids may work better or last longer than others)
- check that materials are not being used incorrectly, wasted or stolen
- budget and organise the finances of the home.

Monitoring supplies usually means that staff have to sign a book, data sheet or other list for materials such as protective gloves for personal use or for the transfer of materials such as toilet rolls. Some items such as drugs have to be monitored with total accuracy – every dose or tablet has to be checked and witnessed, for reasons of health, safety and security.

Cleaning

If you work in a service user's own home it is important to find out about the service user's routine and methods of cleaning so that as far as is reasonable you can work to his or her standards. If you work in a care setting there will be an established routine for regular cleaning in all areas. This is often organised in two ways: regular cleaning happens every day, e.g. for toilets, and periodic cleaning happens at longer intervals, e.g. for curtains and paintwork. You could ask your supervisor to clarify this routine for you.

Regular cleaning will take place in the following areas:

- **Kitchen** Dirty cutlery, crockery and cooking utensils will be washed with an appropriate solution of detergent (washing-up liquid) as soon as possible. Detergent removes grease and food deposits which could otherwise provide a place for harmful micro-organisms to grow and spread. Dirty plates or glassware might offend service users.

Food preparation surfaces, floors and cooking equipment will be regularly wiped down with appropriate cleaning and disinfectant solutions. This helps to prevent the build-up of dirt in which harmful micro-organisms can grow, and to reduce the number of harmful micro-organisms that can come in contact with food. Cloths used for dishes and plates should be kept separate from those used on floors or other surfaces, to stop cross-infection from one area to another.

- **Bathrooms and toilets** Hand basins, baths, showers, bidets, toilets and commodes should be cleaned on a regular basis using appropriate cleaning and disinfectant solutions. In a care setting this is likely to be done at least once a day, and more often if there is a need to control infection. Disposable cloths are ideal for this cleaning and all cloths and brushes should be cleaned with an appropriate cleaning and disinfectant solution.

Some infections can be spread by skin contact, so regular cleaning of washing and toilet facilities must remove the dirt that micro-organisms can live in. Disinfectants can kill harmful micro-organisms and help to prevent the spread of infections.

Towels should be provided on an individual basis and regularly laundered; in more public settings, disposable paper towels or other systems should be used to make sure that micro-organisms cannot be passed from one person to another.

■ **Bedrooms** Floor surfaces and furniture surfaces should be regularly cleaned to remove dirt and dust. This may involve vacuuming, wiping surfaces with a damp cloth and dusting with a cloth.

Bed linen, e.g. sheets and duvet covers, need regular laundering to prevent the build-up of micro-organisms. Soiled bedding must be removed and cleaned immediately, and should be treated as hazardous.

■ **Halls, lounges and other general areas** Floor and furniture surfaces should be regularly cleaned to remove dirt and dust. Dust can help the spread of harmful micro-organisms, and may also contain particles that cause allergies or asthma for some people. Furniture and equipment must be kept tidy to prevent the risk of tripping or other accidents.

Creating a good impression for service users

Living in a clean environment with polished brass and sparkling glass, and a pleasant, fresh smell, is good for people's self-esteem. There may not be any value for physical health in polishing glassware, but it might have emotional importance for a service user.

Assessing and developing abilities

In a great number of care situations, tidying and cleaning is an activity shared between care staff and service users. When service users' needs are assessed an agreement may be reached that they will do certain tasks – perhaps washing and drying crockery in the kitchen while home carers clean the floor and food preparation surfaces.

In some care settings older children and adults are encouraged to learn independent living skills. In these settings staff will demonstrate the necessary cleaning routines and then help service users to learn how to take over these activities.

Where a service user is agreeing or learning to look after his or her own home it will be important to keep records and to understand how other team members may contribute to the service user's learning and activities. It can be important that different members of staff do not teach different routines and activities.

The importance of a clean, safe and secure environment

People's well-being can be threatened in a number of ways:

■ micro-organisms can attack a person's health

■ safety hazards can cause physical injury

■ intruders or other service users might physically or emotionally abuse service users

■ dirty, unsafe or insecure care settings might make people feel emotionally threatened.

A setting that fits service users' expectations and standards might help service users to feel emotionally safe, and may contribute to increasing their self-esteem.

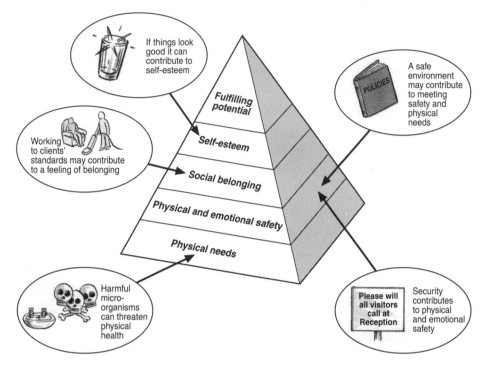

Figure 7.3 *A clean, safe and secure living environment can contribute to different levels of need*

ASSESSMENT ACTIVITY

Describe the safety and security requirements of a care setting and how they can be maintained.

1 While on placement, you should try to get copies of policies with respect to cleanliness, safety and security. Design a table listing the things your work setting does and the equipment it provides in order to ensure a clean, safe and secure living environment. What risks might exist for service users if these services were not provided? You could copy the outline set out below:

Activity	Risks
Cleaning What cleaning routines are there, e.g. clean bathrooms every day?	What could happen if this was not done?
Safety hazards What safety hazards exist, e.g. in food hygiene?	What could happen if hazards were not checked?
Security What security precautions exist?	What could happen if there were no security precautions?

2 Use the table to help you to write a report that describes the safety and security requirements of a care setting.

For a **merit grade** you need to explain, giving examples, the importance of maintaining a clean, safe and secure living environment, and identify techniques and materials for maintaining it. Your report must give detailed examples of cleaning, safety and security procedures and explain what could happen if routines and procedures were not followed.

To achieve a **distinction grade** you need to evaluate the cleanliness, safety and security requirements of a care setting and the effectiveness of policies in your workplace. You might also be able to suggest some ways for improving the quality of cleanliness, safety or security.

Working with other people

Working as part of a team

Being a care worker involves being good at making relationships and understanding other people. It is important to have good relationships with other staff. Usually this will involve working as part of a team, but also developing your role as an individual.

What is a team?

A team is a group of people who work (or pull) together to achieve a task. In some teams everyone works on exactly the same tasks, like a team of horses – everyone pulls their weight doing similar work. An example might be a team of care assistants who all work on the same unit with the same service users – but sometimes on different shifts. Some teams are more like a sports team where different people have different skills and abilities, but they are all working for the same general goal. An example of this might be a day centre, where the manager may spend a lot of time on administration, care workers provide most of the physical care and volunteers lead some activities with service users. People are all working together to improve life for service users – but different people do different jobs.

> **THINK IT THROUGH**
>
> *In your own work or placement setting, how far does your team involve everyone working together on the same jobs, and how far do people in the same team do different work?*

Working teams

The feeling of belonging to a team doesn't necessarily come about because people do the same work. But if teams are going to work effectively in care, individuals within the team have to:

- know who the other members of the team are

- share a common set of values with the other members

- respect and value the differences between team members

- communicate effectively with each other.

Sharing common values

When groups of people get together, they may go through a process of learning to become a working team. This process was described by a researcher called Tuckman as follows:

- **The forming stage:** People introduce themselves and try to learn about others.

- **The storming stage:** People compete with each other to control the group. People may disagree and have arguments. A team could break up and stop working together at this stage.

- **The norming stage:** People develop a set of beliefs and values about how the work should be done and how team members should behave towards each other.

- **The performing stage:** Because people now have common values, they can work together and trust each other. The team can work effectively because there is a feeling of belonging together based on shared values.

In care work, teams are unlikely to work effectively unless staff share the values of respect for each other and concern about each other's rights.

Communicating effectively

When individuals get together to talk it is important that people feel a sense of belonging together and that they can discuss important issues. An effective working team will create the right working atmosphere. This will involve the following.

- **Showing respect and value for each individual** This might be done by welcoming each person by name, asking each person for his or her views, and being sensitive to the emotions and feelings that people express.

- **Creating a feeling of belonging to the group** This might be done by keeping a sense of humour and sharing jokes, encouraging people to speak openly, helping people to say what they feel, being friendly and responsive to others, and helping people to compromise.

- **Keeping people working on important issues** This might be done by organising an agenda for meetings, giving and asking for information

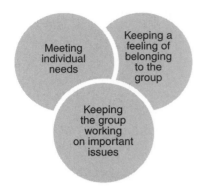

Figure 7.4 *Good team communication will involve a balance of issues*

during the discussion, bringing discussion back to the important issues, and putting ideas forward for other people to discuss.

Good team meetings will involve a balance between meeting individuals' emotional needs, creating a feeling of belonging and keeping people working hard on the business of the meeting.

Develop your own role

Team roles are discussed in Unit 1. Your role within a team will depend on the expectations that other people have of you, and how you wish to develop the way you work. Care work involves continual changes if you are to meet individual service users' needs. As you develop your skills and knowledge of service users, you may be able to discuss the work you do with other members of the team. You may be able to take on increasing responsibilities by negotiating with other members of the team.

Working with visitors

Many service users have a network of people who provide practical and emotional support to them. Visitors can be very important in meeting the social and emotional needs of service users in care. All the communication skills and care skills relevant to service users will also be relevant to service users' visitors (see Unit 4 for discussion of communication skills).

There are some key issues to consider in relation to visitors. These are described below.

Learning about a service user's support network

In order to provide a warm and friendly welcome to visitors, it can be useful to understand who is who in a service user's network of friends and family. Learning to recognise faces and names can help to provide the right atmosphere. Knowing people also helps to maintain security. Information about a service user's network of relatives and friends may be available from other team members or from care plan records. If you are a permanent member of care staff, you will usually have a need to know this information.

Service users' rights concerning visitors

Adult service users have a right to refuse to see visitors. It is important to remember that service users' needs are the first priority of a care service, not the needs of friends or relatives.

Sometimes visits will not go well. It may be that certain visitors seem to upset or distress an individual. If you notice problems, you should report what you have seen or heard to a manager as soon as possible. If an individual appears quiet or withdrawn after a visit, it may also be important to report these reactions.

Helping service users to stay in contact

Sometimes, care workers will take messages from friends and relatives to be passed on to service users. Sometimes, a service user may ask a care worker to pass messages on to friends or relatives or request help in writing a letter. It is important to help people keep in touch with one another, but it is also important to maintain confidentiality and not be drawn into giving information or opinions about a service user.

Confidentiality

It is important not to talk about a service user with relatives or friends unless you have checked with your service user first. It is particularly important not to pass on details of medical matters, health or finances without permission. It is usually possible to suggest politely that friends and relatives discuss issues directly with your service user rather than with you; say something like: 'I expect she would like to discuss that with you.'

Privacy

When visitors arrive it is usually important to have somewhere where they can talk with service users in private. Sometimes this might be the service user's room, or in other settings there might be an office or side room. Having to talk with service users in an open setting causes problems in keeping information confidential, and can make conversation more difficult for service users and visitors.

Helping visitors with enquiries

Sometimes visitors may want to ask about the care services you provide. They may want to know about other services that might be available. Very often, working with visitors may involve suggesting where they might obtain accurate information. It is important, of course, not to give incorrect advice or information.

Welcoming visitors

Use your communication skills to make visitors feel relaxed and welcome. It is important to look interested in visitors and to smile. If you can remember visitors' names and who they are visiting, it will help to make them feel welcome. You may be able to develop particular ways of welcoming visitors by watching other staff and copying the good practice you see.

Coping with emotions

Visitors may experience a wide range of emotions when they visit. They may be anxious or worried about what is happening to a person they love. They may feel angry about things that have happened, or guilty because they feel they should be helping more. Care workers need to be sensitive to this and to recognise and understand the emotions that visitors experience. Skills that enable you to stay calm, listen, show concern and calm others are an important part of the work that carers undertake.

Abuse

Preventing abuse is a very important part of care work. Abuse can take the following forms.

- **Physical abuse.** Hitting, pushing, pulling, restraining or causing pain or distress by other physical actions.

- **Sexual abuse.** Sexually exploiting or humiliating others.

- **Emotional abuse.** Bullying, blaming, threatening and damaging others' feelings of self-worth and self-esteem (this is sometimes called psychological abuse).

- **Financial abuse.** Taking others' property or money, theft or exploiting other people's resources.

- **Neglect.** Not giving enough food or physical care, not giving attention.

- **Self-abuse.** Damaging or harming oneself. People who are distressed might cut themselves or seek to harm themselves in other ways. Self-abuse can sometimes happen when a person has been abused in other ways.

Abuse and the ways of identifying abuse are covered in more detail in Unit 4.

Conflicts in care settings

People in care can become angry or refuse to co-operate with you, causing a 'limitation' to what you can do or achieve together.

Why do people become angry or refuse to co-operate? Some reasons include the following.

- **Illness.** When we are ill it can become harder to control what we say and do. Conditions like dementia can mean that people are unable to control their emotions and responses.

- **Pain.** When we are in pain it can be difficult to control emotions. We may get angry because of the pain.

- **Fear.** Some people in care do not know what to expect. Not being able to understand a situation could make people feel afraid and angry.

■ **Frustration.** Some people become frustrated because they cannot do things as easily as they used to. This stress can lead to anger.

■ **Feeling vulnerable.** Some people may be afraid of losing their dignity. Others may become angry because they feel 'got-at' by others.

■ **Past learning.** Some adults and children may have learned that being angry is the way to get things they need. Some people may be used to arguments and fighting as part of their way of life.

What happens when people get angry?

It often looks as if someone suddenly loses his or her temper. Perhaps a person who is learning to cook suddenly throws things across the kitchen. Perhaps an older resident who finds someone else sitting in what he sees as 'his chair' suddenly seems to explode with rage.

In many situations, a person already feels stressed before becoming angry. People may feel stressed because of pain or fear, or because they feel vulnerable. A person may be stressed because he or she is frustrated about not being able to do something. Feelings of emotional tension can grow as the person feels more stressed.

When a person feels stressed it takes only a single remark, or some little thing that has gone wrong, to tip him or her into an angry outburst. People who feel stressed need a trigger to set off the explosion of anger that has built up inside them.

After an explosion of anger, stressed people can still feel tense. Very often, they may feel that it is someone else's fault that they have been made to feel so angry. Anger can flare up again if the person is not given respect and encouraged to become calm. As time passes, tension may reduce if the stress can be relieved.

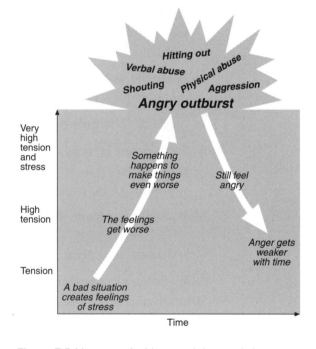

Figure 7.5 *How anger builds up and then explodes*

Not all anger follows this pattern. Some people learn to use aggression to get their way, and some can switch aggressive emotions on and off as they wish. Being angry can sometimes be a reaction that a person has chosen. But it is wrong to assume that all aggression and anger are deliberate. Most anger in care settings will involve the build-up of bad feelings described above.

Coping with anger and disagreement

If possible, try to prevent angry outbursts. If you understand the people you work with, it may be possible to spot when they are feeling tense. You may be able to calm people before an angry outburst happens, perhaps by using your conversation skills to get the person to talk to you. Talking may prevent anger if the person trusts you.

- Watch for things that might trigger anger in another person.

- Be careful not to make demands, or tell other people what to do. Try not to increase feelings of stress.

If an angry outburst happens:

- stay calm

- do not put yourself at risk

- do not blame the person, get angry, or try to 'get your own back'

- try to calm the angry person

- try to talk with the person if possible – but avoid arguing

- try to sort out differences and arguments after the other person is calm and willing to talk with you.

Staying calm

Witnessing anger, shouting, hitting out or abusive words will make a care worker feel stressed. The natural instinct in everyone makes us want to either run away or fight the person who is being aggressive. The ability to stay calm is a special skill that care workers need.

Like all skills, staying calm can be learned, but it may take time and effort to become good at it. An ideal way to learn to stay calm is to watch people who have this skill. Some ideas which may help are given below.

- Try to understand how stress can cause service users to become angry. Don't regard anger as a personal attack on you.

- Use assertiveness skills – know how to express yourself clearly and calmly without becoming aggressive or looking weak.

- Feel confident in your own skills and self-esteem. If you feel good, you are less likely to feel threatened.

- Know how to relax the muscles in your face, shoulders, arms and hands, so that you look and feel calm. It is possible to improve your calmness by practising muscle control.

Risk

If you don't think you can cope, or you think you might be attacked, then you should leave and report the situation immediately. If you are working with someone who you think may become aggressive, you should always check that you will be able to move out of reach and leave the room or house. It is important not to work alone with a service user who may become aggressive; if you think you could be at risk, this should be discussed with your manager. Your health and safety are vitally important.

Getting angry

Any angry behaviour, insult or verbal abuse can be hurtful. If we feel hurt we may want to 'get even' by hurting the person who has caused these feelings. It is an important caring skill not to let this happen to you. If a carer does lose control, he or she might verbally or physically abuse a vulnerable person. Carers should not have to 'bottle up' their feelings, though. If you work with people with challenging behaviours, there should be someone with whom you can talk your feelings through. You should be able to talk to a supervisor or a manager during supervision, or perhaps talk to a counsellor.

Calming others

If you can develop your own skills of staying calm, you may be able to use these skills to calm others. Once again, calming skills are best learned by watching other people with the skill and copying what they do. Their skills may involve:

- keeping face, shoulder, arm and hand muscles relaxed
- showing respect and valuing the other person
- using a calm tone of voice
- speaking normally and clearly
- offering to listen to the other person
- keeping an appropriate distance from the other person
- avoiding fast or jerky movements
- keeping eyes, head and shoulders at a slight angle to the other person – rather than appearing to 'face down' the person.

Talking

When a person has thrown things across the room or shouted, it is natural to ask the person why he or she has done these things, and to discuss the issue. But it is best not to do this straight away, as it may lead to more stress and arguments. Carers should try to build a sense of trust before going on to discuss the reasons why a person feels angry.

Resolving conflicts and disagreements

It is important that an angry person becomes calm and begins to trust you before going on to try to sort out problems. Sometimes it may be important to leave the person for a short period before coming back to talk things through. Sometimes it may be appropriate to ask the person to sit down with you or agree something with you before trying to resolve the conflict. If the angry person agrees things with you, then you have probably developed a sense of trust, which may be enough to enable you to talk about the reasons for the anger. It is important not to argue with the person and not to demand things or threaten him or her. Try to see other people's side of the situation, and help them to see your side.

The role of family and friends in care

As well as having physical needs, people have social, emotional and intellectual needs. For many people, family and friends meet most of these social, emotional and intellectual needs.

Close family and close friends may help us to understand who we are. When people go into care or receive a care service, it may be very important that they can keep in touch with the people who matter to them.

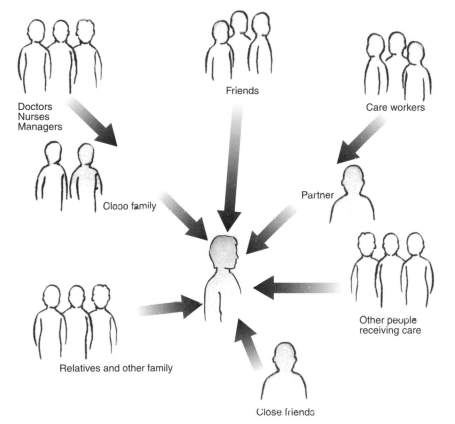

Figure 7.6 *People who meet our needs*

Helping service users to keep in touch

Care workers may be able to help service users stay in contact with friends and family by helping with:

- written communication
- telephone communication
- arranging visits
- getting to know friends and family during visits.

Written communication

A care worker may offer to write a letter for a person who finds this difficult. It is important to write what the person wants to say, and not to put in different ideas. Letters need to be read back to service users before they sign them.

Telephone communication

Some service users need help with making calls. This may involve taking a telephone to them, checking the number to dial and dialling for them, adjusting the volume of the telephone, or finding a private place to make a call.

Visits

Care workers may be able to send messages to help to organise visits. Working with visitors was discussed earlier in this unit.

Getting to know friends and family

Care workers may learn to recognise friends and family when they visit, and something of their feelings and concerns. If friends and family feel welcome and understood, it may help them to maintain contact with relatives.

Involving friends and relatives in a service user's care

Where service users enjoy good relationships, it may be possible to involve close friends and relatives with activities that take place in a care home. Sometimes friends or relatives may be prepared to help or join in with social activities or outings.

Where care is provided to people with a learning disability, it is often vital to explain activities and learning programmes to close family members who also provide care. Care plans for many service users may need to be jointly organised with family members so that the service user's needs are fully understood by everyone, and to ensure that the service user is not treated in different ways by family and carers. If close family are not involved in care it can be possible for a service user to be treated inappropriately. For example, an

Asian person may be used to eating certain foods with his or her fingers when with the family. If a care centre failed to understand this, staff might try to encourage the service user to use cutlery. Involving the family might help to prevent inappropriate care or teaching.

ASSESSMENT ACTIVITY

Identify ways for care settings to promote a positive environment.

Work with others in order to design two posters. One poster should identify ways in which a care setting can create positive physical health and safety; and one poster should identify ways in which a care setting can create a positive setting which meets service users' social and emotional needs. Discuss the posters that have been created and use this work in order to write a report that identifies ways to create a positive environment.

To achieve a **distinction grade** your report should analyse your role as a care worker and explain ways in which you can help to create a positive environment. You might like to look back at the values and the GSCC Code of Practice in Unit 1 together with the theory of working with other people set out in this unit to help you write a report that can meet the distinction criteria.

Dealing with emergencies

Your work setting will have policies and procedures for responding to emergencies, and it will be important to find out about and understand these policies and procedures. The settings in which you provide care are generally covered by the Health and Safety at Work Act 1974. This has been updated and supplemented by many sets of regulations and guidelines, but those most likely to affect care workplaces are:

- Management of Health and Safety at Work Regulations 1992
- Control of Substances Hazardous to Health Regulations 2003 (COSHH)
- Reporting of Injuries Diseases and Dangerous Occurrences Regulations 1985 (RIDDOR)
- Manual Handling Operations Regulations 1992.

Health and Safety at Work Act

Many regulations, laws and guidelines exist to ensure health and safety, and you do not need to know the details of all of them, but you do need to know how the Health and Safety at Work Act is likely to affect what happens in care settings. The Act is the main piece of legislation, and all the guidelines and regulations either add to it, support it, explain it or extend it (see Figure 3.4 on page 121).

The effects of the law

The laws that govern health and safety place certain responsibilities on employers, and also on workers – you need to know what they are. For example, the employer must provide a safe place in which to work, but the employee (or student) also has to show reasonable care for his or her own safety.

Employers have to:

■ provide a safe workplace

■ ensure that there is safe access to and from the workplace

■ provide information on health and safety

■ provide health and safety training.

Workers must:

■ take reasonable care for their own safety and that of others

■ co-operate with the employer in respect of health and safety matters

■ not intentionally damage any health and safety equipment or materials provided by the employer.

Each workplace where there are five or more workers must have a written statement of its health and safety policy. The policy must include:

■ a statement of intention to provide a safe workplace

■ the name of the person responsible for implementing the policy

■ the names of any other individuals responsible for particular health and safety hazards

■ a list of identified health and safety hazards and the procedures to be followed in relation to them

■ procedures for recording accidents at work

■ details for evacuation of the premises.

Control of Substances Hazardous to Health

What are hazardous substances? There are many substances hazardous to health: nicotine, many drugs, even too much alcohol! In this context, however, the Control of Substances Hazardous to Health regulations (COSHH) apply to substances that have been identified as being toxic, corrosive or irritant. This includes cleaning materials, pesticides, acids, disinfectants and bleaches. Each workplace may have other hazardous substances because of the nature of the work carried out.

Every workplace must have a COSHH file. This file lists all the hazardous substances used in the workplace, and should detail:

- where they are kept

- how they are labelled

- their effects

- the maximum amount of time it is safe to be exposed to them

- how to deal with an emergency involving one of them.

What to do in the workplace

If you have to work with hazardous substances, make sure that you take the precautions detailed in the COSHH file. This may involve wearing gloves, or protective goggles. It may involve limiting the time you are exposed to a substance, or using it only in certain circumstances.

The COSHH file should also give you information about how to store hazardous substances. This will involve using the correct containers as supplied by the manufacturers. All containers must have safety lids and caps, and must be correctly labelled.

Never use the container of one substance for storing another, and *never* change the labels.

The symbols in Figure 3.6 on page 126 indicate that these are hazardous substances – the signs are there for your safety and that of those you care for. Before you use any substance, whether it is liquid, powder, spray, cream or aerosol, take the following simple steps:

- check the container for a hazard symbol

- if it has one, consult the COSHH file

- look up the precautions you need to take with the substance

- make sure you follow the procedures carefully – they are there to protect you.

Emergencies that may arise in care settings

People who work in care have to be able to deal with a wide range of emergencies. They can include:

- health emergencies

- intruders or other security emergencies

- escape of chemicals or other hazardous substances

- fires

- explosions

- floods.

How to prevent emergencies

It is precisely because emergencies are unpredictable that they can be difficult to avoid, but following basic safety precautions and procedures will help.

Type of emergency	Actions to prevent it occurring
Health emergency	Trained first aider on duty Check for 'slip and trip' hazards Check safety of all equipment Check all drugs and medications are safely locked away
Fire	No smoking Check safety of electrical equipment Use all fire doors correctly Do not use naked flames
Intruders or security emergency	Have a system for checking visitors Ensure valuables are secure Have an alarm system and use it
Explosion	Regularly check gas appliances Be aware of unattended bags or packages
Escape of chemicals or hazardous substances	Store all chemicals and hazardous substances according to instructions Never put them in different containers Dispose of hazardous substances safely and correctly
Flood	Check the water system regularly Do not allow pipes to freeze Never leave plugs in baths or basins

What to do in an emergency

There are a few simple rules which apply in all emergency situations, no matter what the circumstances:

- keep calm – panic is infectious

- send for help, or get someone else to do so

- be clear if you are giving information or instructions – speak slowly and calmly using simple, short sentences

- act quickly but safely – speed is often very important in dealing with an emergency

- attempt only what you can safely do, not something you are unsure of – summon help and wait for it to arrive.

Health emergency procedures

Summoning help

In the majority of cases, calling for help will mean telephoning 999 and requesting an ambulance. This will depend on the setting in which you work – clearly this is not required if you work in a hospital! But it may mean calling for a colleague with medical qualifications, who will be able to make an assessment of the need for further assistance. If you work in the residential sector, there may be a medically qualified colleague available. If you are the first on the scene at an emergency in the community, you may need to summon an ambulance for urgent assistance.

If you need to call an ambulance, keep calm, and give clearly all the details you are asked for. Do not attempt to give details until they are asked for – this wastes time. Emergency service operators are trained to find out the necessary information – let them ask the questions, then answer calmly and clearly.

Assist the person dealing with the emergency

A second pair of hands is invaluable when dealing with an emergency. If you are assisting someone with first aid or medical expertise, follow all that person's instructions, even if you don't understand why they are necessary. An emergency situation is not the time for a discussion or debate – that can happen later. You may be needed to help to move a casualty, or to fetch water, blankets or dressings, or to reassure and comfort the casualty during treatment.

Make the area safe

Often an accident or injury will have taken place in an unsafe area. At other times, it may be that the accident has made the area unsafe for others. For example, if someone has tripped over an electric flex, there may be exposed wires or a damaged electric socket; a fall against a window or glass door may have left shards of broken glass in the area; or there may be blood or other body fluids on the floor. You may need to make the area safe by turning off the power, clearing up broken glass or dealing with a spillage.

It may be necessary to re-direct people away from the area of the accident in order to avoid further casualties.

Fire emergency procedures

All workplaces must display information about what action to take in case of fire. The fire procedure is likely to be similar to the one shown in Figure 7.7.

There are specific fire extinguishers for fighting different types of fires. It is important that you know this, but you do not have to memorise them as each one has clear instructions on it. Make sure that you read the instructions before use.

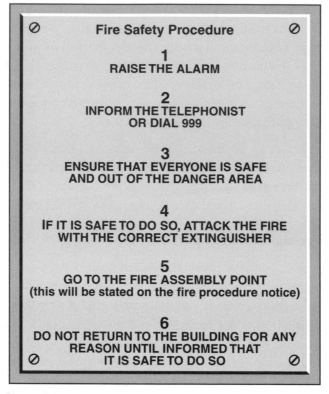

Figure 7.7 *Action to take in case of fire*

Remember

- Read the instructions on fire extinguishers before tackling the fire – the extra few seconds will be well spent making sure you are using appropriate equipment in the correct way. Modern fire extinguishers are all coloured red.

- Check that you have the right extinguisher for the blaze you are tackling.

- Tackle a fire only if you can do so safely – otherwise leave the building and wait for help to arrive.

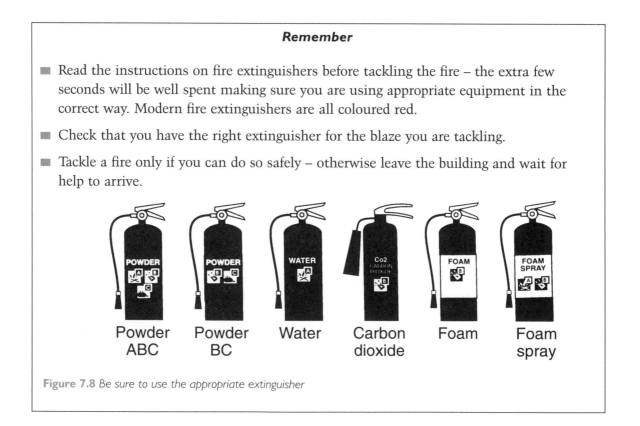

Figure 7.8 *Be sure to use the appropriate extinguisher*

Evacuation procedure

Some other emergencies, such as explosions or the leaking of chemicals, may mean that a building has to be evacuated. Each workplace will have its own procedure, but they are likely to include the following points:

- stay calm, do not shout or run
- do not allow others to run
- organise people quickly and firmly, without panic
- direct those who can move themselves and assist those who cannot
- use wheelchairs to move people quickly
- if necessary, move a bed with the person in it.

First aid box

The essential items that should be in all first aid boxes are shown in Figure 7.9.

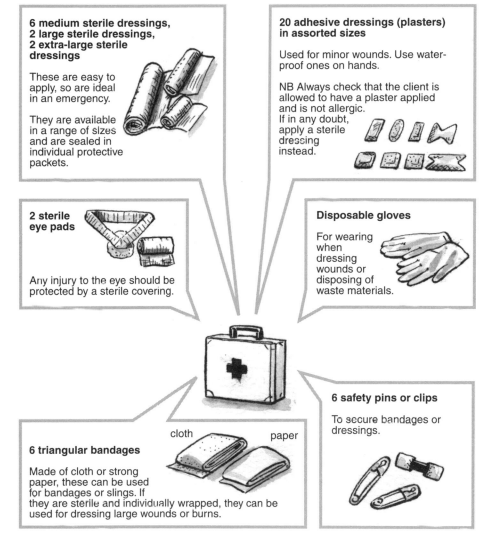

6 medium sterile dressings, 2 large sterile dressings, 2 extra-large sterile dressings

These are easy to apply, so are ideal in an emergency.

They are available in a range of sizes and are sealed in individual protective packets.

20 adhesive dressings (plasters) in assorted sizes

Used for minor wounds. Use water-proof ones on hands.

NB Always check that the client is allowed to have a plaster applied and is not allergic. If in any doubt, apply a sterile dressing instead.

2 sterile eye pads

Any injury to the eye should be protected by a sterile covering.

Disposable gloves

For wearing when dressing wounds or disposing of waste materials.

6 safety pins or clips

To secure bandages or dressings.

cloth   paper

6 triangular bandages

Made of cloth or strong paper, these can be used for bandages or slings. If they are sterile and individually wrapped, they can be used for dressing large wounds or burns.

Figure 7.9 *What you would expect to find in a first aid box*

ASSESSMENT ACTIVITY

Describe current health and safety requirements in the workplace, including the Health and Safety at Work Act 1974 and COSHH regulations.

Design a leaflet that could be given to a student on his or her first placement. The leaflet must give information about the Health and Safety at Work Act and COSHH regulations.

For a **merit grade** you need to explain the importance of current health and safety legislation and guidelines in preventing emergencies and dealing with any which arise. You should also give examples of ways in which policies guide care workers' actions when they deal with emergencies.

To achieve a **distinction grade** you need to evaluate the effectiveness of current health and safety requirements in the workplace, making reasoned comments on improving health and safety in your own workplace.

Emergency conditions

It is important that you can recognise the major signs and symptoms of the main health conditions that may require emergency action.

Severe bleeding

Causes

Severe bleeding can be the result of a fall or injury. The most common causes of severe cuts are glass, as the result of a fall into a window or glass door, or knives from accidents in the kitchen.

Symptoms

There will be apparently large quantities of blood from the wound, and in some very serious cases the blood may be pumping out. Blood, even in small amounts, can be very frightening, both for you and the casualty. Remember that a small amount of blood goes a long way, and things may look worse than they are – stay calm. Severe bleeding requires urgent medical attention in hospital, because although people rarely bleed to death, extensive bleeding can cause shock and loss of consciousness.

Aims

- to bring the bleeding under control

- to limit the possibility of infection

- to arrange urgent medical attention.

Action

1 Apply pressure to a wound that is bleeding. If possible, use a sterile dressing. If one is not readily available use any clean, absorbent material, or even your hand. Apply direct pressure over the wound for ten minutes (this can seem like a very long time) to allow the blood to clot.

2 If there is any object in the wound, such as a piece of glass, *do not* try to remove it – simply apply pressure to the sides of the wound.

3 Lay the casualty down and raise the affected part if possible.

4 Make the person comfortable and secure.

5 Dial 999 for an ambulance.

Protect yourself

You should take steps to protect yourself while dealing with casualties where there is bleeding. Your skin provides an excellent barrier to infections, but you must take care if you have any broken skin such as a cut, graze or sore. Wash thoroughly in soap and water, and seek medical advice if blood comes into contact with your mouth or nose or gets into your eyes. Blood-borne viruses (such as HIV or hepatitis) can be passed only if the blood of someone who is already infected comes into contact with broken skin.

- If possible wear disposable gloves.

- If this is not possible, cover any areas of broken skin with waterproof dressings.

- Take care with any needles or broken glass in the area.

- Use a mask for mouth-to-mouth resuscitation if the casualty's nose or mouth is bleeding.

Cardiac arrest

Causes

Cardiac arrest means the stopping of a person's heart. Cardiac arrest can happen for various reasons, the most common of which is a heart attack. A person's heart can also stop as a result of shock, electric shock, a convulsion or other illness or injury.

Symptoms

- no pulse
- no breathing.

Aims

- to obtain medical help as a matter of urgency
- to start resuscitation to get oxygen into the collapsed person's lungs using mouth-to-mouth resuscitation, and stimulation on the heart by chest compressions. This is called cardio-pulmonary resuscitation – CPR. You will need to attend a first aid course to learn how to resuscitate – you cannot learn how to do this from a book, because you will need to practise on a special dummy.

Action

1 Check whether the collapsed person has a pulse or is breathing.

2 If there is no pulse or no breathing, call for urgent help from the emergency services.

3 Start methods of resuscitation if you have been taught how to do it.

4 Keep up resuscitation until help arrives.

Figure 7.10 *Mouth-to-mouth resuscitation and chest compressions*

Shock

Causes

During shock, blood is not properly pumped around the body. This can occur as a result of the loss of body fluids through bleeding, burns, severe vomiting or diarrhoea, a sudden drop in blood pressure, or a heart attack.

Symptoms

The signs of shock are easily recognised:

- the person will look very pale, almost grey
- the casualty will be sweaty, and the skin will be cold and clammy
- the pulse will be very fast
- the person may feel sick and may vomit
- the breathing may be very quick.

Aims

- to obtain medical help as a matter of urgency
- to improve blood supply to heart, lungs and brain.

Actions

1 Call for urgent medical assistance.

2 Lay the person down on the floor. Try to raise the feet off the ground to help the blood supply to the vital organs.

3 Loosen any tight clothing.

4 Watch the casualty carefully, and check the pulse and breathing regularly.

5 Keep the person warm and comfortable – but *do not* warm the casualty with direct heat, e.g. a hot water bottle.

Do not

- allow casualty to eat or drink
- leave the casualty alone, unless it is essential to do so briefly in order to summon help.

Loss of consciousness

Causes

Loss of consciousness can happen for many reasons, from a straightforward faint to unconsciousness following a serious injury or illness.

Symptoms

- reduced level of response and awareness

- this can range from being vague and 'woozy' to total unconsciousness.

Aims

- to summon expert medical help as a matter or urgency

- keep the airway open

- note any information which may help to establish the cause of the unconsciousness.

Action

1 Make sure that the person is breathing and has a clear airway.

Figure 7.11 *Open the airway*

2 Maintain the airway by lifting the chin and tilting the head backwards.

3 Look for any obvious reasons why the person may be unconscious, i.e. a wound, an ID band telling you of any medical condition. Many people who have medical conditions that may cause unconsciousness, such as epilepsy or diabetes, wear special bracelets or necklaces giving information about their condition.

4 Place the casualty in the recovery position, *but not if you suspect a back or neck injury,* until the emergency services arrive.

Do not

- attempt to give anything by mouth

- attempt to make the casualty sit or stand

- leave the casualty alone, unless it is essential to leave briefly in order to summon help.

The recovery position

Many of the actions you need to take to deal with health emergencies will involve placing someone in the recovery position. In this position, the casualty has the best chance of keeping a clear airway, not inhaling vomit and remaining as safe as possible until help arrives. This should not be attempted if you think someone has back or neck injuries, and may not be possible if there are fractures to limbs.

1 Kneel at one side of the casualty, at about waist level.

2 Tilt back the person's head to open the airway, with the casualty on his or her back and making sure that limbs are straight.

3 Pull the arm on the far side over the chest and place the back of this hand against the opposite cheek.

4 Use your other hand to roll the casualty towards you by pulling on the far leg, just above the knee.

5 Once the casualty is rolled over, bend the leg at right angles to the body. Make sure the head is well tilted back to keep the airway open.

Figure 7.12 *The recovery position*

Epileptic seizure

Causes

Epilepsy is a medical condition that causes disturbances in the brain, resulting in sufferers becoming unconscious and having involuntary contractions of their muscles. This contraction of the muscles produces a fit or seizure. The person does not have any control over the seizures and may come to harm by falling when he or she has a seizure.

Aims

- to ensure that the person is safe and not injured during the fit

- to offer any help needed following the fit.

Action

1 Try to make sure that the area in which the person has fallen is safe.

2 Loosen clothing.

3 Make sure that the person is safe – particularly try to prevent head injury.

4 If the fit lasts longer than five minutes, or you are unaware whether the casualty is a known epileptic, call an ambulance.

5 Once the seizure has ended, make sure that the person has a clear airway and place in the recovery position.

Do not

■ attempt to hold the casualty down, or put anything in the mouth

■ move casualties until they are fully conscious, unless they are at risk where they have fallen.

Choking and difficulty with breathing

Causes

Choking is caused by something (usually a piece of food) stuck at the back of the throat. It is a situation that needs to be dealt with quickly, as people can rapidly stop breathing if the obstruction is not removed.

Symptoms

■ red, congested face at first, later turning grey

■ unable to speak or breathe, may gasp and indicate throat or neck.

Aims

■ to remove obstruction as quickly as possible

■ to summon medical assistance as a matter of urgency if the obstruction cannot be removed.

Action

These guidelines apply to adults and children over eight years old.

1 Try to get the person to cough, but if that is not immediately effective, move on.

2 Bend the person forwards, slap sharply between the shoulder blades up to five times.

3 If this fails, stand behind the person with your arms around him or her. Join your hands just below the breastbone. One hand should be in a fist and the other holding it.

4 Sharply pull your joined hands upwards and into the person's body at the same time. The force should expel the obstruction.

5 Alternate backslaps and abdominal thrusts until you clear the obstruction.

Figure 7.13 *Action to alleviate choking*

Fractures and suspected fractures

Causes
Fractures are a break or crack in a bone. This is usually caused by a fall or other type of injury. The person will need to go to a hospital as soon as possible to have a fracture diagnosed correctly.

Symptoms
- acute pain around the site of the injury
- swelling and discoloration around the affected area
- limbs or joints may be in odd positions
- broken bones may protrude through the skin.

Action
1 The important thing is to support the affected part – help the casualty to find the most comfortable position.

2 Support the injured limb in that position with as much padding as necessary – towels, cushions or clothing will do.

3 Take the person to hospital or call an ambulance.

Do not
- try to bandage or splint the injury
- allow the casualty to have anything to eat or drink.

Burns and scalds

Causes
There are several different types of burn; the most usual are burns caused by heat or flame. Scalds are caused by hot liquids. People can also be burned by chemicals or by electrical currents.

Symptoms
- depending on the type and severity of the burn, skin may be red, swollen and tender, blistered and raw or charred
- people are usually in a great deal of pain and may be in shock.

Aims
- obtain immediate medical assistance if the burn is over a large area (as big as the casualty's hand or more) or if it is deep
- stop the burning and reduce pain
- minimise the possibility of infection.

Action
1 For major burns, summon immediate medical assistance.

2 Cool down the burn. Keep the burn flooded with cold water for ten minutes. If it is a chemical burn, this needs to be done for twenty minutes, and you must ensure that the contaminated water used to cool the burn is disposed of safely.

3 Remove any jewellery, watches or clothing that are not sticking to the burn.

4 Cover the burn if possible, unless it is a facial burn, with a sterile or at least a clean dressing. On a hand or foot, a clean plastic bag or cling film will protect from infection until it can be treated by an expert.

5 If clothing is on fire, remember the basics: *stop, drop, wrap* and *roll* the person on the ground.

Do not

- remove anything that is stuck to a burn

- touch a burn, or use any ointment or cream

- cover facial burns – keep pouring on water until help arrives

- allow anyone with burning clothes to go outside or run around.

Remember

- *Stop* someone with burning clothes from running around.

- Get them to *drop* on to the ground – push them if you have to and can do so safely.

- *Wrap* them in something to smother the flames – a blanket or coat, anything to hand. This is better if it is soaked in water.

- *Roll* them on the ground to put out the flames.

Poisoning

Causes

People can be poisoned by many substances: drugs, plants, chemicals, fumes or alcohol.

Symptoms

The symptoms will vary depending on the poison.

- the person could be unconscious

- the person may have acute abdominal pain

- there may be blistering of the mouth and lips.

Aims

- to remove the casualty to a safe area if he or she is at risk, and it is safe for you to do so

- to summon medical assistance as a matter of urgency

- to gather any information that will identify the poison

- to maintain a clear airway and breathing until help arrives.

Action

1 If casualties are unconscious, place them in the recovery position, which should ensure that the airway is clear, and they cannot choke on any vomit.

2 Dial 999 for an ambulance.

3 Try to establish what the poison was and how much has been taken – this information could be vital in saving a life.

4 If a conscious casualty has a burned mouth or lips, he or she can be given small sips of water or cold milk frequently.

Do not

- try to make the casualty vomit.

Electrical injuries

Causes

Electrocution occurs when an electrical current passes through the body.

Symptoms

This can cause cardiac arrest and burns where the electrical current entered and left the body.

Aims

- to remove the casualty from the current when you can safely do so

- to obtain medical assistance as a matter of urgency

- to maintain a clear airway and breathing until help arrives

- to treat any burns.

Action

There are different procedures to follow, depending on whether the injury has been caused by a high-voltage current – such as overhead power cables or rail lines. In this case:

1 Contact the emergency services immediately.

2 *Do not* touch the person until all the electricity has been switched off.

3 If person is unconscious, clear the airway.

4 Treat any other injuries, such as burns.

5 Place in the recovery position until help arrives.

If the injury is caused by a low-voltage current, such as those that power kettles, computers, drills, lawnmowers, etc., the steps to follow are slightly different.

1 Break the contact with the current by switching off the electricity at the mains if possible.

2 It is vital to break the contact as soon as possible, but if you touch someone who is 'live' you too will be injured. If you are unable to switch off the electricity, stand on something that can insulate you, such as a telephone directory, rubber mat or pile of newspapers, and use an object such as a broom handle to move the casualty away from the current.

3 Do not use anything made of metal, or anything wet to move the casualty from the current. Use a wooden pole or broom handle, even a chair.

4 Alternatively, drag the casualty with a rope or cord, or, as a last resort, pull by holding any dry clothing that is not in contact with the body.

5 Once the casualty is no longer in contact with the current, follow the same steps as with a high-voltage injury.

Figure 7.14 *Move the casualty away from the current*

ASSESSMENT ACTIVITY

Describe the types of emergency that could happen in care settings, measures which can be taken to avoid them, and how to deal with emergencies which do arise.

1 Design a table that uses one column to list possible emergencies associated with fire, security, gas escape, escape of chemicals, escape of water or health emergencies within your placement setting. Use one column to describe what could be done to prevent these risks. Use another column to describe how to deal with each emergency.

2 Identify the signs and symptoms of common medical emergencies, and the basic first aid procedures to deal with them. Design a second table that uses one column to list common medical emergencies, one column to list the signs and symptoms associated with each emergency, and one column to list the first aid procedures needed for each emergency.

For a **merit grade** you need to explain the role and responsibilities of a care worker in dealing with medical or any other emergencies in a care setting. You should add a report to your work on the tables above. This report must explain the procedures you would follow, including your role and responsibilities, if you were to deal with various different emergencies. You also need to give examples that explain how medical emergencies are dealt with in your own care setting.

Answers to Think It Through on page 251

Safety hazards in the kitchen:

- Crockery is left unwashed, with particles of decaying food around.

- Electrical safety – the kettle lead is near water, creating a risk of electric shock. The electrical point might be overloaded with too many connections. The toaster is too near the sink and water supply.

- Fresh food is left uncovered – flies can land on it and spread micro-organisms from the decaying food in the sink and bin. Micro-organisms from the air can also contaminate the food.

- Bleach can be hazardous – it should not be stored near food. Here the lid is off and there is a risk of spillage or even food contamination.

- Food preparation surfaces have not been cleaned, allowing micro-organisms to build up and transfer to fresh food.

- Knives are not stored in a safe way.

- Decaying food is left in a broken pedal bin, encouraging flies and the spread of micro-organisms.

- Fresh food is placed near decaying food, encouraging the spread of micro-organisms.

- The dishcloth is contaminated with micro-organisms from the (dirty) floor area – separate floor and dishcloths should be used.

- The dirty floor might create a hazard of slipping and falling, as well as encouraging the spread of micro-organisms.

- The mop and bucket might be tripped over.

UNIT EIGHT

Promoting Activity

In this unit you will learn about:

- identifying the factors involving service users' mobility

- supporting service users during development programmes and activities

- assisting service users in their recreation and leisure activities.

This unit is about helping service users to remain active. This involves supporting service users' mobility, and helping them to participate in activity programmes. The focus throughout is on maintaining good practice when supporting mobility, and when choosing and supporting development programmes and activities.

Service users' mobility

This section deals with the factors that can affect service users' mobility. Most of us take it for granted that we can move about freely and can choose to take part in different recreation and leisure facilities that we enjoy. It can be difficult to appreciate how frustrating it would be to have restricted mobility, even if it were only for a short time.

Service users whose mobility is restricted will need help and support to gain access to recreational and leisure facilities that are available. It is important to be aware of the legislation and policies that must be considered, the services and products that are available to help, and the need to maintain good practice when assisting service users.

Legislation and policies

The legislation and policies that are discussed in this section have different aims. We will be looking at aspects of them that are relevant to the themes of mobility and safety. This means safety for the service user, for other people and for you.

The legislation and policies include:

- Health and Safety at Work Act (1974)
- Community Care Act (1990)
- infection control policies
- Manual Handling Operations Regulations (1993)
- risk assessment.

Health and Safety at Work Act (1974)

This is a collection of regulations and guidelines designed to make places of work safe. The Act is being constantly updated and added to, to ensure that any potential dangers are covered. Some of the duties in the Act are absolute, which means that they must be followed, while others are qualified by the words 'so far as is reasonably practicable'. This means that if there was a risk that would take great time, expense and difficulty to reduce or avoid, then it might be considered unreasonable to do so.

The Act is described as 'umbrella legislation' because it covers many regulations. These are discussed in Unit 3 on page 121 and are shown in the table below.

Name of regulations	Purpose
Control of Substances Hazardous to Health Regulations 2003. (COSHH)	To ensure that hazardous substances are stored and used safely
Reporting of Injuries, Diseases, and Dangerous Occurrences Regulations 1985 (RIDDOR)	To identify notifiable diseases, and to make sure that injuries and dangerous occurrences are reported and recorded
Manual Handling Operations Regulations 1993	To minimise the risk of injury due to carrying and handling at work
The Management of Health and Safety at Work Regulations 1992	To ensure that employers assess any risks that are associated with work activities

If you are helping service users to make journeys and visits, the requirements of the Act go with you, in the sense that you are still at work and have responsibilities towards yourself, the service users and the public.

Community Care Act (1990)

This Act came into force in 1990 and had two main aims:

- To allow people who need nursing care or help with daily living, but are not acutely ill, to be cared for in their own homes.

- To keep down the national costs of long-term care.

This was a marked change from previous practice, where people requiring high levels of care needed to go into residential homes. In residential care, specialist services can be bought in, and services like hairdressing or dental care can be provided as the number of service users being served at once makes it worthwhile. In a home care situation, the service user is expected to travel to use these services, and to take advantage of social facilities the service user needs to travel to a day centre.

This shift to home care means that service users have to travel much more to access the services they need. As a result, community transport schemes have been set up, and vehicles with adaptations are used to transport people with severe mobility problems. Generally, the Community Care Act aims to help people to live as normal a life as possible as members of the community. Supporting mobility is part of this.

Infection control policy

Infection control needs to be considered if you are supporting a service user with mobility problems. You need to find out whether service users are suffering from infectious conditions, and take the proper precautions to prevent disease being spread to you or to other service users. If you know or suspect that a service user is infectious, you should wear disposable gloves and protective clothing, use clean equipment and make sure that you follow the workplace policy for the disposal of waste materials. Service users who are suffering from infections should not normally be taken on journeys and visits. If you are not sure, check with your workplace supervisor when you are planning trips.

Manual Handling Operations Regulations (1993)

Helping service users with mobility can mean helping them physically. This means that the Manual Handling Operations Regulations (1993) are likely to affect you. These are discussed in Unit 3, page 124. The most important thing to remember when you need to lift or handle a service user is that you should avoid doing it manually. There is guidance published by bodies such as the Royal College of Nursing and the European Commission that advises people to avoid manual lifting at work. The regulations require employers to avoid manual handling where there is a risk of injury, 'so far as it is reasonably practical'. Employers must provide aids to lifting, such as hoists, and these should always be used.

THINK IT THROUGH

The biggest cause of injuries at work for health and care staff used to be the lifting and handling of service users. A quarter of care workers took time off due to back problems created at work, and it was the greatest cause of people having to give up a career in care.

Risk assessment

Under the Management of Health and Safety at Work Regulations, employers have a duty to assess the risks associated with work activities, and to provide safeguards and equipment. This includes the need to move and handle service users in health and care situations.

Although this provides general protection in the workplace, it is up to you to assess the individual risks in any work-based situation. You need to make sure that you have thought through the procedures that will be carried out before you begin, and if you have any doubts, stop and ask advice from senior staff.

Services and products required

A range of services and products are available to help service users to become more mobile. We will look at the modes of transport that service users can use to get around, personal mobility aids and equipment, and prostheses for those who have suffered the loss of a limb.

Modes of transport

The ability to get from place to place is something that we all need for shopping, going to work, visiting family and friends, or taking advantage of the variety of leisure pursuits that are available. The methods of transport we use include cars, taxis, buses and trains. But disabled people could be faced with problems in using any of these methods.

Ordinary cars

Some people with disabilities may find it difficult to get into and out of a normal saloon car. However, modern cars do have features that could be used to make this easier. Car seats today often move up and down as well as sliding backwards and forwards, which could provide more room. Small adaptations could be made, such as buying a revolving pad. By using this, the service user can sit on the seat and then could be swivelled into place simply by lifting and moving the legs over the sill of the car door. Remember that you must always consider the risks involved in such movement and carry out a risk assessment beforehand if necessary.

Adapted cars

Some disabled people are quite capable of using cars, and have cars of their own. Vehicles can be adapted to the needs of an individual both in terms of

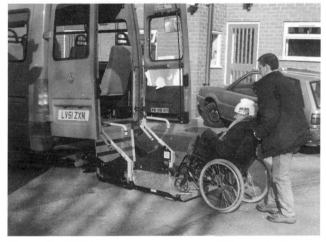

getting in and out, and in methods of control. Adaptations can be made to allow total hand control, so that there is no need for foot pedals. Wheelchairs can be stowed in the rear seat area, or on the roof, and special equipment is available to hoist them into place. There are schemes to help disabled people to buy and adapt cars, such as the Motability scheme. There are also organisations, such as the Disabled Drivers Association, who offer support and advice on matters like insurance and vehicle adaptations.

Figure 8.1 *Vehicles can be adapted to meet the needs of individuals*

Taxis

Taxis may be used for transport. Black cabs are spacious inside and some have adaptations to accept wheelchairs, including ramp facilities. Some taxi firms have a policy of providing transport for disabled people and contracts with local health authorities and social services departments to provide this service. But many taxis are not appropriately fitted, so check before using one. Another problem is cost, as taxi fares are not cheap.

Buses

Most local bus services are difficult for disabled people to use. There is often a high step to climb in order to get onto the bus, and sometimes more steps inside. Seating may be cramped, and there could be none available on crowded routes. Generally, there is no access or support for wheelchair users. The need to get to the bus stop and queue could also be a problem. Some local bus services do have special provisions, however. Some buses are designed to be lowered to kerb level when stopped at a bus stop, so that people can get on and off easily, and some have wide aisles and an open space for wheelchairs near the front.

Trains

Trains may have arrangements to accommodate wheelchairs but this is not always the case. For wheelchair users, getting around some stations and changing platforms often involves getting help, and may be difficult. Train carriages have narrow aisles and wheelchair users may be confined to less comfortable parts of the train.

Special transport

Many disabled people rely on the transport provided by social services departments. Mini-buses are often used, with special adaptations for the needs of the service users, such as ramps, lifts and handrails. There is also the advantage that they are driven by experienced staff who can offer assistance to passengers in getting on and off. The disadvantage is that there is usually a high demand for social services transport and it needs to be booked in advance.

Prostheses

Prostheses are items that are artificial replacements for natural parts of the body. They include substitutes for teeth, eyes, breasts or limbs. So far as mobility is concerned, prosthetic limbs are the important kind. Service users who have recently had prosthetic legs fitted may need additional support initially as they learn to walk steadily. Some people with prosthetic limbs regain nearly full mobility.

THINK IT THROUGH

Look at the design of the buses used by your local bus service. Do they have any features that would make it easier for a disabled person to use them? What features would make them hard or impossible to use? Also look at the facilities at bus stops. Is there any shelter or seating?

Equipment and mobility aids

A wide range of equipment has been designed to help disabled people to keep mobile. The list includes:

- walking sticks

- crutches

- walking frames

- wheelchairs.

Walking sticks are the most common form of mobility aid. They can be made of wood, metal or plastic, and handles can be curved or straight. They are fitted with a rubber end cap to prevent slipping, and this is an important feature that is prone to wearing out. For people who have a lot of difficulty in walking on one side, there are walking sticks with three feet, called tripods, or four feet, called quadrupeds. These are useful if a person has considerable disability on one side only, such as may occur after a stroke. On these sticks, each foot needs to have a rubber end cap. Many sticks, particularly the metal type, are adjustable in length.

Crutches are used when a person cannot put any weight on one leg, but is otherwise fairly fit. They are not usually seen as a long-term aid to mobility but are used when a person has a temporary disability while an injury is healing, or while they wait for a prosthetic limb to be fitted.

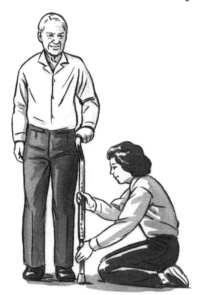

Figure 8.2 *You will need to measure each individual for a walking stick*

Walking frames, sometimes called Zimmer frames, provide a lot more support than a stick. They are used when a person needs constant support to walk safely, and is too unsteady to use a stick. Most walking frames are made of lightweight metal and have four feet. They are adjustable in height, so as to suit a range of service users. Some designs can be folded to allow storage, such as when travelling on a bus. Others have attachments from which to hang shopping bags, or deep trays to allow objects to be carried around. There are models with wheels fitted in place of the front pair of feet, for service users who are too frail to lift the frame forward between steps.

Wheelchairs are used to help people who cannot move around using their legs. There are many different designs, including chairs that have to be pushed, chairs that people can move by themselves, and motorised chairs. Chairs with small wheels are designed to be pushed by a carer. They are used in situations where the service user cannot propel the chair safely, such as a very frail service user or one who is very confused. They are also found in hospital wards, where patients are not expected to move themselves around. Service users who are more able will be supplied with a chair that they can propel. These chairs have large rear wheels with pneumatic tyres, like a bike, with a slightly smaller pair of wheels attached that the user grips to move along. Wheelchairs are available in a wide variety of colours and styles, including specialised chairs for sporting and athletic activities.

Motorised wheelchairs use an electric motor to power the rear wheels, and have batteries on board. They are steered using a small joystick mounted on one of the arms. Very little strength or mobility is needed to steer a motorised wheelchair safely, and they are ideal for service users who are unable to turn the wheels by hand.

Factors influencing good practice

Promoting independence and autonomy

> ## Case Study – John
>
> John is an elderly disabled person who has moved into residential accommodation following the death of his wife, who used to care for him at home. He has been using a small-wheeled chair at home for two years, and has become used to being moved around by his wife and other carers.
>
> Following an assessment of John's needs and abilities, the physiotherapist suggests that he is given a large-wheeled chair that he can propel himself. At first, John is resistant to the suggestion, fearing that he will not be strong enough to move far by himself. Staff suggest an activity programme that will gradually help John to develop his strength and confidence in using the chair, and he agrees to give it a try.
>
> A few months later, John is using his wheelchair regularly to get around the home, and he is now able to choose where he spends his time without having to ask for help.

Promoting the independence and autonomy of service users is about helping them to do things for themselves. This could be through a formal process such as the development programme described in the case study above. Perhaps more importantly it includes the ways in which care is carried out at a day-to-day level. In this sense it is a principle that should guide our judgement whenever we assess how to help a service user.

There are many occasions when it would be quicker and easier for the carer to take over a task that a service user finds difficult. It can be

Figure 8.3 *Achieving independence*

frustrating to watch a person struggling to perform a task when you could easily do it for them. But you need to hold back unless the service user asks you for help. This policy means that you must often expect things to go at the pace of the service user. Accompanying a service user who is using a stick and walking fairly slowly may take longer than pushing him or her in a wheelchair, but it is allowing the service user to be independent.

People being cared for may tend to become accustomed to being dependent on others – this is particularly the case in residential care. Service users will have been admitted to residential care because of their level of need, and their feelings about themselves may change because of their new situation. They can begin to see themselves as more dependent than they really are. Carers need to counter this by helping service users to do things for themselves. Successes need to be built on, and encouragement regularly given.

Service users who are getting used to unfamiliar new equipment, such as a walking frame or sticks, should be supported by encouragement and reassurance. Holding on to the service user to make him or her feel more secure is not likely to help, however. You can be most helpful by making sure that equipment is adjusted to the exact needs of the service user, such as by checking that aids like walking frames and sticks are set at the correct height.

Record-keeping

Keeping records is important in care situations. It is one of the key ways of ensuring continuity of care. In other words, records help carers to find out about work done by other carers and how the service user is progressing.

For service users who are being helped to become more mobile, carers should record progress in a form that allows other carers to access it easily. As with all written records, the issue of confidentiality should be considered. If it is considered to be sensitive information, the record should be kept securely. Different care settings will have their own rules about how records are kept and you need to become familiar with the methods operating in the setting where you work.

The type of information to be kept will depend on the particular needs of the service users and the mobility programme that service users are following. This should be agreed by the caring team so that the right information is recorded.

There are some rules of good practice that apply to any records, and these are shown overleaf.

> ### Good practice: record-keeping
>
> - Handwriting needs to be legible. Most of the records we are discussing are handwritten and they are useful only if they can easily be read. Take your time filling in records, however rushed you feel.
>
> - Information needs to be clear. Use short sentences and simple language to make your point.
>
> - Include all important points. Make sure that you record everything that is necessary, but don't ramble off the point.
>
> - Use bullets if you need to make a list of points, as they can make information easier to read.

Assessment of service users' needs

Part of good practice is the assessment of the needs of service users as they are helped with mobility. Along with accurate record-keeping this is a key process in a programme to improve a service user's mobility. Initial assessment of need may involve professionals such as physiotherapists, and a programme to improve mobility. The carers carrying out that programme need to maintain an ongoing assessment of the service user's progress.

Service users who are beginning to get used to new aids need to be listened to and observed so that their progress can be assessed. Carers can adjust the level and type of support offered in line with their assessment of service users' level of need.

Service user choice

An important aspect of good practice is the recognition that service users can make choices about the care they receive. There may be occasions when carers feel that a particular course of action would be for the best, but the service user does not wish to go along with it. This may happen when a service user does not feel ready to try a new mobility aid, or has a particular fear of using it.

Situations like this can be frustrating for care staff who may feel that they are serving the service user's best interests. There may be a temptation to keep on trying to convince a service user, but this could lead to distress and damage your relationship with the service user. Carers need to show sensitivity and judgement, and give the service user room to say no. If it is seen as important, a strategy might be developed to help the service user realise the benefits of the recommended procedure. For example, the service user could be introduced to other users, who may be better able to reassure and convince the service user than an able-bodied carer. Whatever the outcome, remember that service users have a right to choice and that they must never be bullied into doing something they don't want to.

Health and mobility

The service user's state of health and level of mobility place limitations on the help that can be given. Service users who have severe illnesses or very debilitating conditions may have serious restrictions on their mobility. This places limitations on how much support carers can offer to improve mobility and independence.

Carers may wish to discuss the issue of mobility with medical staff, to assess whether limited improvements in mobility can be planned and worked towards. There may be ways that very disabled people can be helped to be mobile; for instance, motorised wheelchairs can be operated by very light hand movements, though they need co-ordination skills for control. In some cases, however, the health of a service user makes it difficult to promote independence.

ASSESSMENT ACTIVITY

Describe relevant legislation, policies and good practice related to enabling service user mobility.

Legislation and policies are introduced to ensure that service users receive good-quality care that will enhance their lives in many ways. Explain how such legislation and policies have influenced good practice when enabling service users to achieve maximum mobility. Pay particular attention to legislation and policies that relate to health and safety when enabling mobility. Ensure that you address all legislation, policies and good practice that have an impact on mobility.

To achieve a **merit grade** you must explain how the relevant legislation and policies have influenced good practice in enabling service user mobility.

Development programmes and activities

This section is about assisting and supporting service users during development programmes and activities. Development programmes are important for the improvement of service users' quality of life. Through development programmes, service users are helped to retain their existing skills and to develop new ones. The aim is to help service users to cope better with their disability or impairment and to enable them to do as much as possible for themselves.

Policy and good practice

It is important as a carer that you are aware of how to ensure good practice when assessing the needs of service users in development programmes, and when supporting them during the programme's delivery. To maintain good practice you need to be aware of:

- the role of activity within care plans

- service user involvement and choice

- assessment

- monitoring progress

- offering feedback.

The role of activity within care plans

Care plans are statements of how a particular individual's needs are to be met. These needs may be physical, intellectual, emotional and social, and a programme of activities may be planned to meet some of these needs.

A development programme can take many forms, depending on the needs and abilities of the service user and the resources carers can use to help meet these needs. Development programmes are structured, monitored approaches to improving service users' skills, health, or abilities. They include specific goals so that progress can be monitored. For example, a person who has suffered a heart attack may benefit from a programme of physical development as part of the recuperation process. A programme of supervised exercises could be devised so that the service user can improve fitness, and reduce the risk of further heart attack. This is likely to involve regular visits to a gym or fitness centre over a period of several weeks. The service user would be assessed before the programme and guided to exercise at a safe level for his or her physical condition. He or she would be monitored during the exercise programme to ensure safety and to record progress. Other types of development programme may be very different – a programme to develop a service user's communication skills could involve meetings with a speech therapist, together with regular support from care workers during normal daily activities.

People with physical needs may benefit from a programme of activities designed to maintain and increase mobility and dexterity. Activities may involve becoming used to using aids, such as walking frames or wheelchairs. They could be aimed at service users developing skills in dressing or bathing themselves.

A care plan can include a programme of activities designed to encourage intellectual and social activity. Activities that stimulate the imagination or encourage conversation might be included, such as looking at a newspaper, doing a crossword, or taking part in discussions. Service users who are suffering from a mental impairment may need a lot of help to overcome their confusion or disorientation. A programme of activities designed to provide mental stimulation could form an important part of their plan of care.

Service user involvement and choice

For any activity it is important that service users feel a part of the process and fully committed to it. This means that they need to be involved in the planning and carrying out of the development programme, and that their choices are listened to and respected. There are two good reasons for this to be included as an element of good practice. First, service users have a right to be consulted and involved in the planning of activities that they are to carry out and this includes the right to choose not to participate in an activity if they so wish. This leads on to the second good reason, which is that it is no use planning a programme of activity if service users do not want to participate. Even if they go along with it to please you, it is unlikely that they will get much benefit from the programme unless they are really committed to its success.

How do you help service users to become involved in their development programmes? First, you need to make sure that the programme leads to goals that the service user recognises as useful to him or her. The best way to make sure of this is to discuss the activity with the service user at the planning stage. If an individual is reluctant or is worried about any part of the programme this will be revealed at an early stage. It could be that the programme needs to be altered to accommodate the service user's wishes, or perhaps some worries could be eased by explaining the potential benefits and the support that will be available. Service users could be shown the possible advantages by being introduced to people who have benefited from similar programmes in the past. Talking to people in a similar position may have more influence on them than the views of a fit young carer.

During the course of the activity, it is important to involve service users in what is happening to them as far as possible. What you are trying to achieve is a feeling in service users that they 'own' the programme, and that it is for their benefit. One way to help this process is to allow the service user to have a role in recording progress. If simple measurements are made, such as the distance walked or the number of repetitions of an exercise, they can be recorded on a chart by the service user – of course the carer should discreetly check that accurate records are being kept. Also simply asking the service user how a session went can help to keep the service user involved in the activity. If someone expresses the wish not to continue with a development programme, accept that and don't try too hard to persuade the service user to change his or her mind.

Assessment

Assessment of need is one of the first stages of the care planning process. A care manager will be responsible for the assessment process, and for the organisation and delivery of the care package agreed. There are basic principles of good practice upon which an assessment should be based, and these are shown overleaf.

Good practice: assessment

- The service user must give consent before an assessment is made.

- The service user should understand what the assessment is for.

- The views of carers and family should be taken into account.

- Service users should be given as much choice as possible in the services they are offered.

- Assessment should be seen as a partnership between the professionals carrying out the assessment and the service user.

An assessment is made so that a service user's abilities and needs can be established, and care planned to meet those needs. The professionals involved in the assessment will vary depending on the needs and history of an individual service user. People with specialised skills such as a physiotherapist, speech therapist, social worker and GP are likely to be involved. The care plan that emerges from the assessment process will usually include a variety of services and provision. One part of this may be a development programme, which is likely to have been set up by a physiotherapist, possibly with input from medical specialists.

Monitoring progress

Assessment is not a once-and-for-all process, but one that is part of the cycle of care planning. After the assessment process, a care plan is designed that will aim to meet the needs of the individual service user. Next the plan is put into practice, and during this stage the progress of the service user needs to be monitored. This means that the people carrying out the care must make regular checks on how the service user is responding to the care being offered. Monitoring involves making a judgement about the progress made by the service user and keeping useful records of the results.

Since providing care is a team effort, it is important that the records of the monitoring are usable by other carers. These records of progress will help in the reassessment of need which takes place at a later stage of the care planning cycle. It is likely that a physiotherapist or other professional responsible for designing a development programme will have specified the things that need to be measured and recorded as part of the monitoring process. The carers who carry out the monitoring need to keep records that can be easily read. In most care situations, standard methods of record-keeping will be in use, and these should be followed.

Feedback

The purpose of monitoring and record-keeping is to help both carers and service users to see just how well the care plan is working towards its goals. This means that the results need to be fed back.

Figure 8.4 *Feedback is important to both carers and service users*

Feedback is important to both service users and carers as it allows for reassessment and revision of the care plan. It is important that service users see that progress is being made as this encourages them to keep going and helps to boost their self-esteem. If little or no progress is being made the care plan can be revised to allow a different approach to be made or different activities to be tried. Remember always to discuss and agree any possible changes with a service user or to report to senior staff if a service user has mentioned something to you that you think might affect the care plan. Feedback is a two-way process; service users will tell you if they are not happy with their care, and carers keep service users informed about progress and may be able to suggest changes that could be made. If a service user were not able to make decisions for him or herself, relatives or an advocate would need to be consulted.

Materials and products

This section is about using materials and equipment safely. We will look at the safe use and storage of equipment and materials, and at the implications of using dangerous and defective equipment.

Use and storage of equipment and materials

Carrying out activities with service users means using equipment and materials, and this in itself leads to safety issues. A wide variety of types of equipment could be used in a development programme. This could include mechanical devices such as mobility aids or exercise equipment, and it could also include electrical or motorised equipment. Each piece of equipment will have been designed to do a particular job and will have correct methods of operation. In institutional settings, equipment will also have a place for storage.

To make sure that you use and store equipment safely, follow this 'do and don't' list:

Do

- make sure that you know exactly how a piece of equipment is used safely – this means that you need to know how and when to make adjustments if necessary.

- make sure that the service user knows how to use the equipment – this means passing on your knowledge about the equipment to someone else, which is possible only if you have a good understanding yourself

- use equipment only for the purpose that it was designed for; any equipment can become dangerous if it is used in the wrong way

- talk to your supervisor if you feel unsure about the use of a piece of equipment, because it is far better to seek help than to carry on without understanding what you are doing

- store equipment in a safe way – make sure that equipment is folded away correctly, and that items such as electrical leads are safely stowed

- replace equipment in its normal storage area, remembering that others may need to find it later. If you are not sure where things go, then ask.

Don't

- ever use any equipment until you have been shown how to use it safely

- ever let electrical leads trail across the floor or become wrapped around furniture – this could be dangerous for passers-by, as well as you and your service user

- leave equipment lying around after use – make sure you store it away safely.

These rules also apply to materials you may use. In addition, you should bear the following points in mind.

- Some materials are dangerous. Make sure you are aware of any dangers presented by materials you use. Read the labels, and ask a supervisor if you are not sure.

- Some materials have a limited shelf life. Check the age of materials if they need to be fresh.

- Materials often run out. Make sure that you report it when stocks are running low.

- Materials need to be stored safely. Never stack things too high if they are likely to overbalance, and never put heavy items on top of fragile ones.

- Dangerous or hazardous materials require specialised storage. Make sure that you follow the system operating in your workplace.

Implications of dangerous and defective equipment

Equipment that is broken or damaged presents a real risk to safety. The type and level of danger depends on the nature of the equipment, and on the use to which it is being put. Some faults, such as damage to electrical equipment, can be life-threatening.

It should be obvious from this that faulty or defective equipment must never be used. It presents dangers to yourself, the service user and others. If you use faulty equipment knowingly, you are breaching health and safety regulations, and if an accident does occur it would be impossible to defend this way of working.

It is important to be able to spot when a piece of equipment is faulty. You should check any equipment before you use it and examine it for damage or defects. This does not mean carrying out a battery of tests, but you should be sufficiently familiar with the equipment you use to be able to assess its condition quickly. Remember that it is not your job to repair any faults you find, and if you try to do so you could make the situation even more dangerous. If there is a problem that involves more than making a few regular adjustments, the equipment should not be used.

Another aspect of your responsibility is to report any faulty equipment that you find. Your workplace will have a procedure for the reporting of faults and you must make sure that you follow it. Reporting faults is also a responsibility covered by health and safety legislation. Make sure that equipment found to be faulty is stored and labelled so that it is not used unwittingly by others – your workplace should have a system to ensure that this happens.

- Always check equipment before use. If you are in doubt about its condition, don't use it.

- Don't try to repair faults yourself.

- Always report faults. Make sure that you know the procedure for reporting faults in your workplace, and follow the rules on labelling and storage of defective equipment.

Factors influencing practice

The role of staff

Offering support and encouragement is vital to ensure that service users are committed to the development programme and benefit from it. Service users need to feel that the programme has a point to it, and that they are getting benefits from it. Staff need to be sensitive to the feelings and reactions of service users, and able to respond to them. It is important to spot when a service user is becoming frustrated or disillusioned through an apparent lack of progress. Doubts need to be worked through with them, without pressure being put on service users to continue unwillingly. An important feature of support is praising and recognising success, and service user commitment may be improved by recalling things that have gone well in the past.

Facilitating the programme means making sure that the physical resources needed are ready for the service user, and that suitable staff and space are provided. This organisation may be carried out by a senior member of staff, or it may be set up initially by a specialist such as a physiotherapist and then administered by a carer.

Factors influencing development

Another part of the role of staff is to offer guidance and instruction in how the activities of the programme are to be carried out. Staff need to be confident in their knowledge of the activity and able to help service users to carry it out successfully and safely. This means that staff must have the training and experience to help service users effectively, and an understanding of what the programme is setting out to achieve.

If the aim of the care plan is to develop greater mobility or independence, then it may be very important to encourage the service user to learn about the use of any equipment or the specific procedure of any activity. As the service user becomes more able to cope with less support and supervision, he or she may prefer to work alone as long as it is safe to do so.

Service users' needs and interests

Another factor that affects the outcome of a development programme is the service user's needs and interests. As already stated, service users need to be involved in the programme if it is to be really effective. The service user's attitude to the programme will have a big influence on its success.

The programme will have been devised in response to needs identified for the service user. The level and type of need will partly determine the nature of the programme and the goals it sets. The interests of the service user also play a part in the choice of activity planned – the activity needs to be appropriate in terms of the things that the service user likes to do. Good practice involves making sure that service user's needs and interests are reflected in the activities chosen for a development programme.

Desired outcomes

A number of factors are important in determining whether development programmes achieve their desired outcomes. These include the assessment methods and equipment used, the co-ordination of the activities, the preparation of service users, and the level of service user satisfaction achieved.

Assessment methods and equipment

The methods and equipment used to assess service user progress need to be appropriate and adequate. Assessment can take many forms, and the methods and equipment used to measure progress are just as varied. There may simply be a logging of the time taken to complete a task, or technical equipment may be used to measure results. The important thing is that the methods and equipment fit both the activity being carried out, and the service user's needs and expectations. The choice of methods and equipment used should be made at the same time as the programme is devised. Choice may be restricted by the availability of equipment and of staff with appropriate training and experience. If problems occur during the programme, such as assessment methods that are difficult to implement or equipment with which the service user feels unhappy, they should be reported as part of the monitoring and review process.

Co-ordinating activities

To ensure that continuity of care is taking place it is important that activities carried out with service users are well co-ordinated. Care is a team effort and it is vital that the input of an individual carer blends smoothly with that of the others.

Responsibility for co-ordination usually rests with the care manager who oversees the care plan of a service user, but all staff have a part to play in ensuring that things run smoothly and tasks fit together. Sharing information is one aspect of this. All carers who work with a particular service user need to keep the others informed about developments that are relevant to the activity. This means making sure that record-keeping systems are used, and that information is available to those who need it. There are confidentiality issues to bear in mind here, and only relevant information should be passed on. Also, information should be made available only to people who need to know it.

Preparation of service user and environment

For the desired outcomes to be achieved, service users need to be properly prepared for the activity taking place. This means that service users should have an understanding of the process they are taking part in, and be prepared for what is to happen. It also means that they should be physically prepared for the activity. If the development programme involves mobility or exercise, service users should arrive in suitable clothing. Loose fitting, comfortable clothes are best if movement is a part of the activity.

Programmes may require service users to bring aids and equipment that they normally keep with them. For example, a service user who normally wears a hearing aid may need to bring it when attending a development programme session. It is important that service users are forewarned if they need to bring along any equipment.

The preparation of the environment is also important. If an activity requires an open space, it should be cleared before the service user arrives. Any equipment that needs to be located, assembled or adjusted also needs to be prepared in advance. Another aspect of preparation is to make sure that any relevant information is consulted. This could be records of progress, or notes made during previous sessions by other carers. Being aware of the current situation of a service user is as important as making sure that equipment is prepared.

Service user satisfaction

Service user satisfaction with the development programme and its results is the main goal. It would be hard to claim that a programme had succeeded if the service user were dissatisfied with the outcomes.

Figure 8.5 *For activities involving exercise, loose-fitting, comfortable clothes are best*

It may be hard to measure service user satisfaction, and perhaps the best way is to talk to the service user and try to gain an understanding of his or her feelings. Some service users will be able to explain precisely how they feel about their experiences, while others may find it hard to convey their feelings. This may be due not to illness or disability, but to a desire to seem helpful or uncritical. Many service users feel grateful towards carers and do not want to bother or upset them. This can lead to misrepresentation of their true feelings about the care they are receiving, or the situation they find themselves in. In these cases it is important that carers use their communication skills to find out the truth as best they can.

ASSESSMENT ACTIVITY

Investigate and identify a range of services and products available to enhance service user mobility.

1   Using a range of research methods and resources such as the Internet, catalogues and service providers, produce a booklet for service users that provides a comprehensive list of services and products that are available for differing levels of need. You should explain how the services and products are used and what benefits they may provide. Identify the risks and benefits of activities involving service users, and of any equipment or materials used during these activities.

2   Choose three different activities that could be enjoyed by service users and identify the risks and benefits associated with the activities. Also identify the risks and benefits of any equipment or materials used during the activities. Pay particular attention to health and safety, not only to the service users but also to others who may be involved.

3   Using the three different activities that you have written about, evaluate the risks and benefits of service users undertaking the activities, including any equipment or materials that could be used. How would you decide if the risks outweigh the benefits or vice versa? Would you decide not to

organise any of the activities on the grounds of health and safety, or for any other reason that might create too great a risk for the service users?

To achieve a **merit grade** you must explain how the risks and benefits of activities involving service users are assessed.

To achieve a **distinction grade** you must evaluate, using examples, the risks and benefits of activities involving service users, and of any equipment or materials used during these activities.

Recreation and leisure activities

This section is about assisting service users in participating in recreation and leisure activities. It includes:

- the requirements of legislation that may influence the choice of activity
- elements of good practice in helping service users to take part in activities
- factors that influence the choice of activity
- factors that influence the achievement of outcomes in leisure activities.

Legislation, policy and good practice

Effects on health and safety legislation

Recreation and leisure include an extremely wide range of activities, in fact practically anything that people take up as a hobby or spare-time interest. In practice, the range of options open to service users is restricted. A number of factors limit the choices of activity available, and one of these is the health and safety legislation that applies to situations where professional carers are helping service users to carry out an activity.

One of the main legal influences on activity is the Health and Safety at Work Act 1974 (HASAWA). The details of this Act have already been discussed, but we can recap the main points. Under the Act employers must provide:

- a safe workplace
- safe access to and from the workplace
- health and safety training and information
- a named person who is responsible for health and safety
- a list of identified health and safety hazards and procedures for dealing with them
- procedures for recording accidents at work.

Also under the Act, employees must:

- take reasonable care for the safety of themselves and others

- co-operate with their employer in matters relating to health and safety
- follow workplace procedures for reporting injuries and dangerous occurrences.

The HASAWA is a broad umbrella (see Figure 3.4 on page 121) and includes a variety of different legislation. It is intended to apply to a huge variety of work situations. To assess the implications of the Act for helping service users to participate in recreation and leisure activities, it is necessary to think about the particular activity and the service user who will be carrying it out. The relationship between these two factors is important. For example, a service user who is unsteady on his or her feet may face more risk when carrying out some activities than one who is more stable. People with co-ordination problems may face more risk than those with steady hands when using craft tools and equipment.

An assessment of risk needs to be made when considering the activities that may be appropriate for a particular service user. This sort of assessment should be carried out by a senior carer who has the skills to take the different issues into account. These will include:

- the service user's needs and abilities
- the demands that the activity will place on the service user
- whether the activity can be safely carried out with the resources available
- possible hazards from materials and equipment used in the activity.

This last point relates to the Control of Substances Hazardous to Health (COSHH) Regulations 2003. A surprising number of items contain substances that are potentially dangerous. Some items contain hazardous solvents, such as certain types of paint, adhesive, and varnish; and some materials are highly flammable. All such products should carry warnings on the label. Be sure to read the labels on any materials you are providing for service users doing craft work.

Personal beliefs and preferences

Good practice in helping service users to take part in activities includes taking into account their personal beliefs and preferences, discussing activities with service users and recording their responses.

These elements are essential in supporting service users' rights to choose and to have their ideas and feelings respected. Service users need to feel that they have been involved in making decisions about the things they do – when planning an activity this means that you need to talk carefully with the service user.

Discussing and recording responses from service users

A structured approach involves planning the questions, or the topics, that you intend to discuss. Writing down questions could make the discussion seem too formal and restricted, making it hard for the service user to relax and open up to you. But you could make a list of topics to be discussed, writing down a description of the areas you want the discussion to cover. When the discussion takes place you can use your own words to introduce the topic, so that the communication feels more like a natural conversation. Responses can be written down in a space under each topic heading.

You will need to make notes and record the responses of the service user during the discussion, even though this may stop the flow of the conversation. Making notes shows service users that you are genuinely interested in what they are saying and may encourage them to consider their answers more carefully and give more accurate responses.

Factors influencing choice of activity

We have already looked at how health and safety legislation can influence the choice of a recreation or leisure activity to be carried out with a service user. Other factors will have an influence on the activity chosen, and these include: the role of recreation and leisure, the potential difficulties and dangers of activities, the resources available, and therapeutic effects.

The role of leisure and recreation

Recreation and leisure has a part to play in everyone's lives. We all use our leisure time to follow interests and activities, and get a variety of benefits from doing so. These activities help us to relax. We may find that they help us to forget day-to-day problems as we become absorbed in what we are doing. They allow us to feel we are doing something for ourselves, and they often give us a sense of achievement and accomplishment. Our recreation and leisure pursuits are part of our view of ourselves, and they can help to reinforce our self-confidence and sense of identity. Any activity that involves exercise will also have positive health benefits. Exercise raises the heart rate and helps to keep the heart healthy and can help to strengthen muscles and ligaments. Exercise also releases chemicals in the brain, which help to bring about a sense of well-being.

People receiving care are likely to have restricted opportunities for leisure and recreation pursuits, but it is important to remember that they are able to get similar benefits from recreation and leisure. The role of recreation and leisure as part of a care plan should reflect these benefits. It is not just a matter of keeping service users entertained or preventing boredom – positive emotional and social developments should be the aim.

Potential difficulties and dangers of activities

Whether a particular activity is dangerous or difficult depends partly on the nature of the activity and partly on the needs and state of health of the service user carrying it out. An activity may be safe for one service user but hazardous for another. The conditions under which the activity is carried out also affect how difficult or dangerous it is likely to be – the support of specialist equipment and staff can turn a potentially hazardous activity into one that is safe to carry out.

When you are considering the potential difficulties and dangers of a particular activity with service users, it is best to carry out an organised assessment. First, write down a description of the activity and list any equipment needed. Next, think about what a service user has to do when carrying out the activity. This means being specific about the physical demands made by the activity. For example, these demands could include the need to lift or bend, or move quickly. Now you can list the physical demands of the activity below your description of it.

You need to consider the needs and abilities of service users in relation to the demands that will be placed upon them by the activity. Look at the notes you made when you analysed the activity and check this against the abilities and state of health of the service users you intend to work with. This process should help you to gauge the danger that an activity may present. Your analysis of the demands of the activity, set against the abilities of the service user, is a form of risk assessment. This assessment should help you to make an informed choice about the suitability of a particular activity with a service user group.

Conflicts of choice

If you are working in a residential setting where you are caring for a group of people, you must always remember that they will have come from different backgrounds and will have different interests. As a result it can be difficult to provide leisure and recreation activities that will suit everyone. A well-planned activity programme with different events being planned for different days will allow plenty of choice and good communication with service users that keeps them informed of what is available should help to avoid conflict of choice. Activities for individual service users may produce fewer conflicts because making arrangements for one person can allow some element of flexibility. If a clash of events occurs, it can often be possible to change one of them without too much disruption. For example if you have agreed with a service user that you will take them shopping on a particular day, then they are sent a hospital appointment for the same time, the shopping could be rearranged (probably much easier than trying to arrange another hospital appointment).

If you are planning an activity with a group of service users, it is possible that there will be some conflict about what is planned. Remember, even though you may be working with a group of people who are in the same age group, this does not mean that they will all like the same thing.

Helping service users to express their ideas and feelings may not always be easy. You need to use your skills in communication, including listening skills and showing interest and support. Planning an activity may not be as sensitive as other more personal areas of discussion, but you should nevertheless be aware of possible barriers to good communication. A way to help make the communication more effective is to record the responses of service users. This could be done as part of a structured approach to finding out service users' preferences and interests. You may wish to talk to a service user about such areas as previous interests and hobbies, views on different activities and the sorts of people who do them, the service user's own ideas for activities, and activities that have been tried in the past but disliked by the service user.

Of course, it is important that the activities you plan for service users reflect the beliefs and preferences they have expressed in their discussions with you. If they have told you that they hate to watch competitive sport, do not take them to watch a football match! Respecting a service user's right to choose means following his or her wishes as far as possible. It is also important to be aware of any cultural beliefs that may affect service user choice. For example, a female service user whose beliefs include not removing clothing in public places where men are present may not wish to undertake an activity such as swimming. This might be overcome if she could be assured that women-only sessions are available.

Available resources

Another factor that can influence the choice of activity is the availability of the resources necessary to carry it out. Some activities may be a lot easier to resource than others, and many can be carried out with a few, easily obtained materials. Activities like drawing, painting, and writing don't need specialised equipment or a lot of space, but other activities may be less easy to provide for. Some, like computing, need specialised technological equipment. Other activities, such as sports, need space.

Resources also include human resources – people. Many activities need more than one person to run them safely, and this may mean other carers will need to be available. Some activities require the support of people with specialised skills. For instance, some craft activities may need the help of a person with skills and experience in order to be run effectively, and some sporting activities may benefit from the help of skilled specialists, both in terms of getting the most out of the activity and in terms of safety.

You will need to assess the level and type of resources that are available, and take this into account when planning an activity. Remember that most resources have a financial cost, including the cost of your own time. Though you may be able to identify where you can obtain the equipment and materials that you need, you still have to find a budget to pay for them. Often, with a little ingenuity and imagination it is possible to assemble the resources you need.

Figure 8.6 *Taking part in a creative activity can be an absorbing experience*

Therapeutic effects

An important part of the value of recreation and leisure activities to service users is the therapeutic value that it has for them. At the beginning of this section we looked at the value of recreational activities to everyone. For people with restricted opportunities for leisure and recreation pursuits, the activities you help to provide are likely to be even more welcome and beneficial. Carrying out an activity can help people to feel more capable and confident. It reminds service users that they have skills and abilities, and taking part in an activity can be an absorbing experience that helps to distract service users from their daily worries and concerns.

Service users may also be able to gain specific therapeutic benefits if the activity chosen helps to support their medical needs. Maintaining mobility and co-ordination is an important part of the care offered to many service users, and recreation and leisure activities can help to promote these skills. Many craft activities involve co-ordination skills, and mobility can be supported by sporting activities.

The possibility for therapeutic benefits will depend on the needs of the service user. Think about the activity being considered and assess the skills it calls for. These should then be matched with the therapeutic needs of the service users, and it should be possible to decide upon an activity that has a therapeutic effect for the service user group.

The achievement of positive outcomes

Effective communication

Effective communication is important in all your work as a carer. You need to be able to communicate with service users, supervisors and other staff verbally, and to be able to communicate in writing when making notes and completing records.

Communication is also important when assisting service users to participate in recreation and leisure activities. Your communication skills will be needed at all stages of planning and carrying out an activity.

- During the planning stage you will need to explain to service users what the activity entails, and what they will be doing. You also need to listen to their responses, and to interpret their views in the context of the planning you are doing.

- During the activity you need to be able to communicate to the service users what is expected of them. Helping service users understand what is expected of them is important if they are to get the most out of their participation. You also need to use communication skills to help you to understand how service users are responding to what they are doing. If a service user is finding the activity difficult or not enjoyable, you need to be able to understand that this is happening. You may decide to discuss the service user's feelings, and perhaps offer encouragement to continue.

If you do not communicate effectively with service users the outcomes expected of the leisure activity may not be achieved. Activities might be badly chosen, and service users may be unsure of what they are expected to do or what benefits they could gain.

Communication with fellow carers and other people might also affect the success of an activity. It is often necessary to make arrangements with outside agencies, such as transport providers or the staff who work in the facilities you hope to use. It is vital that these arrangements are made properly, and your skills in effective communication will help with this.

Dealing with conflict of choice

In practice, people are fairly flexible and conflicts of choice are usually resolved fairly easily. Sometimes, though, you may find that members of a group have strong ideas about what they want to do and these could conflict with the choices of other group members.

Dealing with conflicts again calls upon your communication skills, as well as your skills in showing sensitivity to the feelings and needs of others. Do your best to allow the conflict to be solved within the group, by participating in a discussion and helping to keep it structured and under control. Your aim is to provide an activity that as many service users as possible want to do and can benefit from. This means helping all service users to express their feelings effectively, and helping service users to understand the views of other members of the group.

If the majority of people are in favour of a particular activity and one or two don't like the idea of it, try talking to the minority and explaining how they could benefit from participation. If they are unconvinced, you could remind them how important they are to the other group members, and how much their presence would add to the occasion. The argument that 'it won't be the same without you' can often win people over and persuade them to join in.

As the provider of the activity, you must make the final choice. You have to balance the need to respect the wishes of service users with the need for the whole group to do things together. If you find you have to choose an activity that some service users don't want to do, make sure that you talk to them individually and explain how you came to your decision. It may be possible to compromise and offer to arrange an activity that they would prefer in the future.

Evaluating activity

An important part of offering recreation and leisure activities is to evaluate how things went. All activities should have been planned with a particular set of goals in mind, in other words there should have been goals that the activity set out to achieve. An evaluation is the process of looking at how successful the outcome has been.

There are different ways in which an evaluation could be done, and a range of sources of information could be used to help it. The type of information you use to evaluate an activity will depend on the goals you expected the activity to achieve. An evaluation can be an informal process or a more structured one. In practice, an evaluation often has both formal and less formal components.

One way of evaluating is to write down your own impressions of how things went. Your observations can be important in gauging the overall success of an activity. Talk to other staff who where involved and record their views also. Any evaluation should of course include the feelings of the service users who participated. How you go about collecting this information will depend on the particular group you are dealing with and your relationship with them. It could be appropriate to hold a group discussion, where service users can make their views known.

It may be more appropriate to carry out your discussions on a one-to-one basis, speaking with each service user in turn. This would be better if some service users have difficulty communicating and need help and time to express themselves. It could also apply in situations where one or two group members usually tend to dominate group discussions, making it difficult for others to make their views heard.

Other criteria may need to be included in an evaluation of the activity. If there were therapeutic goals, it may be possible to make measurements, which can then be taken into account.

An evaluation is important with any activity, as it helps to inform everyone's planning for future activities. Things that went wrong can be avoided next time, and successful aspects can be built on. An evaluation also helps to demonstrate the value of the activity to others who may question whether it was worth while. It is a way of ensuring that your work is achieving its goals, and that service users' needs are being met.

Risk assessment

Completing a risk assessment is an essential part of the planning process when organising leisure or recreational activities. How detailed the risk assessment is will depend on the type of activity that is being planned. For example, an outing for a large group of people will require an extensive risk assessment, as you will need to take into account the risks associated with transport and the available facilities at the venue to be used.

It may well be that a risk assessment will highlight factors that you may not have taken into account when planning the activity. In order not to disappoint service users who may have been looking forward to having the opportunity to do something different, it is vital that you take this into consideration in the planning stage so that unrealistic events are not offered. You would certainly have wasted a lot of time and let down many people if, for example, you planned a theatre trip for a group of people who use wheelchairs, and discovered on arrival that they could not access the auditorium, or that the theatre had few or no seating or toilet facilities for people with disabilities.

Success or failure will depend on taking all the above factors into consideration during planning and carrying out activities. Remember that something that may seem quite insignificant to you might be very important to some of your service users and may make the difference between enjoyment and disappointment.

ASSESSMENT ACTIVITY

Identify factors that may influence the participation of service users in activities, and factors that may affect the achievement of outcomes.

1 What reasons may there be for service users choosing or refusing to take part in activities that are planned? Consider service users' needs and interests. What factors might affect the success or failure of the activities?

2 Use examples of different activities or the same activity for different service users to show how different factors will influence how service users participate in activities. Remember to consider the physical, intellectual, emotional and social needs of service users and how these may influence whether or not they choose to participate.

3 Develop a set of criteria that you could use to judge how beneficial planned activities are for service users. What criteria do you think would be most useful and how would you ensure that the criteria would measure accurately the benefits of any activities? Would you be able to use the same criteria for every type of activity and every service user?

To achieve a **merit grade** you must show, using examples, how service users' participation in activities can be influenced by a range of factors.

To achieve a **distinction grade** you must develop a set of criteria that can be used to judge the benefits of activities for service users.

INDEX